MISCELLANEOUS ALABAMA NEWSPAPER ABSTRACTS

VOLUME 1

COMPILED BY
Michael Kelsey
Nancy Graff Floyd
Ginny Guinn Parsons

HERITAGE BOOKS
2018

HERITAGE BOOKS
AN IMPRINT OF HERITAGE BOOKS, INC.

Books, CDs, and more—Worldwide

For our listing of thousands of titles see our website at
www.HeritageBooks.com

PPublished 2018 by
HERITAGE BOOKS, INC.
Publishing Division
5810 Ruatan Street
Berwyn Heights, Md. 20740

Copyright © 1995 Michael Kelsey,
Nancy Graff Floyd and Ginny Guinn Parsons

Heritage Books by Michael Kelsey, Nancy Graff Floyd, Ginny Guinn Parsons:

Marriage and Death Notices from the South Western Baptist Newspaper

*Miscellaneous Alabama Newspaper Abstracts
Volumes 1 and 2*

*Miscellaneous Texas Newspaper Abstracts: Deaths
Volumes 1 and 2*

Texas Masonic Deaths with Selected Biographical Sketches

Heritage Books by Michael Kelsey:

The Southern Argus*: Obituaries, Death Notices and Implied Deaths,
June 1869 through June 1874*

All rights reserved. No part of this book may be reproduced or transmitted in any form or by any means, electronic or mechanical, including photocopying, recording or by any information storage and retrieval system without written permission from the author, except for the inclusion of brief quotations in a review.

International Standard Book Number: 978-0-7884-0238-8

MISCELLANEOUS ALABAMA NEWSPAPER ABSTRACTS --- VOL 1

ABSTRACT

The newspaper abstracts for this volume were gleaned from microfilmed copies obtained from the Alabama Department of Archives and History in Montgomery, Alabama. The newspapers were originally published during the years 1823 through 1869. Even though the newspapers that comprise this first volume of abstracts were restricted to the counties of Dallas, Green and Talladega, the genealogical information found within the notices are, by no means, limited to central Alabama. Many notices include the surrounding counties of Perry, Autauga, Wilcox, Bibb, Sumter, Montgomery, Shelby and Tuscaloosa.

The abstracts consist of marriage, death, legal and slave notices, advertisements, and a great number of names in lists of letters left unclaimed in the local post offices. The lists of letters are of particular importance to the researcher as many of the names found in the lists do not appear on census indexes, making them an excellent addition to census and tax records.

Every attempt was made, by the compilers, to extract a substantial amount of genealogical data believed to be pertinent to the researcher. It is the intention of the compilers that this and future volumes complement a vital area of research into early Alabama newspapers.

Questions pertaining to this work may be addressed to Michael Kelsey or Nancy Graff Floyd, 1015 North 1st Street, Temple, TX 76501.

ACKNOWLEDGEMENT

We owe considerable appreciation to Shauna Michelle Mowery, Ginny's daughter, for her assistance in preparing this volume. She expended numerous hours making helpful suggestions and comments, preparing the indexes, and placing the finishing touches on the work. Thank you, Shauna.

MISCELLANEOUS ALABAMA NEWSPAPER ABSTRACTS --- VOL 1

TABLE OF CONTENTS

Newspaper Abstracts
SOUTHERN DEMOCRAT	1
THE CAHABA DEMOCRAT	31
SELMA COURIER	60
THE SELMA FREE PRESS	108
CAHAWBA PRESS AND ALABAMA STATE INTELLIGENCER	148
ALABAMA STATE GAZETTE	150
AMERICAN WHIG	151
SEMI WEEKLY DALLAS GAZETTE	152
THE CAHABA GAZETTE	155
EUTAW WHIG AND PUBLIC ADVERTISER	155
THE ALABAMA WHIG	158
AMERICAN WHIG	161
ALABAMA WHIG	167
EUTAW WHIG AND OBSERVER	168
SELMA WEEKLY MESSENGER	173
THE DEMOCRATIC WATCHTOWER	177
ALABAMA REPORTER	187

Glossary	214
Name Index	218
Slave Name Index	254

MISCELLANEOUS ALABAMA NEWSPAPER ABSTRACTS --- VOL 1

SOUTHERN DEMOCRAT

Published at Cahawba, Alabama by Fambro & Clark

ISSUE 7-1-1837, Vol. 11, No. 1

A man by the name of Watts, overseer of T.P. White, near this place, on Monday last, killed a negro of Mr. White and has fled from justice.

LAND FOR SALE: I will sell, at private sale, my plantation; containing 240 acres of timbered prairie land, one hundred of which are cleared, fenced, well watered and under cultivation. This land lies on the waters of Talachie, three miles from Athens, being the E. half of the N.W. quarter of section 17, township 15, range 7; the N.W. quarter of the S.W. quarter of section 17. township 15, range 7; the E. half of the S.W. quarter of section 18, township 15, range 7; and west half of the N.W. quarter of section 17, township 15, range 7, of the district of lands offered for sale at Cahawba. 1-28-1837, Greer Johnson

Committed to the jail of Dallas County, on the 25th day of March, 1837, a negro fellow who says his name is Charles, and that he belongs to James Cooper, a speculator, who was, at the time the boy left, at Montgomery, Alabama.... April 8, 1837, J. Love, J.D.C.

NOTICE: The copartnership heretofore existing under the firm of Thomas Moreng & Co. was dissolved on the 14th September last, in consequence of the decease of one of the copartners. The affairs of the concern will be settled by the undersigned, surviving partners, who will continue the business.... Edward M. Perine, Richard C. Chocheron, whose future business will be conducted under the firm of Perine & Crocheron Cahawba July 2, 1836

NEGROES IN JAIL: Taken up and committed to the jail of Dallas County, on the 16th of September, a negro boy who says his name is Bill, and that he belongs to John Colbert, of Mississippi. Said negro says that Colbert bought him of the estate of John Philips, 25 or 30 miles from Richmond, VA. in the neighborhood of Henry Gee, some time in the winter of 1832. He also states, that he ran away from said Colbert while at Memphis, Tenn. in the spring of the same year. Bill is about 6' high, light complexion, young and likely, stammers when speaking in haste. Said negro says he has been out about 3 years.... October 7, 1836, J. Love, Jailor, D.C.

Whereas Letters of Administration were granted to the undersigned on the 5th of December last, by the honorable Orphans' Court of Dallas County, on the

MISCELLANEOUS ALABAMA NEWSPAPER ABSTRACTS --- VOL 1

estate of W.T. Hooper, deceased, late of said county.... John Hooper, Adm'r

NEW STORE IN CAHAWBA: The undersigned respectfully inform the public that they are now opening, in the store house formerly occupied by Mr. McElroy, next door to Harvey & Craig's.... Cole & Dunham, Cahawba October 29th, 1826

At a meeting of the Cahawba and Marion Railroad Directors, in the town of Marion, on the 6th day of May, 1837, the following Directors were present viz: James B. Clarke, President; Levi Langdon, Henry House, Joseph Bancock, John Hartman, John Lockhart, ---- Blassengame, and James D. Craig, Directors

ISSUE 7-8-1837

A list of letters remaining in the post office at Cahawba, July 1st., 1837, which if not taken out by the 1st. of October will be sent to the General Post office as dead letter.

Mrs. Margaret D. Alison, Mrs. Elizabeth Adams, Alexander Alexander, Solomon Adams

J.S. Beers, Horatio Boxley, Jesse Beene, Mrs. Ann Beckman, Burwell Boyken, Elihu J. Boothe, R. Bohannon, Grady Birdsall, Martha P.J. Beale, Col. R.E.B. Baylor, James Baxter, Doct. F.A. Badger, Miss E.M. Beck, Eleazer Baldwin, Joseph Babcock, William Brenere

Clerk of County Court, Claudus M. Cochrin, Durant Cox, Miss Elizabeth Crumpton, William Cortes, James Craig, Elijah Coker, Rev. Robert Carson, John Cobb, S.D. Cochran, James Cothran, Joel M. Cross

John S. Dewey, Wm. C. Donald, Miss E.A. Diggs, J.P. Donnelly, Shubael Downes

Miss Susan Edwards, Miss Rachael Etherage, Wm. Edwards, Dr. Paul H. Earle

Barnet Frazee, Peter Flurenoy, John C. Fizzle, Flemming Freeman

Thomas Gibson, G.W. Gayle, Matt. Gayle, Mrs. E.G. Goodwin, John Grumbles, Thorton B. Goldsby, Mrs. Margaret Graham, Jacob Gurham, Samuel Goodman

P.W. Herbert, Benj. R. Hogan, Josiah Harroll, Samuel Holloway, Miss Martha

MISCELLANEOUS ALABAMA NEWSPAPER ABSTRACTS --- VOL 1

Hays, Miss Ann Hays, Col. Carter B. Harrison, Isaac Hutcheson, Daniel B. Hough, Jacob Hoss, Miss Rosina M. Hearne, Isaac Howard, Rev. Jesse Hartwell, Harvey & Craig, James Hardaway, Mrs. Elizabeth Hogan

I.M. Jackson, Mrs. Sarah M. Johnson

Hon. Wm. R. King, Warren E. Kannedy, Thos. K. Kornegay, E. Kervin

Miss Harriet R. Lee, James Logan, E.H. Lide, John Lapsey, Isaac Langston

A.P. McCurdy, Wm. Minter, Thomas Mara, Wm. Mathews, Ezekiel Mathews, Martha A. Marshal, Miss Susan W. Martin, P. Muray, H.B. McDonald, A.F. Moss, James S. Moss, Wm. McGlen, Mrs. Mary Morgan, Daniel McFarland

Col. Nuniley, Naghil, Capt. S.W., Mrs. Martha Norwood

A.L. Overton

A.G. Porter, Jesse Pulley, Dr. W.B. Powel, Beymore B. Powell, Levi Parkes, Wm. Pye, Edward Pye, James Petty, John Pearson, John D. Parker, Reuben Pearse, Enoch Parsons, A. Punderson, Geo. Possenby, Rev. Solomon Perkins, Miss Elizabeth Pledger, Mrs. N.A. Pickens, Miss Jane Bolton Peake,

Messrs. Roberts & Walker, Jesse D. Rountree

Mrs. Susan P. Calhoun, John Shearer, Charles Stewart, Samuel M. Stewart, James Sandlin, Robert L. Sargent, Mrs. T. Saunders, James M. Saffold, Allen Stephens, Henry Stanton, James Smyley, David Smyley, Mrs. Lucinda Smiley

Dr. Wm. B. Townsend, Leroy H. Traylor, R.E. Thompson, Col. Clark Taylor

Dr. Wiley J. Underwood, Green Underwood

Dr. John E. Vaescr, Joseph Vann

George J.S. Walker, Beverly Walker, Mrs. Mary Ann Walker, Miss Virginia L.C. Walker, Elijah Wilson, Martin O. Whatley, Conner B. Watts, Thomas Watts, Wm. B. Weaver, Thomas D. Williams, Thomas Wright, Marshel Wren, John Y. Watts, Wm. White, Uriah West

Benj. C. Yancey, W.L. Yancey

TOWN PROPERTY FOR SALE; The subscriber will depose of his property in the town of Cahawba, consisting of one Town Lot and the half of another.

Miscellaneous Alabama Newspaper Abstracts --- Vol 1

On the premises are a good two story dwelling house with all necessary outhouses, an excellent garden with all sorts of fruit trees, and a spring of good water. The above are adjoining B. Halmes' and Dr. Herbert's premises. B. Robeson

Hamilton Stone and Alpin Stone, Executors of Joshua Slone, deceased vs Parmelia, Emiline, Indiana, Angeline, and Trammel children and legatees of the said Joshua Slone, deceased, petition for a sale of Real Estate, for the purpose of making a division among the heirs and legatees. Wilcox County, May Term, 1837, Orphans' Court

ISSUE 7-15-1837

FROM THE BATON ROUGE GAZETTE...."Stabbing. A man named Martin was accused of stabbing another individual last Sunday, named Baptiste Coti, at the plantation of Mr. W.H. Buckner, in this parish."

FROM THE BROWNSVILLE BANNER; ...For some time past a slight misunderstanding had existed between Mr. Henry W. Anderson, of Bolivar, and Mr. Richard H. Jones, Merchant of this place. Near, the close of the week, Mr. Anderson came to Brownsville, and, according to custom, placed his name on the Hotel Register. Shortly afterwards he discovered a remark immediately under his name, impugning his character, and bearing the signature of R.H. Jones. He then wrote a reply, attaching his proper signature. On Monday morning last, at an early hour, Mr. Jones called at the hotel, and seeing the appended remark, became much enraged, and declared he would have satisfaction. He walked across the square to the corner of a store, into which Mr. Anderson had just entered, and called to him to come out. He complied, when Mr. Jones demanded of him whether he had written the remark alluded to above or not. Mr. Anderson answered in the affirmative, at which moment each resorted to a pistol, standing about 4 feet apart, in an instant they fired. Mr. Jones' ball lodged in the muzzle of his adversaries pistol (three balls) lodged in Mr. Jones' breast above the right nipple. He expired in two or three hours, leaving a wife and two or three children....

Committed to the jail of Wilcox County, on the 29th June, a runaway negro man, who says he belongs to a widow Adams of Mobile. Said boy is about 27 years of age; about 6' high; quite black, quick spoken and intelligent; no other marks visible. D. Rosser, Sh'ff, W.C.

NOTICE: In pursuance of a mortgage given to me by Benjamin Adams, I will expose to sale to the highest bidder, at Athens in Dallas County, on Saturday, the 12th day of August next, a negro woman named Morning, the said negro is a good field hand or cook. Athens, July 8th, 1837, James A. McElroy

SHERIFF SALE: Will be sold before the court house door in the town of Cahawba, on the first Monday in August next, the following land, to wit: The West half of North-East quarter of section 23, township 17, of range 8, levied on as the property of Wm. Bolton, to satisfy an execution in favor of Turner & Lewis, and others in my hands for collection. July 8th, 1837, W.T. Minter, Sh'ff

Committed to the jail of Wilcox County, a negro man who says his name is Peter, and that he belongs to Samuel Pickering of Demopolis, Alabama. Said negro is about 4'6" high; quite black, and wanting in intelligence.... July 15th, 1837, D. Rosser, Sh'ff W.C.

NOTICE: I forewarn all persons from trading for a note given by me to Daniel M. Crosland, for $2,000, due April 15th, and dated January 18th, 1837. As the consideration for which said note was given has in part failed, I will not pay it unless compelled by law. July 15th, 1837, Samuel Letters

Committed to the jail of Wilcox County, on the 16th inst., a negro man, who says his name is Ellick, and that he belongs to Col. Root of Mobile. Said boy is about 27 or 8 years old; rather under the common size; quite black, quick spoken....

Will be sold before the court house door in the town of Cahawba, on the 1st Monday in August next; a part of Lot #21, lying and being in the plan of the town of Selma, containing one acre of land, known as the house and lot whereon William E. Gorman formerly lived. Levied upon as the property of James W. Gibson, to satisfy sundry executions in my hands against him for collection. W.T. Minter, Sh'ff

TO MY CREDITORS: You will please take notice that I am a prisoner in the hands of D. Rosser, sheriff of Wilcox County, at the suit of Benjamin W. Saxon, survivor &c., which debt I am unable to pay, and that I have applied to Joseph A. Hall, Judge of the County Court of Wilcox County, for the benefit of the law passed for the relief of insolvent debtors... July 15th, 1837, W.H. Anderson

Committed to the jail of Wilcox County, on the 25th inst., a negro man slave, taken up as a runaway, who says his name is Abram, and that he belongs to a man by the name of Lucas living below Montgomery, Alabama. Said negro was going down the river in a boat in company with two others, who made their escape, and who belong to the same man if the statement of the one taken can be believed. Said boy is about 25 or 30 years of age, stout and well made, a little yellow complected, very well clad in homespun.... 7-15-1837, D. Rosser, Sh'ff W.C.

Two, slaves, Abram and Reuben, belonging to Dr. Meek of Tuscaloosa, who were arrested on a charge of being concerned in shooting Col. Dent, with an intention to kill him, were convicted on Wednesday the 12th inst., and sentenced to be hung on Friday, the 21st inst. (yesterday)

ISSUE 7-22-1837

Committed to the jail of Dallas County, on the 13th day of July, 1837, a negro fellow, who says his name is Jim, and that he belongs to John Erwin of Mobile...

Committed to the jail of Dallas County, on the 13th day of July, 1837, a negro fellow, who says his name is Silas, and that he is the property of John Erwin of Mobile...

Committed to the jail of Dallas County, on the 19th July, 1837, a negro fellow who says his name is Bill, and that he belongs to William F. Daniel and hired to Shumate, near Athens, Dallas County...

Committed to the jail of Dallas County, on the 26th inst., a negro man, who says his name is Reuben, and that he belongs to Dr. Long..... 8-5-1837

The State of Alabama, Dallas County, Lewis Ethridge vs his creditors

The State of Alabama, Dallas County, Richard Allday vs his creditors

The State of Alabama, Dallas County, A.J. Morgan vs his creditors

The State of Alabama, Dallas County, Jorden Holoway vs his creditors

The State of Alabama, Dallas County, Henry McElroy vs his creditors

NOTICE: There will be a barbicue [sic] given at Mr. Jesse Johnston's Mill, on Bogue-Chitto, by the members of the Bouge-Chitto volunteer company, on Saturday, the 5th day of August next.

ISSUE 8-12-1837

Married, in Columbus, Ga., on Tuesday morning, August 1st., by the Rev. Dr. Goulding, John Johnson to Miss Hannah Briggs, all of that city.

MISCELLANEOUS ALABAMA NEWSPAPER ABSTRACTS --- VOL 1

Married, in Plattsburg, N.Y., on the 19th July, by the Rev. Mr. Halse, Asa Hascall, of Malone, to Mrs. Phebe A. Smith, of the former place.

SHERIFF'S SALE.... levied on as the property of Silas Morgan, to satisfy sundry executions in my hands, for collection, against said Morgan, Viz: the N. 1/2 of the S.W. 1/4, and the S.E. 1/4 of N.W. 1/4 section 27, township 14, range 7. August 12th, W.T. Minter, Sh'ff

SHERIFF'S SALE: ....on the described land; levied on as the property of Hugh Lamb, to satisfy sundry executions in my hands against said Lamb, Viz: the E 1/2 of SW 1/4 of section 21, township 17, range 7. Aug 12th, W.T. Minter, Sh'ff

SHERIFF'S SALE: by virtue of a wit of fi fa, from the Circuit Court of Dallas County, against Benjamin Adams to satisfy Deury McMillam, I shall, at the court house door in Cahawba, on the first Monday in September next, expose to sale to the highest bidder, the following lands; levied on as the property of said Adams, Viz: The W. 1/2 of the N.E. 1/4 and the W. 1/2 of the S.E. 1/2 of section 30, township 16, range 7.   Also the W. 1/2 of the N.E. 1/4 of section 23, and the N.W. 1/4 of the N.E. 1/4 of section 11, both in township 15, range 8. August 8th, W.T. Minter, Sh'ff

Will be sold before the court house door in the town of Cahawba, on the first Monday in September next: A part of Lot #21, lying and being in the plan of the town of Selma, containing one acre of land, known as the house and lot whereon William E. Gorman, formerly lived. Levied upon as the property of James W. Gibson, to satisfy sundry executions in my hands against him for collection. August 12th, W.T. Minter, Sh'ff

Committed, to the jail of Dallas County, on the 9th, Aug., a negro man, who says his name is Aaron, and that he belongs to John Waldron (residence not known) said boy has been badly torn with dogs.

Committed, to the jail of Dallas County, on the 8th day of August, a negro man, who says his name is Reuben, and that he belongs to Dr. Robert Williams living near Greenville, N.C. and has been on a plantation in the Cane Brake, under the charge of Ivey Smith, about 8 miles from Greensboro, Ala... J. Love, Jailor D.C.

Committed, to the jail of Dallas County, on the 8th, day of August, a negro man, who says his name is Harry, and that he belongs to Dr. Robert Williams, living near Greenville, N.C. and has been on a plantation in the Cane Brake, under the charge of Ivey Smith, about 8 miles from Greensboro, Ala... August 8th, J. Love, J.D.C.

Miscellaneous Alabama Newspaper Abstracts --- Vol 1

$10 Reward: strayed, from the subscriber, living near Thomas Craig's, and 8 miles north-west of Cahawba, two mules... Cahawba, Aug. 5th, 1837 Hamilton Flaniken

ISSUE 8-19-1837

Married, in this village, on Saturday evening (12th inst.) after an acquaintance of two days, by G.G. Brooks, Mr. Phillip Vogelin to Mrs. Polly Pinson.

Died, on Sunday, the 6th inst., at his residence in Pleasant Valley, Maj. Michael J. Kenan, in the 52nd year of his age, after a painful illness of about 2 years.... The subject of this tribute was born in Dublin Co., N.C., 25th March, 1779. During the late war with Great Britain, he was distinguished as an officer, and held an important trust at Charleston, S.C. Early in 1818, he emigrated to, and has since remained a citizen of Alabama.... Died, on Tuesday the 15th inst., Col. Joab Pinson, an aged and respectable citizen of this county.

SHERIFF'S SALE: .... Levied against Solomon Adams, Aug. 5th W.T. Minter, Sh'ff D.C

ISSUE 8-26-1837

Married, in this county, on Monday evening last, by the Hon. Geo. R. Evans, Mr. David R. Bell, of this town, to Miss Caroline A. Davis.

Notice: The co-partnership formerly existing under the firm of Peck, Ward & Co., was dissolved on the 8th inst., in consequence of the death of one of the partners. The business will be continued under the firm of Peck & Dunham... June 24, 1837, Norris Peck, William P. Dunham

Ad for Perine & Crocheron, Dry Goods, Cahawba
Ad for Joseph Babcock, Groceries, Cahawba

Law Notice: The undersigned have formed a copartnership to practice law, under the firm of Gayle, Van De Graff & Safford, in the several courts in Mobile County.... John Gayle, Wm. J. Van De Graff, G.W. Gayle, J.P. Safford

Ad for William B. Safford, Attorney at Law, office in Hayneville

Land for Sale: .... This land lies on the waters of Talachie, three miles from Athens.... Greer Johnson

MISCELLANEOUS ALABAMA NEWSPAPER ABSTRACTS --- VOL 1

ISSUE 9-2-1837

We regret to learn by the last *Southern Argus*, published at Columbus, Miss., that one of the editors of that paper, Thomas J. Forbes, died on the 21st ult., after an illness of 10 days. Mr. Forbes was a native of Bangor, Maine.

Married, on Wednesday the 23rd ult., near Pleasant Hill, in this county, Mr. Joseph R. Ramsey to Miss Elenor Goodwin. In St. John's Church, Unadilla, N.Y., on the 1st. ultimo, by the Rev. N.H. Adams, Mr. Henry Howard, to Miss Harriet, daughter of the late Mr. Curtis Noble, of the former place.

Committed, to the jail of Dallas Co., on the 27th August, 1837, a negro fellow who says his name is Nathan, and that he belongs to James Sprate, of Lowndes Co. said negro is 5" 9 1/2" high, bright complexion, moderate size, about 26 years of age. September 2, J. Love, J.D.C.

Committed, to the jail of Dallas County, on the 29th August, a negro man, who says his name is Scott, and that he belongs to William Aldridge, near Statesville, Autauga County. Said negro is 5' 8" high, dark complexion, stout and well built, and about 25 years of age....

Land For Sale: Whereas the undersigned, were, at the August term 1837, of the Orphans' Court of Dallas County appointed commissioners to sell the real estate of which John Comelander died seized and possessed.... The purchaser giving notes, with approved security to Daniel Comelander, Adm. of the estate of John Comelander, deceased. September 2, 1837, Hamblin Quarles, Lorenzo Roberts, John Moseley Commissioners

Land For Sale: The subscribers will offer at public sale.... on the 16th day of Sept. next, their tract of land, containing 320 acres, 160 of which is swamp and the balance upland near Barboursville, a flourishing village, and a healthy and pleasant location in Wilcox County, Ala.... Also their store in Barbourville, together with their stock of merchandize.... Sept 2, 1837, Hinson & Patterson

ISSUE 9-9-1837

Died, on Monday the 27th ult., 5 miles south of Selma, in about the 25th year of his age, Mr. Spencer Johnson, next eldest son of our very worthy and respected citizen Lewis Johnson. Having taken but a short time since to his paternal charge a consort for life, he has left this dear partner and only infant son to mourn their loss.... (see issue 9-23-1837)

Died, in Selma, on the 26th ult., of congestive fever, Mr. William C. Baxter, a native of Leith, Scotland, aged 33. His property is in the hands of R.D.

Baxter, of this town, to whom letters in relation to the deceased may be addressed.

Died, in Pleasant Valley, on the 20th ult., Mrs. Hannah Cormichael, at an advanced age.

ISSUE 9-16-1837

Executors Notice: Take notice that letters of testamentary have been this day granted to the undersigned, on the last will and testament of Linda Lee, late of Dallas County, deceased.... September 11, 1837, Eaton Lee, Samuel Moore Executors

ISSUE 9-23-1837

Taken up by Samuel Dehay and strayed before Wm. DeVaughan, a Justice of the Peace in and for the County of Wilcox, an iron gray mare about five years old.... J.P. Fairly, clerk

Taken up by Ephraim J. Vernon.... a sorrell mare, about 4 years old. J.P. Fairly, clerk

Ad for William E. Bird, Attorney at law, may be found at the office of Beene & Fambro, Cahawba
Ad for the Mansion House, Mineral Springs, Talladega Co., Ala, W.C. Batchelor

Dr. Miles has located himself at Mr. Henry Avyrett's on Bague Chitto, one mile from Bridge, on the Marengo road, and will attend to the duties of his profession.

Died, on Saturday evening, the 2nd inst., in the 18th year of her age, Jenette, relict of Spencer S. Johnson, who departed this life on the 26th of August in the 27th year of his age; only one week intervened and she followed him to his long home. (see issue 9-9-1837)

The subscriber having retired from the mercantile business in the town of Benton will remove to the city of Mobile, in October next, for the purpose of making sale of cotton, and purchasing goods for those who may entrust their business to his care. John H. O'Neal

Administrator's Notice: Letters of Administration on the estate of Spencer S. Johnson, deceased.... (see issues 9-9 & 9-23)   Lewis Johnson, Adm

MISCELLANEOUS ALABAMA NEWSPAPER ABSTRACTS --- VOL 1

Committed to the jail of Dallas County, on the 17th day of September, 1837, a negro woman, who calls herself Phillis, and says she belongs to Mrs. Ann Mashiere living on the Tombecbee river. Said negro is about 35 or 40 years of age, light complexion and likely for her age; about 5' 5 or 6 inches high.... Sept 23, 1837, J. Love J.D.C.

Taken up by Abraham Hillyard.... a yellow mare....

Taken up by Hezekiah Erwin.... a deep bay horse....

ISSUE 9-30-1837

Administrator's Notice: The undersigned has been appointed administrator of the estate of Phoedras Rutherford, deceased.... September 27, 1837, Max. Rutherford, Adm.

State of Alabama, Dallas County: To Washington J. Outlaw, Wm. Chapman and Brother, Jacob Brown, Benj. F. Adams, F.H. and B. Gustin, John D. Adams, Spencer Adams, Weaver & Stone, Andrew Niolin, Ezekiel Pickens, James P. Lee, Vincent J. Grigsby, Wm. Browning, Erasmus Parker, Julius Norton, and ____ Sellzer, and to all others, the creditors of John Hughes: You are hereby notified that the said John Hughes did on the 28th day of September, inst., apply to us two, acting Justices of the Peace in and for the County of Dallas, for the benefit of the several acts of the legislature of this state passed for the relief of insolvent debtors, and that we have appointed the 12th day of October next, at the hour of 12 o'clock, meridian, at the office of W.W. Fambro in Cahawba, to hear and determine the said application. W.W. Fambro & G.G. Brooks, Justices of Peace

ISSUE 10-7-1837

A list of letters remaining in the Post Office at Cahawba, on the first day of October, 1837....

Henry Adams, Leo. Abercromby, Nith. Alilard, James Alexander, Alfred Averyt

Joseph Babcock, G.N. Bassett, James Battle, Miss Helen C. Beck, Wm. Bower, Edward Blackwood, Mrs. C.R.S. Beers, Samuel J. Bolling, Wm. Beasley, John Brown, G.W. Bolls, Mrs. Rachael Bell, John P. Blann, Maj. Boykin, L.L. Bass

Clerk of Co. Court, Joel C?rtis, Capt. Wm. Curtis, John Crumpton, John C. Caldwell, Wiley Collins, William Coleman, John Callilan, Dr. Willis Carr, Carter Cleveland, Jas. G. Covan, Levi Comeandler, James W. Craig, John

Miscellaneous Alabama Newspaper Abstracts --- Vol 1

Campbell, W.H. Cardy, John Conts, Andrew Crawford, David Chambers, Charles Cobb

Joseph Derry, T.F. Deckinson, Wm. Daniel, Nancy Denson, Nancy A.D., Pa?? Howell, A. Denham, Suthern Democrat

Vm. W. Gayle, V.G.M. Godhame, Francis J. Garrett, Archibald Glen, Thomas Graham, H?ups Gayle

Maj. F.C. Heard, Thomas Hogg, John M. Henry, E.B. Holloway, H.E. McKenny, John Hill

Levi Jordan, John G. Johnson, John Johnson, James Johnson, T.T. Jones

Thos. S. Keets, Mrs. Nancy Kimble, Samuel Kendal, Isaac King, James W. Kelly, Miss Eliza King, H.J. King

Miss Lemar, Wm. Lee, John S. Ledbetter, Mathew Locke, David Laugher, Adam S. Ledlow, E. Lyde

Dr. Robert Miles, L. Moore, Dr. B.H. Mitchell, A.H. Melstead, T. Morong & Co., Dr. Morgan, Jesse Moye, Mrs. J.C. Morong, John McGill, Ira Meador, Mrs. D. Mathews

Benj. Newton, James F. Nunn

A.L. Overton, Lewis Owen, Theodrick Oliver

Theo. M. Porter, John B. Pouncey, Mathis A. Perry, Wm. B. Powell, John Parnall, Miss Jane B. Peake, Ezekiel Pickens, Ira V. Parker, P. Philips, Porter & Pool, A. Punderson

Chas. Ross G?ge

Sheriff of Dallas, John Sulivan, Hon. R. Safford, Alfred Smith, Samuel Stewart, Jas. G. Sheppard, Abner Stone, Mrs. M. Spensby, Wm. Scott, D. Saltonstall, Henry Stanton, Miss Ann Speed, James Sandlin, John Short, John Smiley

Robert Thompson, Clark Taylor, E.R. Th?rp, R.E. Thompson, Mrs. S.T. Torrans, Robt. A. Thompson, James Thomas, Leroy H. Taylor, Mr. Talene

Doctor Ulmer, Wiley J. Underwood

MISCELLANEOUS ALABAMA NEWSPAPER ABSTRACTS --- VOL 1

P. Veglen, Green Vickers, J.W. Vedge

William Whitted, J.P. Waugh, Jas. E. Whitten, James Woodruff, S.A. Watts, Wm. N. Williams, G.J.S. Walker, Elisha Webb, T.O. White, Alexander M. Ward, James H. Wilson, Thomas Wilson, Moses Watkins, Miss A.S. Watts, Wm. Wadsworth, Thos. M. Williams, Mrs. G.A. Walker, A.C. Walker, Ferd. Williams, Joshua Watson, James Welch, Thos. Whitlock, Manning Walton

ISSUE 10-14-1837

Married, at Selma, on Tuesday evening, 10th inst., by the Rev. S.M. Nelson, Dr. Thomas Smith, to Miss Sarah L., daughter of Col. Thomas Kenan.

Died, in Selma, on the 6th inst., after a short illness, Mrs. Charlotte T., consort of James Cannte, aged 23 years and 6 months.

Died, on Monday the 9th inst., Mrs. Matilda, consort of Mr. Wm. Blevins, of Pleasant Valley.

Died, on Sunday, the 7th inst., at his residence in Monroe County, of a lingering illness, Mr. Johnathan English, aged 57 years.

Notice: Robert West is duly authorized to transact my business, during my absence from this place. Wm. West

Legal Notice: Dallas County, October 14, 1837, Littleton Chambless vs his creditors.

State of Alabama, Wilcox County, May Term 1837: Ezekiel Gaskins vs attachment, David Logan....the defendant is a non-resident.

Committed to the jail of Dallas County, on the 8th day of October, 1837, a negro woman, who calls her name Amey, and says she belongs to the estate of Maj. Michael J. Keenan, of Pleasant Valley, Dallas County, Ala. Said negro is about 34 or 35 years of age, stout and likely, dark complexion, one of her front teeth out and another defective....

ONE CENT REWARD: No charge will be paid on delivery of Robert Clement, an indented apprentice to the blacksmith business, about 17 years of age. And Washington Blakely, an apprentice to the Tanner's trade.... Carlowville, Ala., Sept. 22nd.

Committed to the jail of Dallas County, Ala., on the 11th day of October, a negro man who calls himself Lewis; said negro says that he ran away from

MISCELLANEOUS ALABAMA NEWSPAPER ABSTRACTS --- VOL 1

a man by the name of Henry Mets, who lives in Lexington, South Carolina, about 3 weeks ago; that he had been living with said Mets about three years to whom he was sold by a man who undertook to carry him from North Carolina to his real owner Charles Sewel, Mobile, Ala., and to whom he says he properly belongs. Said negro is of a black complexion, between 25 and 30 years old, 5'8" high, stout and well built...

ISSUE 10-28-1837

Married, on Thursday evening, the 26th inst., by the Rev. P.S. Graves, Mr. William J. Norris, merchant of Selma, to Miss R. Louisiana Rutherford, daughter of Col. William Rutherford of this county.

(Married) On the 12th inst., by the Rev. Mr. Parks, Mr. Joseph E. Norris to Miss Marian Sewell, all of Perry County.

Died, at Mobile, on Monday morning last, of yellow fever, Mr. John Chandler, a highly respectable citizen, formerly of this county.

(Died) In the town, yesterday morning, Mr. Mathew Locke, about 35 years of age.

ISSUE 11-11-1837

The undersigned having on the 16th day of October, 1837, by the Orphans' Court of Wilcox County, been appointed Administrator of the estate of Doct. Wm. N. Baker, deceased.... Prairie Bluff, Oct 24, 1837, James H. Wilson, Adm.

Committed to the jail in Monroe County, on the 13th inst., a negro man, who calls himself Alfred, and says he belongs to Laben Warren, of Lowndes County; near 23 or 25 years of age, 5' 8 or 9 inches high, of a pleasant countenance...

Administrative Notice: Dallas County on the estate of Jonas McCoullough, late of said county, deceased.... James V. Pettibone, Adminis'r Valley Creek, Nov. 4, 1837

Auction Sale: Will be sold on the 15th inst., to the highest bidder, the remaining stock of dry goods belonging to the late firm of Peck, Ward & Co. P.R. Pritchard

Ad for land for sale: Situated in Autauga County; Phillip Voegelin, Cahawba; Fred'k. Voegelin, Selma

MISCELLANEOUS ALABAMA NEWSPAPER ABSTRACTS --- VOL 1

ISSUE 12-2-1837

Married, on Thursday, the 23rd November, by the Rev. Flemming Freeman, Mr. Young F. Bohannan, to Miss Peninah A. Murray, all of this county.

Taken up by John McLeod.... a black mare mule.

Land For Sale: The plantation on which the subscriber lives, containing 360 acres, with about 200 acres in a state of high cultivation, situated on the Cahawba and Selma road; 7 miles south-east of Marion, Perry County; will be sold on accommodating terms, by immediate application. December 2nd, Lewis Howell

Dallas County legal notice: Rufus W. Greening, vs casa Nathan Ethridge: Gentlemen: Please take notice that I have applied to A.C. Mobley and T.G. Rainer, acting Justices of the Peace, for Dallas County, for the benefit of the act for the relief of insolvent debtors.... November 25th. Nathan Ethridge

Notice: The partnership of Morgan & Boykin is dissolved by the health of the senior partner, Wm. J. Morgan. The business will go on and be conducted under the name of Burwell Boykin, the surviving partner... Mobile, December, 2nd

Richard W. Gayle vs casa, David Y. Buck To Richard W. Gayle, William Chapman and brother, William Cockran, Peck, Ward, & Co., John L. Greening, Nathan Ethridge, Joseph W. Outlaw, Rufus Getchell, and Caleb Ethridge. Gentlemen: Please take notice that I have applied...for the relief of insolvent debtors.... Dallas County, November 25th..... D.Y. Buck

Died, in Montgomery, on Wednesday, the 22nd, the Hon. William D. Pickett. We understand that Judge Pickett was taken ill while holding the Montgomery Circuit Court, which attack caused his untimely and lamented dissolution.

Departed this life, at the residence of her father, (Thomas Craig) Mrs. Sarah M., consort of Col. Bernard Johnson, in the 23rd year of her age, after a long and painful illness of eight months....(*Selma Free Press*)

Application For Dower: Notice is hereby given, that we, Flemming Freeman and Nancy Freeman, his wife, in right of said Nancy, will apply to the Hon. the Judge of the Orphans' Court, of Wilcox County, at the Court to beholden for said county, on the 3rd Monday in December next, for Dower in the following lands, lying and being in said county, of which James Wade died possessed of an equitable interest; said Nancy Freeman being the relict and widow of said Wade; Viz: the east 1/2 of southeast 1/4 of section 4, township

Miscellaneous Alabama Newspaper Abstracts --- Vol 1

12, range 9. The west 1/2 of north-west of section 4, township 12, range 9. Also, at the same time and place, application as aforesaid, will be made for Dower in the interest which the said James Wade had and held, and died seized and possessed of, in, and for the following tract of land, lying in said county, as tenant in common with Archibald Cawthorn, deceased, Viz: the southwest 1/4 of section 3, township 12, range 9; which interest has been set apart to the heirs of said Wade, by partition. November 25th

State of Alabama, Wilcox County, Orphans' Court, November Term, 1837: William D. Scull vs William Philew, Administrator of Peter Philew, Sr., deceased.

Cahawba Polemic Society: At the last meeting of the Polemic Society, (Nov. 29th) the following gentlemen were elected officers for the ensuing six weeks: Dr. P.H. Earle, President, G.W. Seaman, Vice President, G.W. Clark, Sect'y, T.P. Harvey, Tres.

LOOK OUT FOR MURREL MEN: Whereas, Nathan Batts, a notorious rascal, formerly of Houston County, Ga., and lately of Dale County, Ala., did, from some time in May last, until October, harbor a negro man belonging to the undersigned....It is supposed he will go to Lee County, Ga., as he has a brother living near Starkville, in that county. He was assisted in harboring the boy by John Stapleton, Seaborn Stapleton, Zenothan Stapleton, and Zeno Stapleton, four brothers, all living in Dale County, Ala., who have also escaped from justice. DESCRIPTION: The Stapletons, are all fiddlers, John is about 5' '7", dark complexion; Seaborn, 5' 10", dark complexion; Zenothen, 5' 9", dark complexion; Zeno, 5' '6" fair complexion; Nathan Batts, about 5' '7", dark complexion, very talkative, laughs very loud and has a very bad countenance. Saml. M. Hill

State of Alabama, Wilcox County, Orphans' Court, November Term, 1837: Gabriel S. Haudley, Administrator of the estate of Mary C. Haudley vs Leonard Haudley, Jackson Haudley, William T. Mathews, Guardian, ad-litem of John Haudley, Benjamin Haudley, and William Haudley, minor heirs of the estate of Mary C. Haudley, deceased. Petition for sale of real estate.

Land For Sale: 325 acres of land, 3 miles west of Cahawba, 100 acres of which are cleared and under cultivation.... Also the east half of the north-west quarter of section 9, adjoining the plantation of Capt. Hendricks. For price & terms apply to W.W. Fambro, Cahawba, or B.R. Hogan, Mobile.

Administrators Sale: Will be sold, on the premises, on the 28th December next, all the personal property of James Johnson, deceased, consisting of Negroes, horses, mules, cattle, and hogs, household and kitchen furniture, corn and fodder. William Johnson, Adm

Sale of Real Estate: Whereas, the undersigned were appointed commissioners of the Orphans' Court of Dallas County, at the November Term of said court, to sell the real estate belonging to Henry McCaghren, deceased.... The purchaser giving notes with approved security, payable to Jane McCaghren, executrix of the last will and testament of Henry McCaghren, deceased. William Carr, John Dudley, Wm. M. Rumph Commissioners

Executor's Notice: Letters Testamentory have been this day granted to the undersigned, on the last will and testament of M.J. Kenan, late of Dallas County, deceased.... September 29th, 1837, F.S. Blount, Thomas Kenan Executors

CAUTION: The public are cautioned against trading for a note given by the subscriber to Kenith B. Murchison for $1,200, dated some time in May, 1835.... Philip C. Hansbrough

The state of Alabama, Dallas County, Orphans' Court, November Term, 1837. This day came Sarah Maples, Administratrix of the estate of Stephen W. Maples, deceased, and reported said estate to be insolvent and unable to pay the debts thereof in full, and applied to have said estate finally settled.

The state of Alabama, Dallas County: Wiley J. McElroy vs his creditors. To John J. Greening, Allen Davis and to each and every other of my creditors.

Ad for J. Babcock, Cahawba
Ad for R.D. Baxter

ISSUE 12-9-1837

Notice: I hereby forewarn all persons from trading for a note of hand, given by me, to Messrs. M. & H. Pruit, of Dallas County, Ala., payable on the 1st day of January next, as the consideration for said note has failed. H. Trippe

Marshall's Sale: Judgment taken April Term, 1837: William A. McCain vs Horatio Baxley & Solomon Adams. By virtue of a fi fa issued from the Clerk's Office, of the Circuit Court of the United States, for the Southern District of Alabama, will be sold to the highest bidder, Monday the 8th day of January, 1838, between the hours of sale, in the town of Cahawba, all the right title, claim and interest, both in law and equity, which Horatio Baxley has in and to the following described tracts or parcels of land; Viz: the SW 1/4 NE 1/4 and W 1/2 of SE 1/4 of section 23 - W 1/2 of SE 1/4 of section 22 - and S 1/2

Miscellaneous Alabama Newspaper Abstracts --- Vol 1

of NE 1/4 of section 24 the E 1/2 of SW 1/4 of section 24, and the E 1/2 of NW 1/4 of section 22, all in township 16, and range 7, in the district of land subject to sale, at Cahawba, Alabama, lying near Athens, Dallas County, levied on as the property of Horatio Baxley, to satisfy an execution in favor of Wm. A. McCain.

Marshall's Sale: Judgment taken April Term 1837: Wm. A. McCain, Wm. P. Gunn vs Horatio Boxley and Solomon Adams

Ad for land for sale, Jesse Beene

Land for Sale: Dallas County, Orphans' Court November Term: The real estate of Daniel Parnell, deceased, consisting of three very valuable tracts of land and including the plantation whereon he resided at the time of his death.... Willis A. Wilcox, Peter Mosely & Jonathan Mosely (Commissioners) Also, at the same time and place all the personal property belonging to said deceased.... Daniel Parnell, Jr., John Parnell, Adm's

ISSUE 12-16-1837

Sale of Real Estate: The undersigned were, appointed commissioners, by the Orphans' Court of Dallas County, at the December term of said court, to sell the real estate belonging to Wm. M. Cato, deceased... H.S. Rawls, W.G. McKeney, John McKeney

State of Alabama, Dallas County, Orphans' Court, December Term 1837: Person Davis Administrator of the estate of Ransom Davis, Jr., deceased.

Died, on Saturday evening the 2nd inst., Mrs. Margaret A. Alison, wife of Capt. Jacob S. Alison, departed this life, in the 34th year of her age.... Her remains were deposited in the cemetery attached to the Baptist Church, near Carlowville.

ISSUE 12-23-1837

Married, at Centreport, in this county, on the 17th inst., by the Rev. Mr. Sorell, Mr. John Stachan to Mrs. A. Vanpelt.

(Married) On Thursday evening last, by the Rev. Mr. Sreaoman, Mr. Joseph Chapman to Miss Mary Ann daughter of Col. B. Johnson, all of this county.

ISSUE 1-13-1838

Married, on Thursday evening, the 4th inst., by the Rev. Mr. Walker, Mr.

MISCELLANEOUS ALABAMA NEWSPAPER ABSTRACTS --- VOL 1

Henry N. Crocheron of Wilcox Co., to Miss Lucretia, daughter of Col. Henry King, of Marengo County.

Administrator's Notice: Letters of Administration, with the will annexed, have been this day granted to the undersigned, from the Orphans' Court of Marengo County, Ala., on the estate of Wm. Cabaniss, deceased... Jan. 1, 1838, Henry King, Adm'r

LOST: Near Craig's Ferry, on Cahawba River, on the 29th December last, a Black Morocco Pocket Book, containing about $600 in money, mostly bills on the merchant bank at Cheraw, S.C.... Greensboro, Jan. 8, 1838. P.W. Kiltrell

Strayed from the subscriber, on the 15th ult., near Mount Moria, Wilcox County, Ala., a yellow sorrel horse.... Edwin Knight.

DISSOLUTION: The co-partnership heretofore existing between the subscribers, under the firm of Fambro & Clark, was dissolved, by mutual consent, on the 1st inst... January 13, 1838, W.W. Fambro & G. Wm. Clark

ISSUE 1-20-1838

Notice: Will be sold, at public auction, before the court house door, in the town of Cahawba, on Saturday, the 10th day of March next, the following described property, Viz: The south east quarter of section 25, in township 16, of range 7, in the district of land subject to sale at Cahawba, Ala. Also, the following described slaves, Viz: a negro woman named Milly and her 6 children, Lucretin, Harriet, Jackson, Jennete, Mary and Sol; sold as the property of Jacob Hoot, under a mortgage to John S. McGuire, bearing date the 3rd day of August, 1835....

Wilcox County, Ala., Joseph A. Hall, Judge of the County Court: Notice is hereby given, that the application to me by Lewis L. Parham, of said county, who claims an undivided third part of all the following parcels of land, Viz: The east 1/2 of the south-west 1/4 of section 23, in township 13, range 7; containing 120 acres. Also the south-west ? of the south west 1/4 of section 23, in township 13, range 7. Each of said parcels of land being in said County of Wilcox, I have nominated Duman C. Smith, Hugh McLean, and Blakely Higginbotham, commissioners, to divide said tracks of land into three equal shares or parts....

Whereas, at the January Term of the Orphans' Court of Dallas County, the undersigned were appointed commissioners by the said court, to sell the lands belonging to the estate of Jacob Hollingsworth, deceased.... John

MISCELLANEOUS ALABAMA NEWSPAPER ABSTRACTS --- VOL 1

Dudley, Willie J. Sorell, Jos. H. Mead Commis's

The undersigned having opened a store at Cahawba invite the attention of the public, and Physicians in particular, to their stock of Drugs & Medicines.... G.W. Seaman & Co.

Ad for Drs. P. Walter Herbert & E.G. Ulmer

Letters of Administration having been granted to the undersigned by the Hon. the Judge of the County Court of Wilcox County, on the estate of James Files, deceased, on the 18th of December 1837.... J.P. Williamson, Adm'r

State of Alabama, Wilcox County: Notice is hereby given, that on application to me, by Charles Cook, of said State and County, who claims an undivided half of the north east quarter of section 11, in township 7, of range 11. I have nominated David N. Saunders, John Snell and James Yeldell, to divide said tract of land into equal shares or parts...

A list of letters remaining in the Post Office, at Cahawba, Alabama on the 1st of January 1838.

Asaph Abbey, Alexander Alexander, Milo B. Abercromie, Milton Acock

J.N. Bohannon, Joseph Babcock, Miss Mary F. Brookes, G.G. Brookes, Thos. H. Bowles, Elihu J. Boothe, Wm. Branch, Miss Helen C. Beck, Warren Brantly

J.D. Craig, Joel Curtis, A. Caldwell, Thomas J. Carver, Thomas J. Carrell, Allen Cochran, G.Y. Cowan, John R. Caldwell, Sheriff of Dallas

John Davis

Phillip Fatherlain, Mrs. M.L. Faulkner, S. Finch

L.C. Graham, Jacob Givhan, Elhannon Garret, Volney Garret, Thomas Gill, R.G. Gordan, James Goree

Rev. C. Hearn, Bethel Holmes, P.W. Herbert, Thomas Harris, Baker Hobson, Harrison Greps, John L. Higgins, Robert H. Hines, Sharp Hughs, Daniel Henry, Howard & Wilson

Wm. Johnson, Mrs. Ann Johnson, James W. Jeter, J.J. Jordan, George H. Jacob

Gen. E. King

MISCELLANEOUS ALABAMA NEWSPAPER ABSTRACTS --- VOL 1

Charles Levard, Benj. S. Logan, Col. Wm. Lawrence, Ananias Luton, W.F. Levie, Wm. F. Luckie, Adam Ledlow, Henry J. Linn, Doct. A. Lancaster

Col. Wm. Minter, Morgan Mills, J.B. Mulder, Abram Mathews, B.H. Mitchell, David Murdock, Wm. P. Molett, James Murr, John Miller, A. McNair, Richard C. Murray, U.G. Mitchell, John E. Mosely

Willis Nunilee

Wm. S. Phillips, Perine & Crocheron, H. Powell, James M. Powell, Jeremiah Prichard, W.S. Patten, Levi Parks, Miss Adeline Powell

Hamblen Quarles

E.T. Rees, David Russell, Linsey Roberts, Jesse Rasco

W.J. Sorrell, Jno. Sorell, James Sanfley, Stephen Smith, Alexander Shaw, Mrs. Sindonia Snow, J. Sneed, Wm. Sanders, John L. Supple, Stephen W. Snow

David Terry, Lucy B. Thomas, Elizabeth B. Thompson, John Tipton

Messrs. Underwood, Garner & Co.

Green Vickers, Wm. J. Verrell, Charles Volly

Col. John Walker, W.B.C. Walker, Alfred Wood, H.S. Wade, Ludwell Watts, A.C. Walker, Rev. Robert Walker, Mrs. A.P. Weaver, G.I. Walker, Moses Wadkins, James E. Whitten, A.R. Ward, Martin O. Whatley

B.C. Yancey, C.C. Young

ISSUE 1-27-1838

Married, on Thursday evening last, by the Rev. Mr. Nelson, Mr. Alfred King, of Burksville, Ky., to Miss Mary Ann Adams, daughter of Mr. Henry Adams, of this county.

(Married) On the same evening, by the Rev. Mr. Crumpton, Mr. Samuel Stewart to Miss Susan Johnson, daughter of John Johnson, all of this county.

Died, in this county, on Saturday morning (20th inst.) after a painful illness of several months, Francis L., youngest daughter of the Hon. J.J. Greening, aged one year, eleven months, and seven days.

MISCELLANEOUS ALABAMA NEWSPAPER ABSTRACTS --- VOL 1

Administrator's Notice: The undersigned having been appointed Administrator of the estate of Richard Ponsonby, deceased.... Wm. Ponsonby, Adm's

Lost or Mislaid: A note of hand, drawn by Robert Parrott, in favor of A. Hurlbert, or bearer, for $60, dated 12-12-1835.... Cahawba, 1-6-1838, Peck & Dunham

ISSUE 2-3-1838

Married, at Athens, in this county, on Thursday evening, 25th ult., by J.R. McElroy, Mr. H.H. Huckaby to Miss Hannah M. Adams.

(Married) On Wednesday evening, 24th ult., by the Rev. James Thompson, Calvin Powe, to Miss Adeline Mary Ann, eldest daughter of Col. Archibald K. Smith.

(Married) At the same time and place, by the same, Rev. gentleman, Thomas Powe to Miss Jane, daughter of Col. Archibald Smith, all of Wilcox County.

Died, at Higganum, Ct., on Saturday, the 13th ult., after several months suffering with the consumption, Samuel W., infant son of Albert M. and Harriet F. Clark.

Administrators Notice: Letters of Administration having been granted to the undersigned, on the estate of George Sage, deceased... Wm. P. Dunham, Adm'r

ISSUE 2-24-1838

$10 Reward: Lost in the town of Cahawba, on the 11th inst., by the subscriber, a calf-skin pocket book, of something more than the ordinary size, containing $43.... J.T. Watkins

Letters of Administration were granted to the subscriber, by the Orphans' Court of Dallas County, on the estate of Mitchell Wood, deceased, on the 20th September last. 1-5-1838, G.W. Thrash

Ad for J.P. Saffold, Attorney at law, office in Cahawba
Ad for house for sale, John S. Carver, Cahawba, 2-17-1838

EXTRAORDINARY OCCURRENCY: Thursday the 15th day of February, 1838, was a cloudy, dark, cold, rainy day, occasionally spiting now. About 3 o'clock P.M. there was heavy thunder, and the dwelling house of Maj. Jesse Beene, in this vicinity, was struck by lightning. It penetrated the comb of the house, about 8' from the west chimney, fractured a few of the shingles, passed down to the plate, without further injury to the roof; from the plate, it was conducted by a piece of scantling in the wall, to which the lathing in the dining room, the room above it, and two shed rooms which are opposite, were nailed, equal distance from the studding, throwing the plastering off, in all four rooms, for the space of 18 inches, on each side of the conductor, until it reached the chair-board; there it passed off, and seized the staff of an umbrella which was leaning against the wall, melted part of the slide, set the cotton covering on fire, which being wet, extinguished itself, passed down to the point, went through the carpet and floor, driving a large nail before it, making a hole the size of a musket ball, and killed a duck, which happened, at the moment, to be under the floor, at that spot. The children were at school, and no persons were near, except, Mrs. Beene, who was sitting in the dining room, and a servant girl in the room immediately above it, who at that moment, was doing something with a feather bed. They each received slight shocks only; Mrs. Beene, as it is believed, being saved by the carpet, and the servant girl by the feathers, both of which, are non-conductors of the electric fluid.

ISSUE 3-3-1838

Another Homicide: A difficulty took place in the southern part of this county, on Friday, the 16th inst., between William Kerr and Elisha Mosely, in the course of which the latter was killed by a pistol shot of the former...... (*Montgomery Journal*)

ISSUE 3-10-1838

Died, at the residence of his son, at Centre Ridge, on the 2nd ult., Mr. James Womack, aged 70 years. Mr. W. had been afflicted with the consumption for 16 years, which he bore with a Christian fortitude.... He has left a large circle of friends in North Carolina and Tennessee....

Ad for Will. Bird, attorney at law, Cahawba, Alabama

Administrator's Notice: The undersigned having been appointed Administrator of the estate of Francis W. Thomas, deceased, by the Orphans' Court of Wilcox County, on the 4th of January, 1838. Bird M. Pearson, Adm'r

ISSUE 3-17-1838

Administrator's Notice, Dallas County, March Term 1838: Joab Hill Administrator of the estate of James Kemble, deceased.... March 17th James D. Craig, Cl'k

MISCELLANEOUS ALABAMA NEWSPAPER ABSTRACTS --- VOL 1

Married, at Selma, on Thursday evening last, by the Rev. Mr. Mortow, Henry Leslie, of Norfolk, Va., to Miss Louisiana M. Stringfellow, of the former place.

MURDER: The village of Washington, Miss., says the Natchez Courier, "has had its ordinary quiet disturbed, by a tragedy, of which we have heard the following account. Some gamblers, on Friday night, the 9th inst., had a quarrel about their games, a encounter ensued, and one of the parties had his throat cut so badly that he expired.... A correspondent of the same paper, gives the annexed item: "I have just been to see the body of Alexander Campbell, who was killed last night, in an affray which he provoked, when intoxicated. He is the last of four brothers, of a respectable family in Westmoreland Co., Pennsylvania. Three of them died last summer, with congestive fever, and he, the last, was rescued by medical aid, from the very verge of the grave, to await a more awful death, by the hand of a fellow creature."

HIGH LIFE BELOW STAIRS: An encounter took place in this city on Friday evening last between two negroes, one owned by Judge Benson and the other by Mrs. Mayhew, both of this city, in which the former received a pistol shot from the latter in his face; his recovery is considered doubtful. Mrs. Mayhew's boy has been committed. *(Montgomery Journal)*

ISSUE 3-24-1838

Wilcox County estray notice: Taken up by James L. Reeves.... an old sorrel horse.
Ad for Centre Ridge Academical Association, Carlowville, Alabama;
Paul S.H. Lee, Pres't

ISSUE 3-31-1838

Married, on Tuesday evening last by _____Campbell, Mr. Gabril H. Harrel to Miss Eliza J. King, all of this county.

LAND FOR SALE: The subscriber being desirous to leave this country, wishes to dispose of his plantation on Bogue Chitto Creek, containing about 1,500 acres choice land, well adapted to the growth of cotton and corn, on which is a good dwelling house, and the necessary out houses; which he will sell at $5 per acre. Also a saw and grist mill, which is at present out of repair. March 31st, Jesse Johnson

Wilcox County estray notice: Taken up by Francis Hinds.....a dark bay pony horse...

MISCELLANEOUS ALABAMA NEWSPAPER ABSTRACTS --- VOL 1

$10 Reward: Lost, on Saturday morning last, either between Col. Barnes, and the Providence Meeting House, a small pocket wallet, containing $40 in cash.... Also 3 notes, one on James D. Craig, for $323.64, payable to Wm. Whitted, or bearer dated Jan. 23, 1836, and due 18 months after date. One on J. M. Mayes, for $100, payable to James Mayes, or bearer, dated Jan. 1838, and due one day after date. One on Jesse ?????? payable to James Mays, for $17.50 dated Jan. 1st., 1838, and due one day after date.... March 31st, James Mays

ISSUE 4-7-1838

Executor's Notice: Letters testamentary on the last will and testament of Samuel W. Oliver, deceased, having been granted to the undersigned..... Orphans' Court of Dallas County, on the 23rd day of March, 1838.... Elizabeth Oliver, Execu'x Henry Hunter, Executor

ISSUE 4-14-1838

Orphans' Court, April Term, 1838, Dallas County: This day came Mrs. Sarah Maples, Adm'x of the estate of Ann Williams, deceased, and applied for a final settlement of said estate....

Notice: The following persons have taken out license for retailing spirituous liquors in Dallas County, since the 1st January, 1838, for one year: Feb. 12, 1838, Israel B. Bigelow, Selma, Feb. 12, 1838, R.D. Baxter, Selma, Feb. 13, 1838, S. Crosby, Tavern & bar, Cahawba, Mar. 12, 1838, J.H. High, Retail Country, Mar. 12, 1838, Henry T. Jones, Retail Country, Mar. 12, 1838, Benjamin B. Ellis, Retail Country, Mar. 12, 1838, Raiford & Har?, Retail Country, Mar. 13, 1838, Moses Jones, Retail Country, Mar. 14, 1838, Wm. Hendrick, Retail Country

Wilcox County estray notice: Taken up by John Helman...a small brown mule, about 18 or 20 years of age....

Wilcox County estray notice: Taken up by Charles Satterwhite....a chesnut sorrel horse....

Wilcox County estray notice: Taken up by John H. Dekle....a black mare, with long tail....

Dallas County, Orphans' Court, April Term 1838: Dr. Edward Gantt, Administrator of the estate of Samuel Garett, deceased.

Wilcox County Administrator's Notice: on the estate of Agnus McIntosh, late

25

MISCELLANEOUS ALABAMA NEWSPAPER ABSTRACTS --- VOL 1

of said county, deceased... Jennet McIntosh, Adm'x, Alex. McLeod, Admr

Married, on Thursday, the 23rd November, by the Rev. Flemming Freeman, Mr. Young F. Bohannan to Miss Peninah A. Murray, all of this county.

Died, in Montgomery, on Wednesday, the 22nd ult., the Hon. William D. Pickett.

Departed this life, at the residence of her father, (Thomas Craig) Mrs. Sarah M., consort of Col. Bernard Johnson, in the 32nd year of her age, after a long and painful illness of eight months. *(Selma Free Press)*.

ISSUE 4-21-1838

Erastus Wheeler vs casa Wm. Roberts: To Erastus Wheeler, Messrs. Gayle & Bowers, Douglass Puckett, Wilkerson & Powers, Wm. Chapman & Brother, and Robert Cravens. Gentlemen, you will please take notice, that I have applied.... for the benefit of the act for the relief of insolvent debtors, and they have appointed the 23rd of April next, at Athens, to administer the oath, at which time, you may attend and object if you wish. March 17,
Wm. Roberts

A list of letters remaining in the Post Office at Cahawba, Dallas County, Alabama on the first day of April, 1838:

John Avery, B.F. Addams, John Addams, Sol. Addams, S.J. Addams, G.W. Acker, L.B. Acker

Thomas Butler, James A. Branch, Warren A. Brantly, Berry Bolton, Brantly & Harrell, Aken Brazeal, Charles Backus, Col. Barnes, Ostill Busbee, Blake Bradberry, Elizabeth Barlow, Mrs. S.M.G. Barns, Mrs. Sarah A. Bolton, Mrs. Sarah Booth

Wm. Cochran, Lauchlin Campbell, Amasa Cadwell, Duran Cox, Allen Coleman, J.B. Clark, John Crosby, Levi Comalander, John B. Carson, John L. Crocheron, Richard Cox, Norman Callender, Wiley Collins, Clerk of County Court, Mrs. Mary Clark

Seamon Deas, T. Dickinson, Daniel F. Dupree, Lensie H. Davie, Edward Day

J.J. Ellis, Winston Estes, Spencer Evans, Edw'ds Baylor & Earle, Samuel Edmondson, Samuel Etherage, Oliver Ellis

Miss Louisa Foy

MISCELLANEOUS ALABAMA NEWSPAPER ABSTRACTS --- VOL 1

Francis J. Garret, Wiley Gwyn, Edward Gunter, Wm. Gray, M.G. Gaston, James Gaston, Virgil Gardiner, S.P. Gambia, Jesse Grumbles

Carter B. Harrison, James R. Howie, Charles Holmes, Benj. Harrison, O. Herrington, J.W. Henstis, Samuel Hooper, David R. Heaggard, Wm. Hornbuckle, Wm. Hill, Rev. C. Hearn, B.R. Hogan, Samuel M. Houston, Patrick Hewes

Lewis Jackson

Thomas Kenan, Mrs. M. Kenworthy, Col. Geo. C. King

Issac W. Lenoir, Annias Loaten, C.L. Leer, Dr. Lancaster's Lewis, Benj. S. Logan, Mathew Lock, James W. Lapsley, Henry Lesley, George Leffers

U.G. Mitchell, John Moore, Lauchlin McInnes, Robert R. Minter, Wm. G. McKinney, John G. McLean, Matthew A. Marshall, John McLaughlin, A.B. Moore, McLaughlin & Norwood, John Mitchell, J.E. Matthews, Peter McIntire

E.P. Noble, Samuel New, Mrs. Sarah Nickson, John A. Norwood

Miss M.H. Ogolvie

Perine & Crocherson, Jeremiah Pitman, W.W. Parsons, Dorroh Phillips, Harrison Persons, John S. Pegues, James M. Powell, Hudson Powell, J.V. Perryman, John Paulling, Mrs. A. Potts, Chy Pomroy

George F. Randolph, John Richey, Wm. E. Reid, Dr. Geo. Rieves, Rawlen Raines, Wm. Rutherford, L. Rose, P. Rutherford, Robert Rae, John Roper, Miss Martha Richey, Thomas Rutherford, B.C. Rowan.

Harvey Smith, James K. Smith, Wm. S. Smith, John Short, Sheriff of Dallas, Isaac Stephens, John Stidman

David Terry, Archibald Thompson, A.J. Thompson

John J. Ulmer, Dr. W.J. Underwood

Thomas Vanderslice, Littleberry Vasser

James C. White, Thomas L. Whitlock, George L. Weaver, Wm. Whitted, Richard H. West, Thomas Watts, Harvey J. Wright, James S. Williamson, M.G. Wood, Frederick H. West, Joseph Wilbanks, Matthias Weissinger, Becton Wadkins, J.B. Wilkins, Marshal Wrenn, Wm. Waddle, James Williams,

Miscellaneous Alabama Newspaper Abstracts --- Vol 1

J.M. Wardwell, Dr. J.F. Wallis

Wm. L. Yancey

ISSUE 4-28-1838

Strayed from the subscriber about the last of March, a dark bay horse, six years old, with a blaze face, black main and tail.... S. Finch, Cahawba, Ala., April 21st

Strayed from Selma, a short time since, two sorrel horse... Thomas W. Street, G.O. Ghehegan

Ad from Wm. Wilson, Cahawba, Alabama

Sheriff's Sale: The east 1/2 of the northwest 1/4 & the west 1/2 of the northeast 1/4 of section 18, township 15 of range 7: levied on as the property of Benj. Adams, to satisfy an execution in my hands for collection, in favor of Drury M. Millan.... April 21st

I hereby caution and forewarn all persons not to trade for a promissory note of hand made payable by myself, to James Battle, or bearer, one day after date, for $146 and some cents, dated the 14th of Feb., 1835, as I have an offset against said note sufficient to cove it, and I will not pay said note until I am compelled by law, unless my claim is allowed, then I am ready and willing to pay it, for it is just, otherwise I will not. April 7th, John L. Bulla

ISSUE 5-12-1838

Mr. D'Grafton Flanniken, of this county, was drowned on the morning of the 7th, inst., in attempting to swim the Alabama River. The unfortunate man was intoxicated at the time, and it is probable was taken with the cramp, when within 30 yards of the shore. Our citizens were engaged all the day in dragging the river for his body, but without success. Up to this date (Saturday) the body has not been found.

State of Alabama, Dallas County Circuit Court, Spring Term: Samuel Shaddock vs George W. Willis.... the defendant is a non resident.... May 4, 1838.

State of Alabama, Dallas County Circuit Court, Spring Term: Matt Gayle vs Kinchen W. McKinney, in Chancery....defendant is a non resident.... May 4, 1838.

MISCELLANEOUS ALABAMA NEWSPAPER ABSTRACTS --- VOL 1

Ad for Peter M'Intyre, Cahawba, May 5, 1838
Ad for Wm. Wilson, Cahawba, April 21, 1838

ISSUE 5-19-1838

Notice: Joseph Furr vs His creditors: Messrs. James Clrrk (Clark?) Loyd Burnes, James Chapman, Silas Morgan, Richard Gayle, Jackson M'Elroy, James Jordan, Hiram High, and others concerned. Gentlemen you will please take notice, that Joseph Furr has applied to me, the Judge of the County Court, of Dallas County, for the benefit of the laws passed for the relief of insolvent debtors... May 12th, Will E. Bird

State of Alabama, Dallas County, Orphans' Court, May Term, 1838: This day came Enoch Bell, Administrator of the estate of Wesley A. Jones, deceased, and applied for final settlement of said estate.

State of Alabama, Dallas County, Orphans' Court, May Term, 1838: Vestil J. Johnson, Adm'r vs Richard Blalack's Heirs: Petition to sell land.

Notice: Letters testamentary were this day granted to the undersigned on the estate of William Wren, deceased... May 14th, Lewis B. Mosely, Ex'r

ISSUE 5-26-1838

The body of Mr. D'Grafton Flanniken who was drowned on the 7th inst., in the Alabama, at this place, was discovered floating down the river, on Thursday, the 17th inst., opposite the mouth of Bogue Chitto. A buzzard was standing on the body; and it appeared, had mutilated it, very much, especially about the face. The friends of the deceased, caused the body to be decently interred on the next day.

Married, on Centre Ridge the 20th inst., by J.H.D. Womack, Mr. Andrew A. Elliott to Miss Louisa Parson.

DISSOLUTION: The copartnership, heretofore existing between the undersigned, is dissolved by mutual consent. May 18, 1838, Jesse Beene & W.W. Fambro

Ad for the law office of Jesse Beene & Benj. C. Yancey

Wilcox County estray notice: Taken up by Duncan C. Smith....a small bay mare about 5 years old....

Wilcox County estray notice: Taken up by John W. Daniel....a mouse colored horse mule, about 7 or 8 years old...

Notice is hereby given, that the undersigned having been appointed executors, of the last will and testament of David Pace, deceased, (in which will and testament a certain negro man slave, named Joe, of rather light complexion, about 40 or 45 years of age was ordered to be set free, after all the debts, of the estate of said David Pace, were paid), will petition the Orphans' Court of Dallas County, State of Alabama, of the 2nd Monday of August next, to emancipate said negro man slave, the debts of said estate having been all paid. May 19, 1838   Wm. Hendrick, Tilman Hitt

$50 Reward, strayed or stolen from the subscriber, on or about the 15th inst., a large bay horse, about 5' high... May 26th, Julius Snead

Died, in Montgomery, on the 3rd inst., Mr. William Crosby, a native of Charleston, S.C., aged 30 years; after a painful and lingering illness, which he bore with the utmost fortitude. He left a wife and one child to mourn an irreparable loss.

SHERIFF'S SALE: Will be sold before the court house door in the town of Cahawba, on Monday the 2nd July next, within the usual hours of sale, the south east 1/4 of the north west 1/4 of section 28 of township 16 of range 7; levied on as the property of Solomon Adams, to satisfy sundry executions in my hand for collection. June 2,1838, I.N. Campbell, Sheriff

Will be sold before the court house door in the town of Cahawba, on Monday the 2nd July next.... the east 1/2 of the south east 1/4 of section 16 of township 15 of range 7; levied on as the property of Wm. Chapman and Joseph Chapman, to satisfy sundry executions in my hands for collection. I.N. Campbell, Sheriff

Will be sold before the court house door in Cahawba.... on the 2nd day of July next, the west 1/2 of the north west 1/4 of section 9 of township 13 of range 10; levied on as the property of John W. Goodwin, to satisfy an execution in favor of Thomas W. Holden. June 2nd, 1838, I.N. Campbell, Sheriff

ISSUE 6-16-1838

$100 Reward, Runaway from the subscriber in the city of New Orleans, on the 18th May, the mulatto woman Hester; she is about 20 years of age, small stature, well made, bright yellow color, and likely countenance, speaks English only, but understands a little French when spoken to. She took with her a female child, Harriet, a very bright quarteroon who will pass almost any where for white. The child is between 4 and 5 years of age, has long black eyes [sic], long dark brown curled hair, is of a delicate appearance, extremely small hands and feet, has very interesting handsome features rather small for her age and has the upper front teeth much decayed. It shows considerable intelligence, and will occasionally when asked her name, call herself LoLo.....The above slave was raised by the family of Ravenel, in Charleston, S.C., was bought in March, 1834, in New Orleans, by the subscriber of Thomas Taylor Williamson, a negro trader from Charleston, S.C., now living at Red River, near Alexander, La. She had been living previous to being sold, at the plantation of Mr. Richard B. Harrison, Dallas County, Ala., and as she frequently expressed a desire to return to that place or its vicinity, it is probable that she may have made her way into that neighborhood.... A. Byrenheidt, No. 43 St Louis St., New Orleans, June 1, 1838

Wilcox County, County Court, January Term, 1838: John W. Evans, use &c. vs John Rowell: Attachment levied.

Dallas County Orphans' Court, January Term, 1838: This day came Samuel Chesnut, Administrator of the estate of Elizabeth Ross, deceased.... final settlement of said estate.

Sale of Real Estate: Whereas, the undersigned were appointed at the June Term of the Orphans' Court of Dallas County, commissioners to sell the real estate of which Richard Blalock, died, seized and possessed, to wit: The N.W. 1/4 of N.E. 1/4 of section 27, township 14, range 11. The E 1/2 of S.W. 1/4 of section 26, township 14, range 11, and W 1/2 of N.W. 1/4 of section 36, township 14, range 11.... Green Underwood, John Smiley, Thos. J. Webster, Commissioners

State of Alabama, Wilcox County, January Term, 1838, Cullen & Riley vs John Rowell: Attachment levied.

ISSUE 6-23-1838

Married, on Wednesday the 20th inst., in Cahawba, by the Rev. S.S. Lewis, Mr. Geo. R. Tuthill of Mobile to Miss Phebe Ann Perine of Staten Island, N.Y.

THE SOUTHERN DEMOCRAT
CHANGES NAME TO THE CAHABA DEMOCRAT

ISSUE 7-21-1838

Committed to jail in Monroe County, a runaway negro man who calls himself John, and says he belongs to John Cunningham of South Carolina, and that he made his escape while traveling through this country, at Cahawba; he is about 35 years of age, 5' and 9" high.... Monroeville, July 1, 1838

Dallas County Creditor's Notice: George Ponsonby vs his creditors.

A list of letters remaining in the post office at Cahawba, Ala., on the 1st of July, 1838.

John D. Alexander, Benjamin F. Addams, Solomon Addams, James Anderson, Horatio Allen

Peter Buffington, Jas. M. Blann, Stephen Blann, F.M. Bradly, Eldr. J.A. Butler, Briston & Roper, T.M. Brantly, J. Babcock, John Banone, Elihu J. Boothe, Richard Blackwood, Jesse Beene, Henry Burton

Ezra Cleveland, Clerk of County Court, J.W. Clark, George W. Carvill, John Crawford, Mr. Cayol, H.J. Crocheron, Thomas Cook, Clerk of Circuit Court, Wm. W. Clark

B.P. Drew, Newell Day, Thos. Dawell, Edward Day

Richard T. Forsythe, Wm. J. Falconer, Daniel Fitzgerald, Stephen Fedrick, Solomon Finch, John R. Freman

Jas. Gaston, George W. Gayle, Andrew J. George, James George, T.B. Golesby, Wm. & A.J. Gayle, John S. Gager, John J. Greening, Wm. W. Gayle, Matt Gayle

H.C. Hansborough, Mrs. Ann Hatcher, W.L. Holoway, Richard Hilburn, J.W. Hewstis, Partick Hughs, John J. Heard, Benjamin Harrison, Albert Hulbert, B.F. Witt, Hardiman Harrel, Robert J. Haden, Richard Harrison, Jacob Hammock

Wm. Johnson, G.E. Jones, Archibald Johnson, B.V. Jones

Johnson Kirkland, Benajah King, G.E. King

Jarvis Langford, J.W. Lapsley, James P. Lossy

A.G. Magers, S.D. Miller, Wm. Minter, Alex. McDonald, L.D. McNair, Mrs. M. McCord, G.W. Molkey, John McLaughlin, Geo. Molkey, Hartwell S. Marris, Jas. D. Molkey

Wm. E. Norwood, Sampson Nance, E.P. Noble, John Nye

Miscellaneous Alabama Newspaper Abstracts --- Vol 1

Theo. Oliver, A.M. Otley

Theo. M. Porter, P.M. Crocheron's Landing, Peck & Dunham, Col. C.H. Pickering, Jeptha Parnall, Joseph Pickens, Seymore B. Powell, Abner Paine, Abraham Pearce, Madison Powell, Perine & Crocheron, Jas. A. Prestwood, Stephen D. Pelham, Jas. S. Porter, Wm. Ponsonby

Anderson Rochell

Sheriff of Dallas, Orin Savage, L.H. Sullivan, Mary A.J. Stephens, Thos. E. Smith, Jas. Safford, Jos. P. Saffold, Capt. R.B. Simms, John Smith

David Terry, Josiah Todd

Sarah R. Walker, Geo. J.S. Walker, Agness Watts, Master R.H. West, Mathew E. Walker, Master Geo. White, Jacob T. Wadkins, Thomas O. White, Wm. Wade, C. White, Michael Wessenger, Richard B. Warters, Green Williams, J.D. Williams, B.J. Wright, Ashly Wood

Ad for Drs. J.A. English and P.H. Earle

Sheriff's Sale: .... Levied on as the property of Andrew Niolep to satisfy an execution in my hands for collection in favor of Kissam & Co. Cahawba, June 30, 1838

ISSUE 7-21-1838

Will be sold before the court house door in Cahawba, within the usual hours of sale, on Monday the 6th day of August next, the east half of the north east quarter of section # 6 of township 15 of range 12; also the east half of the south east quarter of section # 31, and the south west quarter of section # 32 of township 16, of range 12, in the district of land subject to sale at Cahawba; levied on as the property of Carter B. Harrison, to satisfy sundry executions in my hands for collection in favor of Wm. May, use of Precilla Reynolds, &c. Cahawba, June 30, 1838, I.N. Campbell, Sheriff

Will be sold before the court house door in Cahawba, within the usual hours of sale, on Monday the 6th day of August next, the east half of the south east quarter of section 36 of township 13 of range 11, containing 80 acres more or less, in the district of land subject to sale at Cahawba; levied on as the property of Morgan Mills, to satisfy an execution in my hands for collection in favor of Caty Riley and others. Cahawba, June 30, 1838, I.N. Campbell, Sheriff

MISCELLANEOUS ALABAMA NEWSPAPER ABSTRACTS --- VOL 1

For Sale: Two latest style buggies, also one Barouche. Inquire of Paten R. Pritchard, Cahawba, June 23rd.

ISSUE 7-28-1838

Died, in Merriweather County, Georgia, on the 17th July, Major James Hatcher, aged 63 years. Maj. Hatcher was a native of South Carolina, but at an early age became a citizen of Georgia, where he resided until 1818, at which time he changed his residence to Alabama, and settled at Hatchers Bluff....

I lost my spectacles, with gold frames, at or near Mr. Jones' Steam Mill west of Cahawba, two weeks ago; my name is engraved on one of the bows.... Jesse Beene

Notice: The undersigned having taken Francis A. Lee into copartnership, on the 29th ult., the Factorage Business for the future will be conducted under the name of Kane & Lee.. Mobile, June 21, 1838, D.D. Kane

Will be sold before the court house door in the town of Cahawba, on Monday the 6th of August next, within the usual hours of sale, all the undivided interest which William E. Norwood holds or has in the following lands, Viz: The east 1/2 of section # 30, northeast 1/4 of section # 29, and the west 1/2 of the southeast 1/4 of section # 20, all in township # 15 of range 9; levied on by virtue of an execution in my hands for collection, in favor of H. McLean & Co. Cahawba, July 2, 1838, I.N. Campbell, Sheriff

MARSHALL'S SALE: Bartlett Davis & Co., vs Dupree & Paulding, Judgment taken April Term, 1838. By virtue of a fi fa issued from the Clerk's Office of the Circuit Court of the United States, for the Southern District of Alabama, will be sold to the highest bidder, on the first Monday in September next, between the usual hours of sale in the town of Cahawba, all the interest of Messrs. Dupree and Paulding in Lots, # 99 1/2 and 100 1/2, and all improvements thereon; said lots situated in the town of Selma, Dallas County. Levied on as the property of Dupree and Paulding to satisfy an execution in my hands. R.L. Crawford, U.S. Marshall by David White, Deputy

MARSHALL'S SALE: Stout Engoldsby, &co. vs Dupree & Paulding, Judgment taken April Term, 1838.

Will be sold before the court house door, in the town of Cahawba, on Monday the 6th August next, within the usual hours of sale, the east 1/2 of the southeast ? of section 16 of township 15 of range 7: levied on as the property of Wm. & Joseph Chapman....

Miscellaneous Alabama Newspaper Abstracts --- Vol 1

ISSUE 8-4-1838

MARSHALL'S SALE: Charles C. Mills, vs B. Adams, & others, judgment taken April Term, 1838....

ADMINISTRATOR'S SALE: By consent of the heirs of the estate of Phoed's Rutherford, deceased, I will offer for sale on the premises at public auction, on Saturday the 25th of August next, the following tract or parcel of land, lying and being in the County of Dallas, and State of Alabama, to wit: The E. 1/2 of the S.E. 1/4 of section #17, township #15, range #8, containing eighty acres and 18 1/2 hundredths of acres. Also the N.E. 1/4 of the N.W. 1/4 of section #21, township #15, containing 40 acres and 18 1/2 hundredths of acres. Also the S.W. 1/4 of the S.E. 1/4 of section #17, township #15, range #8, containing 40 & 9 hundredths of acres. Max. Rutherford, Adm.

Administration on the estate of Starke Hunter, late of Conecuh County, deceased, was this day granted by the Judge of the County Court of said county, to the undersigned.... Aug. 11th, Elizabeth Hunter, Adm'x, Henry Hunter, Adm'r

ISSUE 8-18-1838

For Sale: A first rate work mule both for wagon & plough. Terms cash. For further particulars, apply to L. Lesley, at the subscribers plantation, 2 miles from Cahawba. W.L. Yancey

INFORMATION WANTED: Of one Rudolph Hufford, a Printer, who left Cahawba, Alabama, for Mobile, some time in November, 1836, and not having since returned, his wife is anxious to learn where he is (if living)... Tuscaloosa, July 28, 1838, Sarah Hufford

The State of Alabama, Dallas County: Orphans' Court, August Term, 1838: This day came Isaac Dubose, Administrator of estate of Joseph Baker, dec'd, and applied for final settlement of said estate....

The State of Alabama, Dallas County, Orphans' Court, August Term, 1838: Durant Westbrook vs Lewis B. Moseley, Ex'or, Petition for Titles

The State of Alabama, Dallas County, Orphans' Court, August Term, 1838: This day came Samuel G. Norris, Executor of the last will and testament of Bethada Brown, deceased, and applied for a final settlement of said estate....

The State of Alabama, Dallas County, Orphans' Court, August Term, 1838: John Gildersleeve and Wm. Charlotte, vs John Hooper, executor of Woodley

MISCELLANEOUS ALABAMA NEWSPAPER ABSTRACTS --- VOL 1

T. Hooper, dec'd: Petition for Title. This day came the petitioners by their attorney, and filed their petition, to compel the said John Hooper administrator as aforesaid to make titles to them to a certain tract of land, lying in Autauga County, known as the tract of land which he the said Woodley T. Hooper bought of Archilus Pope and William Swingston, containing six hundred acres; and it appearing to the satisfaction of the court, that said Woodley T. Hooper has sold said tract of land to John Franklin and had given him a Bond for Titles, and that said Franklin had transferred said Bond to the petitioners; and it also appearing that said Woodley T. Hooper had departed this life, without making Titles to said tract of land, and that full payment had been made for said land....

ISSUE 8-25-1838

Died, at L.B. Moseley's, on Monday, the 20th inst., after a short, but severe illness, Mary Jane, daughter of Allen Coleman, in the 12th year of her age. The subject of this notice, having lost her mother, in infancy, was adopted by Mr. & Mrs. Moseley....

The subscriber offers for sale two plantations, or tracts of land, containing about two thousand acres, situated between the two Mulberry Creeks, in Autauga County.... Mulberry, Autauga Co., July 6, 1838, S.H.N. Dickson

ISSUE 9-1-1838

Died, on Thursday, 23rd day of August, in the 14th year of his age, John Warren, eldest son of Hamblin Quarles, of this county.....

ISSUE 9-8-1838

Disease preys not always "on the thorn and brambles of the wilderness, but on the rose and passion flower of human excellence and gentleness." This was exemplified in the death of George Earle, youngest child of Sarah and William L. Yancey, who departed this life, on the 23rd of August, in Greenville, So. Ca. [sic], aged six months....

MARSHALL'S SALE: United States vs Bartrum Robeson, By virtue of a fi fa issued from the Clerk's Office of the United States Court, for the Southern District of Alabama, will be sold to the highest bidder, on the 1st. Monday in October next, between the usual hours of sale in the town of Cahawba, a negro man, named Simon, a woman named Isabella, and a girl Maria. Levied on as the property of Bartrum Robinson, to satisfy an execution in my hands.

Miscellaneous Alabama Newspaper Abstracts --- Vol 1

SHERIFF'S SALE: Will be sold before the courthouse door, in Cahawba, on Monday the 1st day of October next, the southwest quarter and the northeast quarter of section 23 of township 16 of range 7, in the district of land subject to sale at Cahawba: Levied on as the property of Horatio Boxley, to satisfy an execution in favor of William Chapman and brother.

Will be sold before the court house door in the town of Cahawba, on Monday the 1st day of October next....the east 1/2 of the northeast 1/4 of section # 9; also the east 1/2 of the south east 1/4 of section # 31 of township # 16 of range 9, and the east 1/2 of the north east 1/2 of section # 31 of township # 16 of range # 9; levied on as the property of Lorenzo Roberts to satisfy an execution in my hands for collection, favor of Benjamin Adams.

ISSUE 9-22-1838

Died, on the 9th inst., at her fathers' residence in Dallas County, after a painful illness of sixteen days.... Eliza Ann Camp, the only child of Joseph and Eliza Camp, in the 15th year of her age....

State of Alabama, Dallas County, Orphans' Court, Sept. Term, 1838: Merit W. Roberts & Wife, Exparte, Petition for Dower: This day came the said Merit W. Roberts and Lucinda, his wife, (formerly Lucinda Simpkins, widow and relict of John Simpkins deceased), by their attorney, and filed their petition for dower in the lands, tenements, and hereditaments, of which the said John Simpkins, died seized, Viz: The south west quarter of section one, in township thirteen, of range eleven, lying in Dallas County....

ISSUE 9-29-1838

Died, on the 24th inst., near this place, after a long and painful illness, Eliza Ada Saltmarsh, daughter of Alanson and Mary A. Saltmarsh, aged about 14 months.

ISSUE 10-13-1838

The State of Alabama, Dallas County, Orphans' Court, October Term, 1838: E.J. Underwood, vs Joseph Ramsey, Adm'r: Petition for Titles. This day came the said E.J. Underwood, and filed his petitions, to compel the said Joseph Ramsey, administrator of the estate of Hardy Gooding, deceased, to make titles to him to 12 1/4 acres of land, lying in section 36, T. 14, R. 11...lying in Dallas County....

The State of Alabama, Dallas County, Orphans' Court, October Term, 1838: I.N. Campbell, Sh'ff Adm'r. vs Evan Evan's heirs: Petition to sell land: This

Miscellaneous Alabama Newspaper Abstracts --- Vol 1

day came the said Isaac N. Campbell, Sheriff, and administrator of the estate of Evan Evans, deceased, and filed his petition for a sale of the land belonging to the said deceased, and it appearing to the Court that Jeremiah Mills, in right of his wife, and Harvey Mills, in right of his wife, are heirs at law to the estate of said Evan Evans, deceased, and that their residence is unknown to the petitioner....

State of Alabama, Dallas County, Orphans' Court, October Term, 1838: Abram Sheppard vs I.N. Campbell, Adm'r. : Petition for Titles: This day came the said Abram Sheppard by his attorney and filed his petition to compel the said Isaac Campbell, administrator, by virtue of his office of the estate of Aaron H. Milsted, deceased, to make titles to him to the S.W. quarter of the S.E. quarter of section 21, township 14, of range 10, in said county....

The State of Alabama, Dallas County, In Chancery: Benjamin S. Logan & Wife, vs Joshua W. Lockwood, Stephen Lee Lockwood, Regina A. Lockwood, Dangrige C. You, and Mary Lee, his wife formerly Mary Lockwood, Benjamin C. Webb and his wife Alison H. formerly Alison H. Lockwood, and Francis J. Lee.... residence of South Carolina.

Notice: Administration on the estate of Lloyd Barnes, late of Dallas County, deceased, was granted by the Judge of the County Court.... to the undersigned.... Demaris Barnes, Admr'x Henry J. King, Adm'r

Notice: Ranaway from the subscriber about the 15th of August last, one mile from King's Landing, a negro man by the name of Abram, about 5' 8 or 9 inches high, dark complexion, 40 years of age, he is blind in his right eye, but cannot be discovered without close examination, slow spoken, and shuts one eye when spoken to, has a down look, I believe one fore tooth out.... John E. Barnes

<u>A list of letters remaining in the post office at Cahawba, Dallas County, the 1st October, 1838:</u>

Alexander Alexander, John D. Adams

George Barlow, Jeremiah F. Bently, Elihu J. Booth, R.D. Baxter, R.E.B. Baylor, Joseph C. Babcock, Caroline Burkit, Wm. H. Bonneau, B. Bohanan, George W. Barlow

James D. Craig, Isaac N. Campbell, Polly Camble, George W. Clarke, Carter Cleaveland, James Collins, Mary Clarke, Willis Carr, Col. Cuthbert, Wm. C. Clifton

Miscellaneous Alabama Newspaper Abstracts --- Vol 1

Samuel Durraw, John Dudly, Emanuel Deckart, Wm. Davis, A.A. Dexter

Lewis Ethridge, John S. Edmondson, Robert English

George R. Frazer, George Frazer, Samuel Frost, Wm. G. Fisher, Flamin Freeman

Uriah Grigsby, John Gayle, John W. Garrett, Obadiah Gibson, George W. Gayle, Matt Gayle

Silman Hill, Wm. Hendrick, B.R. Hogan, Thomas O. Hollaway, Josiah Harrell, Bethel Holmes, Robert S. Hatcher, Jacob Hoot, Carter B. Harrison, Harvey & Craig, Thomas C. Holloway, Edwin B. Holloway, P.C. Hansbrough, Patrick Hughes

Lewis Jackson, John Johnson, Julius C.P. Jones, Thomas Jordan, James Johnson

Eliza A. Kemp, Alfred King, Andrew King, H.J. King, Vicy Kornegay

Wm. C. Lary, D. Long, L. Love

Bluford, McRight, Lucy McGeehee, Benj. D. Moseley, John S. Morris, John McLean, Neel McLearin, Wily Mason, Andrew McCaton, Wm. P. Molett, James McCrea, Josiah McCants, Isaac W. McElroy

W.W. Olds

T.M. Porter, Peck & Dunham, Elena Parnold, Richmond D. Pegues, Jeremiah Pitman

Jane Russel, A.L. Razer, Joseph Rane, John W. Ross, Henry Randle, R.D. Rice, Drury Ross, John Roper

Rosanna Smith, Grus Small, Henry Stidman, Robt. Sturdivant, John E. Smith, James Saffold, Robert Singleton, John Strachon, Abram Shepprard, James H. Smith, Josiah H. Smith, John D. Saunders, Orrin Savage, Edwin T. Sturdivant, Varnis Smith, Elizabeth Swepson, Thomas C. Sullivan

Parcal B. Traylor, George R. Trarer

Wm. S. Verrell, Bill Varnell, James H. Vail

Elisha Webb, Page R. Windham, John Walker, Thomas Welch, David

Miscellaneous Alabama Newspaper Abstracts --- Vol 1

Weaver, Thos. O. White, James Williams, E.B. Wilson, A.J. Warford, Wm. Whitted, John D. Williams, J.J. Wilson, Joseph B. Wilbanks, D. Wolfe, John Wilder, Osborn White

Land for sale, for the first time: .... situated 5 miles south east of Cahawba, on the Greenville road, on which my son T.B. Sorell, at present resides, is offered for sale, containing 1,280 acres.... adjoins the lands of Mr. P. Millhouse, Doct. E.W. Hamilton, Maj. George Bowie, and R.S. Hatcher. Dallas County, Ala. John Sorell

ISSUE 10-20-1838

Administration on the estate of Stephen Morgan, Sen., late of Dallas County, deceased.... Daniel Morgan, Sackfield Brewer, James J. Morgan Adm'rs

Wilcox County, Orphans' Court in Vacation, October 6th, 1838: Upon the application of Watkins Salter, Administrator of the estate of Samuel Salter, deceased, for a final settlement of said estate....

Sheriff's Sale: ....Levied on as the property of Carter B. Harrison to satisfy an execution in favor of Taylor & Wood

Notice: To Philips & Edwards, attorneys for Beers & Prevost, and Gascoigne & Holly, Bethel Holmes, James B. Clark, attorney for Chas. K. Bullard, Beene & Fambro, and all others concerned. I hereby notify you, that I have made application.... for the benefit of the laws passed for the relief of insolvent debtors.... Silas Morgan

Land Sale: Whereas at the September Term, 1838, of the Orphans' Court of Butler County, the undersigned were appointed commissioners to sell the real estate of Henry West, deceased, in Dallas County.... Thomas M. Matthews, John E. Barnes, James Kelly, commissioners

ISSUE 11-10-1838

Died, at the residence of her father, near Carlowville, in Dallas County, on the 11th of October, Harriet Rebecca Lee, youngest daughter of Maj. Paul S.H. Lee, in the 16th year of her age.

Sheriff's Sale: Will be sold before the court house door in the town of Cahawba, on Monday the 3rd day of December next....the east 1/2 of the southeast 1/4, and the northwest 1/4 of the northeast 1/4 and the east 1/4 of the northeast 1/4 of section 21, all in township 16 of range 9: levied on as the property of T.M. Jackson and P.R. Prichard, to satisfy an execution in my

MISCELLANEOUS ALABAMA NEWSPAPER ABSTRACTS --- VOL 1

hands for collection in favor of Benjamin Adams against Lorenzo Roberts, T.M. Jackson and P.R. Prichard.

Will be sold before the court house door in Cahawba, on Monday the 3rd December next.... lots Nos. 69, 100, 101, and 103 in the town of Cahawba: levied on as the property of Bartram Robeson, to satisfy an execution in my hands for collection, in favor of Matt. Gayle.

Will be sold before the court house door in Cahawba, on Monday the 3rd of December next.... the west 1/2 of the south east 1/4 of section 19 of township 13 of range 10.... levied on as the property of Simeon Nunellee to satisfy an execution in favor of James S. Williams.

Ranaway from the subscriber, residing in the southwestern corner of Dallas County, near McKinley Post Office, on the morning of the 31st of last month, a negro man named Bill 30 or 35 years old, bright complexion, somewhat slow spoken, has a small piece out of each of his ears, and has in time had his left thigh broken, which is quite perceptible in his walking; said boy is about 6' high and tolerably stout built, weighing about 175 or 180 pounds.... it is probable the above boy will shape his course towards Georgia, as he was brought from that state some three years ago.... William Ogletree

STOP THE MURDERS! $1,000 REWARD....for the apprehension of John Step and Solomon Step, who murdered Martin Fraley, Sen'r. on the 8th October inst. near Wolf's Ferry, in Hardin County, Tennessee. John Step is about 26 years of age, 5' 8 or 9 inches high, dark complexion, dark eyes, black hair, inclined to curl, and very low forehead. The middle joint of the fore finger of his right hand is considerably enlarged, occasioned, it is supposed by a hurt. Solomon Step is about 23 or 24 years of age, 5' 11" high, stout built, a little inclined to be stoop shouldered, dark complexion, dark eyes, dark hair, inclined to curl, and very high cheek bones. The bones of his right hand have been broken near the middle of the palm, and occasion a considerable ridge on the back of his hand. The Step's formerly resided in the Cherokee Country in Georgia, and it is thought they will either make their way back to Georgia or strike for Texas.

ISSUE 11-24-1838

Stolen from the subscribers stable, 4 miles west of Marion, Perry County, on the 14th of November, a red chesnut sorrel horse, 8 years old.... Joseph Massey

Dallas County, Orphans' Court, Nov. Term, 1838: This day came Lewis B. Moseley, executor of the will and testament of Jesse Parnall, deceased, and applied for a final settlement of said estate....

Dallas County, Orphans' Court, Nov. Term, 1838: This day came John Howell, administrator of the estate of Thomas Nixon, deceased, and applied for final settlement of said estate...

Dallas County, Orphans' Court, Nov. Term, 1838: This day came William Davis, administrator, of the estate of Henry Barnes, deceased, and applied for a final settlement of said estate...

ISSUE 12-8-1838

Wilcox County, Orphans' Court, Nov. Term, 1838: This day came Charles J. Gee, and applied for a final settlement of the estate of Soseph (Joseph) Gee, deceased....

Wilcox County, Orphans' Court, Nov. Term, 1838: This day came Dr. John Bonner, administrator, of the estate of Isaac Williams, deceased, and filed his account current and vouchers for final settlement of said estate.

Wilcox County, Orphans' Court, Nov. Term, 1838: This day came Dr. John Bonner, administrator, of the estate of Archibald Cawthon, deceased, and filed his account current and vouchers for final settlement of said estate.

Wilcox County estray notice: Taken up by Dr. William H. Flemming.... a small mouse colored mule....

POSTPONED SALE: The sale of the real estate of Henry West, deceased, is postponed until Saturday the 29th day of January next. T.M. Matthews, James Kelly, John E. Barns, comm's

Wilcox County, County Court, July Term, 1838: Francis Bridges vs Richard J. Painter: attachment levied.... the defendant in this case has left the state, and gone to parts unknown....

Wilcox County, County Court, July Term, 1838: J.A. Kimbrough, & Co., vs Richard J. Painter: attachment levied.... the defendant has left the state....

Wilcox County, Orphans' Court, November Term, 1838: This day came Charles W. Gee, of the last will and testament of Mark W. Gee, deceased, and made application for a final settlement of his estate.

Wilcox County, Orphans' Court, Nov. Term, 1838: This day came Charles J. Gee, administrator of the estate of Nevill Gee, deceased, and made application for a final settlement of the estate of said deceased.

Married, on the 24th ult., by J.H.D. Womack, Mr. Peter Shelton to Miss Mary Sorrell, all of this county. By the same on the 29th ult., Mr. Joseph Isgate to Miss Emeline Powell, all of this district.

Wilcox County, County Court, July Term, 1838: James Newberry vs Redic H. Armstrong, attachment levied.... defendant in this case has left the state....

Sheriff's sale: ....in the town of Cahawba.... levied on as the property of Wm. G. Samson, to satisfy an execution in favor of James D. Johnson, use &c.

Will be sold before the court house door in Cahawba, on the first Monday in January next (1839), the southwest 1/4 of the southeast 1/4 of section 21, and the southwest quarter of the northwest 1/4 of section 26 of township 15 of range 8: levied on as the property of Spencer Evans, to satisfy an execution in favor of Maria Hatfield.

By virtue of five orders of sale, issued by the Clerk of the Circuit Court of Dallas County, and to me directed, will be sold before the court house door in Cahawba, on the first Monday of January next (1839), as the property of Samuel Fleniken, the southwest 1/4 of section 23, of township 15 of range 8.

Will be sold before the court house door in Cahawba, on the first Monday in January next (1839) as the property of Thomas Wright, the northeast 1/4 of section 18 of township 15 of range 8.

Will be sold before the court house door in Cahawba...as the property of Edmond Shaffer, the east 1/2 of the northwest 1/4, and the northwest quarter of the northeast 1/4, and the northeast quarter of the southwest 1/4 of section 7 of township 14 of range 8, in the district of land subject to sale at Cahawba.

Will be sold before the court house door in Cahawba.... the west 1/2 of the northeast 1/4 of section 19 of township 13 of range 10.... levied on as the property of Simeon Nunellee, to satisfy an execution in favor of James S. Williams.

FOR SALE: The late residence of Mrs. Elizabeth Bolles, situated 2 1/2 miles from Selma, on the Cahawba road. There is 240 acres attached to the tract.... for terms apply to Doctor Paul H. Earle, at Cahawba.

ISSUE 12-15-1838

Dallas County Orphans' Court, December Term, 1838: This day came

Miscellaneous Alabama Newspaper Abstracts --- Vol 1

Thomas P. Fergerson, administrator of the estate of John P. Boyd, deceased, and applied for a final settlement of said estate....

ISSUE 12-22-1838

Died, in Cahawba, on the 17th inst., Mrs. Ann Eliza Perine, consort of Mr. E. M. Perine, aged 22 years and 20 days.... She had been a member of the small society of our village for only two years....

The subscribers, having been appointed by the honorable the Judge of the County Court of Wilcox County, Commissioners, to audit and determine upon the validity of the claims against the estate of Benton B. Parham, deceased.... William F. Daniel, William F. Gee, Calvin C. Sellers Com'rs

ISSUE 12-29-1838

Married, on Sunday evening, 23rd inst., by the Rev. Mr. Lindsey, Mr. Alexander Steward, of Coneuchaker, to Miss Averilla Jane Dennis, second daughter of Mr. Samuel Dennis, of this county.

ISSUE 1-5-1839

Dallas County Orphans' Court, December Term, 1838: This day came James E. Moss, executor of the last will and testament of Henry Moss, deceased, and applied for a final settlement of said decedents estate....

Letters of Administration de bonis non having been granted to me, on the 17th day of December, 1838, on the estate of Benjamin J. Wright, deceased, late of Dallas County.... Peyton R. Pritchard

Administrator's Sale: By virtue of an order of the Orphans' Court of Dallas County, I shall proceed to sell on the first Monday of February next, at the plantation of the late Benjamin J. Wright, in Dallas County, all the personal property belonging to the estate of the said deceased, consisting of about 20 very valuable negroes, men, women, and children..... Cahawba, Jan. 2, 1839, P.R. Pritchard, Adm'r. de bonis non

TRUST SALE: By virtue of a deed of trust made to me by Joseph H. Mead, to secure the payment by said Mead, to John E. & Thomas Butler, of North Carolina, of the sum of $3,375 with legal interest thereon from 1st. January 1838, till paid, and all cost and charges, expended in and about the collection of said sum and interest; and which deed is dated January 29, 1838, and recorded in the Clerk's Office of the County Court of Dallas County, Alabama the 16th Feb. 1838, I shall sell to the highest bidder at public auction before the court house door, in the town of Cahawba on the first Tuesday or 5th day of February next, between the usual hours of sale, the following described tracts of land lying in Dallas County, and designated and known, as the north east quarter of the south east quarter, the south east quarter of the south east quarter, and south west quarter of the south east quarter of section # 27, in township # 14, of range # 10, containing 120 acres, more or less. Also, the following slaves, Viz: Hagar, a woman about 27 or 28 years of age; Robert, a boy about 7 years of age; Lucy a woman about 23 years old, and her three children, Frank, a yellow boy about 5 years old; Henry, a boy about 4 years old, and Sophia, a girl about 1 year old, and the increase of the females thereof, if any, since date of Deed of Trust.... Matt. Gayle, trustee

ISSUE 1-12-1839

TO MY CREDITORS: Notice is hereby given, that on the second day of February next, I will appear in the town of Athens, before J.R. McElroy and T.G. Rariner, and make application to be discharged from further legal process on all my past liabilities under the law providing for the relief of insolvent debtors. Levi Comelander

Ad for fresh groceries at the Washington Hall, Cahawba, Ala., D. Grant

ISSUE 1-19-1839

Dallas County Orphans' Court, Jan. Term, 1839: This day came John M. Lucas, administrator of the estate of Levi L.T. Lucas, deceased, and applied for a final settlement of said estate....

Dallas County Orphans' Court, Jan. Term, 1839: This day came John E. Vasser, Executor of the last will and testament of Lemuel Vasser, deceased, and filed his account current and vouchers, and applied for a final settlement of decedents estate....

Dallas County Orphans' Court, Jan. Term, 1839: This day came Milo B. Abercrombie, administrator of the estate of Joseph Scripter, deceased, and applied for a final settlement of the estate of said deceased....

Dallas County Orphans' Court, Jan. Term, 1839: This day came Washington J. Outlaw, administrator of the estate of Marshall A. Parnell, deceased, and applied for a final settlement of said estate...

In pursuance of a decree of the Circuit Court of Wilcox County, Exercising Chancery Jurisdiction, I will expose to sale for cash, at the court house door in Wilcox County on the first Monday of Feb. next, the following described

MISCELLANEOUS ALABAMA NEWSPAPER ABSTRACTS --- VOL 1

lands to wit: West 1/2 north east 1/4 section 15, township 12, range 10; south east 1/4 north east 1/4 and north east 1/4 section 14, township 12, range 10; north west 1/4 section 23, and east 1/2 north east 1/4 section 22, township 12, range 10, all of these lands are situated in Wilcox County.... C.C. Sellers, Cl'k

Letters testamentary on the last will and testament of William F. Roper, deceased, late of Dallas County, Ala., having been granted to the undersigned.... William P. Guinn, Exec'r

Marshall Sale, Thomas Butler vs James Degman and others, Judgment taken April Term, 1838...levied on as the property of James Degman....

A list of letters remaining in the Post Office at Cahawba, January 1st, 1839:

Spencer Adams, Pitman & Alexander, Miss Caroline Anderson

Morgan Brown, J.M. Burk, Thos. G. Bailey, John Bowie, John N. Brent, Warren Brantley, Codey Baze, Thomas L. Bradly, Robert Burt, Lenard Butler, Elizabeth Barlow, Miss Francis Brooks, J.B. Bethea

Clerk of County Court, She'ff of Dallas County, Mrs. Mary Crosby, J.B. Clark, Ezra Cleveland, J.G. Cowan, Capt. Joel Curtis, Col. Clifton, James Calhoun, Thomas Craig, Cashier of the Branch Bank of the State of Alabama at Cahawba

Dunham Rutlege & Co., A.C. Duest, James M. Dunaway, Editor of Democrat, Messrs. Demming & Yeldill

Miss Amanda C. Edney, Benjamin F. Ellis, Dr. J.A. English

Stephen Fredrick

Matt Gayle, L.C. Graham, James Gaston, Samuel D. Gaines, James Gardner, Grisby, Thomas Gill, T.B. Goldsby, F.J. Garrett

John J. Heard, Maj. F.J. Heard, Judge Harris, Bethel Holms, Elber J. Hardey, J.F. Huckeby, Thomas Harris, John M. Holms, W.L. Halloway, Joseph Hendrick, Mrs. Ann H. Hays, P.A. Horn

Harberson Jemerson, Robert Ingram, Jesse Johnson, Berryman Johnson

T.K. Kornegay, Samuel Keats, Miss Eliza A. Kemp

MISCELLANEOUS ALABAMA NEWSPAPER ABSTRACTS --- VOL 1

Henry Leslie, Stephen Lockwood, Hardey T. Lewis, Jeremiah N. Laws, El Lockwood, Wm. Langley

U.G. Mitchell, J.B. Moore, Bruce H. Mitchell, John Murry, John Mann, A.C. Myres, Rebecka Murphy, N.B. Mashaw, James McDaniel, James D.W. McKeller, P. Molette

Sampson Nance

Washington J. Outlaw

Austin Punderson, Cristopher Plunket, Levi Parkes, Jesse Pitts

Hamblin Quarles

Wm. Roberts, Ephram Rogers, Anderson Rockell, R.D. Rice, Wm. Rutherford, Alfred Roberts, Mitchel Roberts, Roleing Raines

Stephen Steele, Thos. Smith, Wm. Searle, E.S. Smith, W.J. Sorrell, A. Saltmarsh, Mrs. Mary A.J. Stephens, Col. M. Smyley

Williamson Tarver, Robert J. Travis, Rebecka Tolson, Dr. H. Tomme, Thos. Thurmond

Wiley J. Underwood

Bill Varnell, Capt. James H. Vail

George J.S. Walker, Laird H. Walker, Thomas T. Walker, George A.B. Walker, William Walker, A.C. Walker, W.B.C. Walker, Miss Julia Watts, Wm. Whitted, Jacob T. Wadkins, Henry Welch, J.K. Watson, Watson Wilcox, Edward Watts, Anson Whaples, James Williams, H.H. Womack, Mrs. White, Beverly A. Walker

ISSUE 2-2-1839

By virtue of an order of the Orphans' Court of Wilcox County, we will expose to public sale, to the highest bidder, at Prairie Bluff on Saturday the 16th of February next, at 12 o'clock, of said day the following described tract of land, Viz: Lot A. or fraction east of the Alabama river, in section 34, township 14, range 7, in the district of lands offer for sale at Cahawba, being part of the lands belonging to the estate of Wiley Jones, deceased.... T.M. Matthews, Thomas E. Ellis, Stephen T. Jones Commissioners

MISCELLANEOUS ALABAMA NEWSPAPER ABSTRACTS --- VOL 1

Will be sold before the court house door in Cahawba.... on Monday the 4th February next, one lot of ground lying in the town of Selma, Dallas County.... levied on as the property of Amos H. Lloyd, to satisfy an execution in my hands in favor of Josephus D. Echols and others.

Will be sold before the court house door in Cahawba.... on Monday the 4th February next, two lots of ground lying in the town of Selma, Dallas County.... levied on as the property of Stephen W. Murley....

Will be sold before the court house door in Cahawba.... on Monday the 4th February next, two lots of ground lying in the town of Selma, Dallas County.... levied on as the property of Henry Traun....

Will be sold before the court house door in Cahawba.... on Monday the 4th February next, a part of lot No. 219.... containing one and one-third acres (more or less), all in the town of Selma, Dallas County: levied on as the property of Alexander H. Conoley....

Will be sold before the court house door in Cahawba.... on Monday the 4th February next, part of lot No. 32.... also part of lot No. 1.... all lying in the town of Selma, Dallas County: levied on as the property of Daniel Sanford....

ISSUE 2-9-1839

Wilcox County, Orphans' Court, in vacation, February 2nd, 1839: John W. Bridges vs Martha Dann Admd'x.; petition to compel titles. This day came the said John W. Bridges, assignee of William R. Lenoir, and filed his petition, to compel the Administratix aforesaid to execute titles, in pursuance of the condition of a bond Executed by her interstate Thomas Dann in his life time to William R. Lenoir for the following described real estate, lying in the immediate vicinity of Barborsvile bounded on the north by Calhoun Street, on the west by lands belonging to the estate of said Dann, on the south by lots belonging to Jonathan Kennedy and on the east by Maine Street, containing 12 acres, more or less.....

Wilcox County Notice: All persons holding claims against the estate of Peter Lee, deceased, are requested to come forward and present them... Martin B. Lee, Eaton Lee executors

ISSUE 2-16-1839

Town property for sale: I wish to sell my residence in Cahawba.... J.B. Clark

Law Notice: Having purchased a residence near Eutaw, the new seat of

Miscellaneous Alabama Newspaper Abstracts --- Vol 1

justice of Greene County, I expect to remove to the same in July next, with an intention to permanently reside there, and to follow my profession.... J.B. Clark

Dallas County, Orphans' Court, January Term, 1839: This day came James Williams, adm'r. of the estate of Lewis Etherage, deceased, and applied for a final settlement of said estate....

Dallas County, Orphans' Court, February Term, 1839: This day came German Burnes, adm'r. of the estate of Isaac Durham, deceased, and made application for a final settlement of said estate....

ISSUE 2-23-1839

Died, on the 13th inst., Mrs. Catharine C. Dozier, consort of Mr. Richard M. Dozier, in the 26th year of her age.

Notice: Came to my house about the 26th of January, a large fat HOG, which after two or three weeks, I killed and salted the meat. The owner can have the meat, or its value, by proving property and paying charges. John Johnson

ISSUE 3-2-1839

Ranaway from my house near Cambridge, Dallas County, Alabama, a negro man named Charles, about 40 years of age, slick bald on the top of this head, speaks broken, about 5'4" high, short teeth.... John Adams

$100 REWARD: A negro boy, by the name of Frank, ranaway or was stolen from my place on the first of January 1839. The boy is about 30 years old; 5' high, stout built, rather light colored, and stutters in his speech. The boy formerly belonged to Joseph Camp. Bethel Holmes

ISSUE 3-9-1839

Departed this life on Sabbath evening, the 3rd inst., Mrs. Elizabeth Craig, consort of Thomas Craig, in the 62nd year of her age.

Stolen, on the night of the 2nd inst., from the estate of the late Dr. Thomas Casey, about four miles from Cahawba, on the Alabama River, a small chesnut sorrel stallion, about 5 years old.... Any information given, which will lead to the recovery of the horse, or to the detection of the thief, will be liberally rewarded either by Col. G.J.S. Walker, Adm'r. of the estate, or by the subscriber living on the place. Larkin Lesley, overseer

MISCELLANEOUS ALABAMA NEWSPAPER ABSTRACTS --- VOL 1

Letters of Administration on the estate of Benjamin B. Watson, deceased, have been granted to me this day by the Judge of the County Court of Dallas County.... William Carr, Administrator

Dallas County, Orphans' Court, March Term, 1839: This day came Robert S. Hatcher, late administrator of the estate of William Green, deceased, and applied for a final settlement of said estate....

Dallas County Orphans' Court, March Term, 1839: This day came Lewis Johnson, administrator of the estate of Spencer S. Johnson, deceased, and applied for a final settlement of said estate....

Dallas County Orphans' Court, March Term, 1839: This day came William Day and Marshall Day, executors of the last will and testament of William Day, deceased, and applied for a final settlement of said decedents estate....

Dallas County Orphans' Court, March Term, 1839: This day came Theodrick Olliver and Lucy B., his wife (late widow and adm'rx. of the estate of James Thomas (deceased)) and applied for a final settlement of said estate....

Negro Fellow For Sale: There will be offered for sale, at public auction, immediately after the sheriff's sale on Monday, the 1st of April, a mulatto fellow named Henry, on a credit till the first January next..is to be sold on account of the owner, residing in South Carolina, and not for fault. W.L. Yancey

Dallas County Orphans' Court, March 29, 1839: This day came James Ellis, administrator, of the estate of Thomas N. Gardner, deceased, and Guardian of the minor heirs of said descendant and filed his account current and vouchers, for final settlement....

ISSUE 3-30-1839

NOTICE: The undersigned takes pleasure in informing his old friends and patrons, that he has entered into partnership with Doctor J. Bennett.... Wm. B. Johnson

$100 REWARD Will be given for the apprehension and detection of a man calling himself J. Wilson, who stole from me (in my bed room in Cahawba, $610 on the night of the 20th inst...) J. Wilson is about 5' 6" in height and rather stout and fleshy, has black eyes and a large mouth and florid countenance.... Malcom Brogden

MISCELLANEOUS ALABAMA NEWSPAPER ABSTRACTS --- VOL 1

ISSUE 4-13-1839

A list of letters remaining in the Post Office at Cahawba, March 31, 1839:
Benj. Adams, Mary Arthur

Thomas Butler, Fleming Y. Bohanan, John Barclay, J. Babcock, Connor Betts, Richard D. Baxter, Miss M. Bradford, Sarah Broughton, Thos. H. Bowles, Thos. Butler, Benj. Burge, Jesse Beene, R. Browen, David R. Bell, R. Boles, J. Babcock, Robert Bates, Patrick Brown, Rachel Bell

Jno. Cronondontholigus, Laughlin Campbell, Sheriff of Dallas County, Ira Cole, Wm. Chesnut, James B. Coleburn, William Clark, Eliza Chambers, Messrs. Chapins & Co., Clk. Orp. Ct D.C., James D. Craig, John S. Coleman, J.D. Creigk, Clk. County Court, Ann Cole, J.J. Chrocheron, Circuit Ct. Clk.

John Day, Sen, John G. Dubar, Peter Dubose, John Davis, James Dillett, Louis D. Drumond, Stephen B. Davis, Jackson Dennis

John J. Elmore, Baylor & Earl

Charles Fur, Rachel Flanegan, John J. Foster

T.W. Gill, Dr. Geeghegan, Jese Grice, John B. Galloway, John J. Greening

Hardamon Herrell, John F. Huckaby, W.L. Holloway, Edward Hughs, Thos. Harris, Susan E. Haskew, John M. Holms, Ebenezer Hem, Gabriel Herrell, E.J.L. Haskew, R.S. Hatcher, Thos. M. Hogan, Benj. B. Hogan, Thos. O. Holoway

Enoch Jessup, Benj. B. Jones, T.M. Jackson

Jonathan Knockhimback, James Kirkpatrick

Henry Leske, George Livespers, James Langford, Martha S. Lucas, Loco poco & Hoco poco

Mrs. B. Mosely, Calmn Mathews, Hugh B. Mitchel, Martha McDaniel, B.H. Mitchell, John Brenton Moore, B. Moore, John Man, Miss Nancy Mays, Dr. B. Mashaw, Robt. Mays, Benj. D. Mosely, W.A. McCain, Wm. P. Molett, J.B. Moore

S. Norwood, J.B. Norman

W.W. Olds

Miscellaneous Alabama Newspaper Abstracts --- Vol 1

Theo M. Porter, Wm. Posonby, Susan Parnall, Archl. Paul

Jese Ross, Mrs. Matilda Rogers, John Roper, Temperance Robertson

Mrs. Sarah Sponsonby, Bryan P. Sparrow, Hiram Scott, Constantine Strambler, J.P. Saffold, Stephens the Pump Maker, James Saffold, Nonilia Saxton, Jas. Smyley, Jas. M. Sorrell

Pascal B. Traylon, Hiram Toomer, Tpincutoperitatus

Wiley J. Underwood

John H. Volentine

Geo. J.S. Walker, David White, Jr., Thos. Watts, William Wadsworth, Amassa West, R. Williams, William Whitted, James Williams

James G. Young, James S. Yarnell

ISSUE 4-20-1839

TRUST SALE: On Monday, SIXTH OF MAY NEXT: By virtue of the authority in me vested by deed of trust from G.J.S. Walker, dated 10th of May 1837, and recorded in the office of the Clerk of the County Court of Dallas County: I will proceed, agreeably to the terms of said Deed, (the conditions and stipulations in said Deed not having been complied with) to offer for sale at Public Auction, at the plantation of the said G.J.S. Walker, in said county, on Monday the sixth of May next, between the hours of 10 o'clock,A.M., and 4 o'clock P.M., for cash, the following negroes, Viz: Poydere, Abby, Casy, Lydia, Cyrus, Ann, Mary, John, Lloyd, Martha, Green, Solomon, Jesse Tom, Mary, Louisa, George, Emily, Isobel, Martha, Fanny, Aggy, Biddy, and her child Aggy, Billy Gee, Ben, Hannah, Jeffry, Sophonia, Barbary, Betty, Mariah, George, Jim, Sam, Prince, Henry, Peter, Sam, Jane, Lucy, Judy, Anne, Amy, Daniel, Rachel, Ned, Priscilla, Mary, Jery, Ben, Phoeby, Harriett, Phyllis. J.A. Campbell, trustee

Dallas County, Orphans' Court, April 19, 1839: This day came William P. Dunham, Adm'r. de bonis non, of the estate of George Sage, deceased, and applied for a final settlement of said estate....

ISSUE 5-4-1839

SHERIFF'S SALE: Will be sold before the court house door in Cahawba.... on Monday the 8th April next, the west half of the northeast quarter of section

6, in township # 16 of range # 10.... levied on as the property of James J. Downes, to satisfy an execution in my hands for collection, in favor of John Honeycut.

Will be sold before the court house door in Cahawba..the Southwest quarter of section # 18, in township # 16 of range # 8: levied on as the property of Thos. Wright, to satisfy an execution in my hands for collection, in favor of Warren Brantley.

Will be sold before the court house door in Cahawba.... the west half of the northwest quarter of section 23; and the east half of the northeast quarter of section 22; the half of the northwest quarter and the west half of the southwest quarter of section 14, all of township 16 of range 8, being and lying in Dallas County: Levied on the property of Henry W. Barnes to satisfy two executions in my hands for collection.

Will be sold before the court house door in Cahawba.... the south half of the northeast quarter of section # 2 township # 18 of range # 10, lying in Dallas County, containing 81 and 12/100 acres more or less: Levied on as the property of Edward Murphy to satisfy sundry executions in my hands for collection.

Will be sold before the court house door in Cahawba.... the southwest quarter of section # 26 of township 17 of range 10, containing 160 acres more or less, lying in Dallas County...also so much of lots No's. 13, 14, and 15, lying in the town of Selma, Dallas County.... levied on as the property of Uriah Grigsby to satisfy sundry executions in my hands for collection.

Will be sold before the court house door in Cahawba...the following lots, tracts or parcels of land, being and lying in the town of Selma, Dallas County to wit: a part of out lot # 18.... levied on as the property of Henry Traun to satisfy two executions in my hands....

Will be sold before the court house door in Cahawba.... six lots, tracts, or parcels of land, being and lying in the town of Selma, Dallas County, known and distinguished in the plan of said town as lots No's. 7, 8, 9, 10, 11, and 12: Levied on as the property of Alexander H. Conoley to satisfy an execution in favor of M.G. McKeagg.

Will be sold before the court house door in Cahawba..the west half of the northwest quarter of section 28 of township 15 of range 7: Levied on as the property of Samuel H. Taylor to satisfy an execution in favor of E.B. Seltzer.

Will be sold before the court house door in Cahawba.... the west half of the northwest quarter, and the northeast quarter of the southwest quarter, and the west half of the northeast quarter of section 8, and the west half of the northwest quarter, and the west half of the southwest quarter of section # 9; and the northeast quarter of the southeast quarter of section # 5, all in township 15, of range 8, being and lying in Dallas County: Levied on as the property of Edward Clark....

ISSUE 5-11-1839

It is with regret that we are called upon to record the death of M.D. Simpson, editor of the *Wetumpka Argus*. He died on the 7th inst., after much suffering and long continued disease. He had just disposed of his press to the editors of this paper.

ISSUE 5-18-1839

Married, on Wednesday the 17th ult., at the residence of Louis Bringiet (Surveyor of the State of Louisiana) by the Rev. Mr. Clapp, Major General E.P. Gaines, of the United States Army, to Mrs. Myra Clark Whitney, only daughter of the late Daniel Clark of this city. (*New Orleans Picayune*)

Died, at her residence in this county, on the 11th inst., Mrs. Martha Hatcher, relict of the late Maj. James Hatcher. She had nearly completed the 57th year of her age, more than 20 of which have been spent in this county. Member Methodist Church....

Whereas Leonard H. Handley, late of Wilcox County, by deed, bearing date the 20th day of May, 1838, on record in the office of the Clerk of the County Court of Wilcox County, recorded in book E, page 418 to 420, conveyed to the undersigned with full power to sell to secure him the payment of certain sums of money, to become due as stated in said deed.... also the following negroes, to wit: a negro boy named Charles, one named Stephen, and a negro woman named Hannah, and two horses.... Wm. Thomas Mathews

ISSUE 5-25-1839

Strayed from the subscriber's plantation, near Cahawba, on the 17th inst., a pair of good sized Oxen, about 6 years old.... W.L. Yancey

Taken up, on the 14th inst., on the 3rd section of the Cahawba and Marion Rail Road, a sorrel horse.... George Roach

Notice: Persons wishing to contract for the erection of a meeting house, on the Cahawba road, near Mr. Philip Milhous', will please hand in proposals to the undersigned.... George Bowie, Robert Hatcher, Philip Milhous, Wm. S. Smith, George A.B. Walker

Dallas County Orphans' Court, May Term, 1839: This day came Mrs. Dicey Reisor, administratrix of the estate of James Reisor, and applied for a final settlement of said estate....

SALE: Having it in contemplation to remove to the city of Mobile, I offer for sale a valuable tract of land, on which my plantation is situated, commencing within one mile north east of Selma, containing twenty two hundred and ten acres.... Also, some desirable town land, containing near two hundred acres, on a part of which is a good mill seat near the mouth of Beach Creek, and all my town property.... Edward Gantt

ISSUE 6-1-1839

Married, on Sunday morning the 19th inst., by the Rev. Mr. Crane, Mr. H.W. Watson, to Miss Elenera S.L. Mulder, all of this city. (*Montgomery Journal*)

Died, at the residence of his mother, on Friday the 24th inst., Major M.V. Eiland, in the 25th year of his age.

Died, in the city of Wetumpka, on Saturday morning, the 28th ult., Mr. Lawrence Spinnacuta, Printer, aged 45 years.

Dallas County Orphans' Court, May Term, 1839: This day came James Buanch, administrator of the estate of William Buanch, dec'd., and applied for a final settlement of said estate, which has heretofore been reported insolvent...

ISSUE 6-8-1839

Dissolution: The copartnership heretofore existing between West and Denison, of Cahawba, Ala. is this day dissolved by mutual consent. Wm. West, S.A. Denison

SALE OF LANDS: By virtue of an order to us directed, from the Orphans' Court of Dallas County, appointing us commissioners to sell certain of the real estate of Lloyd Barnes, deceased.... Wm. W. Olds, Jarvis Langford, Wm. Hendrick Commis'rs

Whereas the undersigned were, at the June Term 1839 of the Orphans' Court, appointed commissioners to sell the real estate of which Evan Evans died seized and possessed.... I.N. Campbell, administrator John McLaughlin,

Miscellaneous Alabama Newspaper Abstracts --- Vol 1

John A. Norwood, L.C. Graham Commr's

ISSUE 6-22-1839

Married, by the Rev. Mr. Nelson, on the 18th inst., at the residence of Dr. Saltmarsh near this place, Dr. Richard S. Key, of Canton, to Miss Helen C. Beck of Dallas County.

ISSUE 6-29-1839

The undersigned have united in the practice of law.... J.W. Lapsley, George R. Evans

ISSUE 7-6-1839

Committed to the jail of Dallas County a negro fellow who calls his name Isaac, and says he belongs to Roe Wiggins of Marengo County, Alabama....

ISSUE 2-1-1840

Married, on the evening of the 21st ult., by Rev. E. Hearn, Dr. James Birney, of Hayneville, to Miss Jane E., eldest daughter of Hon. R. Saffold, of Dallas County.

A Ball, to be given at the Cahawba Hotel. The managers have the pleasure of announcing to the public, that a ball will be given in this place at the Cahawba hotel, on Wednesday the 5th instant. MANAGERS: R.S. Hatcher, C.G. Edwards, F. Vaughan, J.A. English, W.R. Thurber, E.G. Ulmer, J.A. Lawrence, G.J. Bowie, J.W. Olds, R.C. Crocheron, W.S. Phillips, W.P. Dunham.

Dr. Earle has established his office one door west of the Store of Perine & Crocheron

Letters of Administration have been granted to the undersigned on the estate of the late Thos. Childers, deceased.... Mary Childers, Admr'x J.H. Willson, adm'r, Prairie Bluff, 1-23-1840

A gray mare, about 7 years old, 15 hands high, and no brands, was taken up on the road between Cahawba and Prairie Bluff, on the 17th inst.... Thomas Dougherty

Notice: The subscribers having been appointed by the honorable the Orphans' Court of Wilcox County, to audit and determine upon the validity of

MISCELLANEOUS ALABAMA NEWSPAPER ABSTRACTS --- VOL 1

the claims against the estate of Benton B. Parham, deceased, give notice that they will, on the second Monday in April next, at Wilcox court house, proceed to audit and determine upon the validity of said claims.... David Rosser, Matthew Flemming, Whitman W. Rives commissioners

A list of letters remaining in the Post Office at Cahawba, January, 1st, 1840:

Aardy Abney, Jeremiah Austil

Joseph Bell, Danie Brooks, Stephen Blann, Amos Bishop, Canon Betts, James M. Boling, J.S. Beers, C.R. Butler, Elizabeth Bell, Sackfield Brewer, Wm. E. Bird, M.E. Beck, Ostill Baylue

I.N. Campbell, James D. Craig, Meredith Calhoun, Allen W. Coleman, Joseph Camp, J. Coleman, Joel Curtis, James B. Clark, J.P. Cook, James M. Calhoun, Henry N. Crocheron, Joseph A. Clark, James Collins, Spilisby Colman

Jackson Dennis, Joseph Dennis, Elizabeth Dennis, John Davis, Mary E. Davis, Wm. Dennis, Edward Day, Thomas J. Due, Jno. Dennison

George R. Evans, Charles G. Edward, Paul U.? Earle

Jackson Flanekin, Jackson Fleniken, Charlotte Forte, James Fleming, Fred. R.F. Foscue, Benji. Franklin

Jacob Givhan, Wm. P. Givhan, John J. Greening, H.M. Grant, Abram Geiger, Benjamine Grumbles, James Grumbles, John Grumbles, Hosey George, Edward Grumbles, Eldridge Gardner

Thos. M. Hogan, R.S. Hatcher, Wm. Hunter, Frema Hughes, John Hill, James A. Hart, Benjamin Hollingshead, J.W. Hustis, Josiah Harrell, Gabriel Harrell, John J. Heard, John Hays, George Hood, Wm. F. Harrell, John Hatcher, Bethel Holmes, Hardyman Harrell

Wm. M. Johnson, James Jorden, Jesse Johnson

Thos. K. Kornega, Henry J. King

John Latourrette, John C. Latourrette, James M. Lenvir

A.P. McCurdy, John McGill, John G. Maull, James A. McCain, Silas Morgan, Napoleon B. Mitchell, Abner McMillan, J.B. Moore, Neill McLaurin, Logan Metts

MISCELLANEOUS ALABAMA NEWSPAPER ABSTRACTS --- VOL 1

George A. Norwood, Martin Nowel

James O'Donell, L.B. Oliver

Eliza Powell, A. Powell, John Parnell, Jeptha Parnall, S.E. Phillips

Alfred Roberts, Benjamine Rennolds, Wm. Rhem

J.P. Saffold, Wm. S. Smith, Susan Swift, John Simpson, Sarah E. Smith, Bryan P. Sparran, Wm. Sanders, Wm. Smiley, John Smith, James Saffold, A. Saltmarsh

Eli Thrash, T. Tueman, Maryann Thomas, M.D. Thompson, John Thompson

Green Underwood, Ally Underwood, E.G. Ulmer

John E. Vasser

Mathias Wisinger, James Wilcox, Wentworth Wyman, James Willson, Wm. Whitted, George J.S. Walker, T. Williams, C.M.C. Walker, Thos. Watts, Richard Whiting, Joseph Walker, Margret White, M. Wanan

Jonathan Yongue

By virtue of a mortgage deed, and the consent of parties, we will, on the 1st Monday of January, 1840, at the house of Isaac W. McElroy, expose to sale, a negro man slave, named Anthony, of the age of 27 years.... Isaac McElroy, James McElroy

Dallas County Orphans' Court, January Term, 1840: Elijah Rigby vs L.C. Graham, and B. Johnson, ex'rs.: Petition for Titles. This day came the said Elijah Rigby by authority and filed his petition to compel, the said Bernard Johnson and Laird C. Graham, executors of the last will and testament John D. Alexander, to make titles to him....

The copartnership heretofore existing between Drs. English and Earle, is this day dissolved...

Ran off on the 9th inst., three negro men, of the following description, viz: Jim: five feet five inches high, of dark complexion, stoutly made, and has upon the small of his back, extending into the right ----- marks of the whip.... about the age of 27.... Isaac: is of the same height, and of rather lighter complexion, not so stoutly built, about 25 years old, and stammers when speaking.... Sam: five feet nine inches in height, quite dark complexion, full frame, pleasant countenance, weighs from 160 to 165 pounds.... Samuel M. Stuart

Lowndes County: Notice is hereby given, that a final settlement of the estate of James Moor, deceased, will take place.... James G. Gowan, Lewis Moor Adm'rs

Whereas, Letters of Administration were granted to the undersigned, by the Judge of the Orphans' Court of Dallas County, on the 11th of October, 1839, on the estate of Tillman Hitt, deceased.... Elizabeth Hitt, Administratix, John McGill, Administrator

The undersigned having obtained Letters of Administration on the estate of William Pelham, dec'd., of Dallas County.... Lewis Johnson, adm'r

Letters of Administration were granted to the undersigned, on the estate of Christopher J. McConnico, deceased,late of Wilcox County on the 16th day of September, 1839, Charles T. McConnico, Adm'r

Dallas County, Circuit Court, Fall Term, 1839: Thomas Williams, administrator, vs Benjamin M. Reynolds

LOST: Between my house and Mr. J. Strothers near Athens, about the first of September, a small black morocco pocket book, containing some money.... Also one note on Jesse Rasco for $56 .... J.H. Harrell

LAW NOTICE: The undersigned having united in the practice of Law, under the firm of Gayle & Saffold.... G.W. Gayle, J.P. Saffold, A.J. Saffold

The undersigned having obtained Letter of Administration on the estate of Jacob Brown, dec'd., will sell at public auction, on the 25th of January next, in the town of Athens, all the property belonging to said estate, consisting mostly of negroes.... T.E.B. Pegues, A. Niolon, Admr's

Taken up near my plantation on Cedar creek, on Wednesday last, one iron grey mare mule, about 5 years old.... H.B. McDonald

Dallas County: Taken up by Philip Milhous.... a gray mare, about 7 years old...

MISCELLANEOUS ALABAMA NEWSPAPER ABSTRACTS --- VOL 1

SELMA COURIER
Volume I, Number 2, printed and published by Thomas J. Frow

ISSUE 11-29-1827

Married on Tuesday the 20th inst., by the Rev. Charles Crow, Mr. Elijah Taber, of Bibb County, to Miss Susannah Simms, daughter of Mr. Reddick Simms, of this county.

(Married) On Thursday last, by James Craig, Mr. Paschall Traylor, to Miss Mary Ann Harrell, daughter of Mr. Gabriel Harrell, all of this county.

ISSUE 12-6-1827

The business heretofore carried on under the firm of Dyke & M'Innis, is this day dissolved by mutual consent.... N. Dykes, Daniel M'Innis

Died, at his residence, in Wilcox County, on Thursday last, Mr. Abner Cleveland, a highly respectable citizen of that County.

Departed this life at Chelatchie Heights in Dallas County on 25 Aug last, in the 87th year, Col. Alexander Outlaw, formerly of Jefferson County, Tenn., but for the last 9 years a venerable and respectable inhabitant of this state....

Notice: John Johnson, Administrator, with the will annexed, of the estate of Robert Greer, Sen., deceased... for final settlement.... Court of Dallas County.

ISSUE 12-13-1827

Married, on Thursday the 29th ult., by William Foster, Mr. Edmund Jennings, to Miss Eliza Smiley, eldest daughter of Mr. James Smiley; all of Cedar Creek, in this county.

Died, in this town, on Saturday morning last, Mrs. Stringfellow, wife of Mr. Robert R. Stringfellow.

Ad for Benj. Smith, dry goods

The subscriber having removed to Montgomery County, offers his plantation, in Dallas County, for sale. It is on the east side of Alabama river, 10 miles above the town of Selma.... For particulars, apply to the subscriber, near Montgomery, or to Gilbert Shearer, of Selma... Nov. 29th, Thomas M. Cowles

Ad for the Washington Inn, Washington, Autauga County, Alabama, John

MISCELLANEOUS ALABAMA NEWSPAPER ABSTRACTS --- VOL 1

Tittle
Ad for McLaughlin's Cotton warehouse, Selma, M. McLaughlin John Simpson having taken Samuel F. Jones into co-partnership, the business will be conducted hereafter under the firm of Simpson & Jones

Lost, between, Selma and Mr. Haine's Mill, about the 25th of June last, a leather pocket book, containing a note on Samuel Murry for $50, payable on the 25th Dec. 1827; a note on Leonard and Chas. Crockor, payable to Daniel Stout; a due bill on James Owens for $7.87 1/2 ; a due bill on Obediah Hewitt for $6. 87 1/2.... Randolph M. Day

ISSUE 1-3-1828

Ad for Geo. G. Brooks, attorney at law.
Ad for Autauga Academy; C.G. Rush, James Howard, Green Hill, Edwin Fay, teacher

Married, on Wednesday evening, the 26th ult., by Bernard Johnson, George G. Brooks, attorney at law, of Cahawba, to Miss Margaret, daughter of Alexander Cathey, all of this county.

(Married) In Pleasant Valley, on Thursday last, by Robert C. Morrison, Mr. Elihu M. White to Miss Mary M. Glass, all of this county.

(Married) On Thursday evening last, by J. Langford, Mr. William Hardy to Miss Tibitha Harvey, all of this county.

List of letters remaining in the Post Office at Cahawba, Alabama, for the quarter ending Dec. 31st, 1827:

Leo. Abercrombie, Thomas Arnold, William Allen

Aiken Breazeal, Abraham Borland, Solomon Boggan, Ralph Blakeslee, James M. Bolton, Wm. Browning, J.G. Bare, Saml. Baskerville, Nancy Bogle, Dr. Bickley, Mary Brown, James B. Blalock, Edwin Bolton

George E. Chisolm, Jno. Carson, W.L. Camp, Emily Cunningham, W.R. Carter, Willis Carr, J.C. Campbell, Richard Covington, Walter Crenshaw, Dred Cooper, Jos. C. Campbell, Partrick Chisom, Wm. Chisholm, Edwin Curtis, Obadiah Coley

Ichabod Davis, Nancy Denson, Wm. Doriah, Ann & Eliz. Denson, Bradley Dear

MISCELLANEOUS ALABAMA NEWSPAPER ABSTRACTS --- VOL 1

A.B.C. Erwin, Jas. Erwin

Mary French, David Franklin, Wm. Fisher, Wm. Fletcher, Francis Ford

Rev. E. Gilmore, Matt. Gayle, John George, R.G. Gordon, Jacob Givham, Thos. Goolsby, John Grumbles, Livingston Gardner, John F. George, Mr. Gascal, Robert Garret, James Gilmore, James Ga?away

Dr. J.W. Heustin, Ob?? Harris, Peter Hare, H. Harold, Bennet Hill, Mr. Hatcher, Rev. E. Hearn, Wm. Higginbottom, John Howard, John Henry, Alexander Hill, Shaderick Howard, Robert Hattox

James Jurnet, Susan Jack???, Vestal J. Johnson, Comfort Johnson, Hastings Jones

M.J. Kenan, B.G. Key

Levi Loyd, Isaac D. Lockwood, James M. Lewis, James H. Lafevre

James Moor, Joseph Murry, Wm. C. Morgan, Lewis M'Gran, James M'Cullough, Abner M'Millan, Nancy Moor, James M'Kinney, Duncan M'Artha, Rachel Mitchell, Charlotte Moss, James M'Bride, John M'Kinley, Wm. M'Cord, Wm. A. Me?on, Richard S. Moor, John M'Coroke, Wm. Moor or J. Ellis, Robt. Melton, M'Neal & Martin

Eli Nobles, Willis Nunnella

James Ormand

Ezekiel Pickens, Enoch S. Phelps, Enoch Phelps, Bird Pruitt, H.G. Perry, Thos. Pierce, J.W. Patton, Wm.H.? Pool, E.U. Purdy, Britain Perry, Henry Pearson

Eli Riggins, James Reynolds, Daniel M. Riggs, John G. Rainer, Joab Reynolds, Lerrin Roberts, John Robinson, Thomas Richardson, John Royle

William Simes, William Smith, James Saffold, Eleanor Sheppard, Hon. Reuben Saffold, Jefferson Smith, Benjamin Skinner, Jack Shackelford, Jonathan T. Sims, Alex Shaw, Moses Shipman, Robert Shephard

John Travis, Edwd. W. Thompson, Abraham Trigg, Hon. John M. Taylor

Lemuel Va?er, Dr. John E. Vasser, J.C. Van Dyke

MISCELLANEOUS ALABAMA NEWSPAPER ABSTRACTS --- VOL 1

William Wallace, Mary Willey, Page R. Windham, Jac? Woods, David White, Joseph Walker, Nancy Wallace, Hezekiah Williford, Thos. H. Willey

Benjamin Young

Ad for cotton cards from B. Smith
Advertisement for sale of land by Lemuel Pruitt

Notice is hereby given that the following described tracts of land will be offered for sale to the highest bidder, on the 3rd Monday in February next, before the door of the court house for Dallas County, in Cahawba.....

Date of Purchase	Names of Purchaser	Residence
05-11-1819	Ethen Melton	Clarke Co.
05-11-1819	Drakeford L. Trammel	Clarke Co.
05-18-1819	Robert W. Carter	Monroe Co.
05-18-1819	Stephen Harvey	Baldwin Co.
05-18-1819	Stephen Harvey	Baldwin Co.
05-20-1819	P.T. Harris	Tuscaloosa
05-20-1819	P.T. Harris	Tuscaloosa
05-20-1819	P.T. Harris	Tuscaloosa
05-20-1819	P.T. Harris	Tuscaloosa
05-13-1819	Richardson Owen	Tuscaloosa
06-09-1819	Aaron Moore	Dallas Co.
06-12-1819	Michael Corley	Edgefield
06-12-1819	Michael Corley	Edgefield
05-05-1819	Thomas Matlock	Clarke Co.
08-05-1819	Sam Davis	Monroe Co.
08-06-1819	James Ingrem	Monroe Co.
08-03-1819	Will. F. Crenshaw	Morgan Co.
08-20-1819	Will. Locklin	Monroe Co.
10-08-1819	Thomas Bullard	Jones Co.
10-08-1819	James Bullard	Jasper Co.
10-27-1819	Bozwell Turner	Morgan Co.
10-27-1819	Bozwell Turner	Morgan Co.
10-27-1819	Bozwell Turner	Morgan Co.
10-27-1819	Bozwell Turner	Morgan Co.
10-27-1819	Bozwell Turner	Morgan Co.
11-06-1819	John Ingrem, jun.	Monroe Co.
11-06-1819	John Ingrem, sen.	Monroe Co.
10-19-1819	Noah W. Nichols	Conecuh Co.
01-11-1820	Richard Hainsworth	Monroe Co.

MISCELLANEOUS ALABAMA NEWSPAPER ABSTRACTS --- VOL 1

01-18-1820	Robert Hill	Monroe Co.
01-18-1820	Robert Hill	Monroe Co.
01-15-1820	Jesse Street	Tuscaloosa
01-14-1820	Will. Walton	Clarke Co.
01- -1820	Hardy H. Keenan	Milledgeville
01-12-1820	Will. Walton	Clarke Co.
01-14-1820	David Hubbard	Cotaco Co. (?)
01-12-1820	James Diven & Ann M'Rae	Monroe Co.
01-14-1820	David Hubbard	Cotaco Co. (?)
01-07-1820	David White	
02-12-1820	Hume R. Field	

Issue 1-10-1828

Ranaway from the subscriber in May last, a negro man, named Tom, about 35 years old, about 5'8" high.... He is a native of Africa but has been in the U. States since a boy.... Wm. P. Molett

Will be sold on the 23rd day of January next, the west half of the east half of the north east quarter of section 1, township 17, range 11, belonging to the estate of Samuel Wallace, deceased. Dallas County Court, J.J. Wallace Adm'r. of S. Wallace, deceased

ISSUE 1-17-1828

Married, on Tuesday evening last, by the Rev. T. Alexander, Mr. David Morrow to Miss Isabella Reid, all of Pleasant Valley.

We copy the following from the *Green County Republican*: Married at Winham, on the 16th inst., by the Rev. Mr. Bennet, Mr. Eli Spencer to Miss Ann Hogeboom.... one for Jackson the other for Adams.... *(N.Y. Enq.)*

Died, yesterday, Ashfield Ellis, infant son of Maj. Edwin Butler. The friends of the family are respectfully invited to attend the funeral, at 11 o'clock, this morning.

(Died) In Tuscaloosa, Ala., on the 30th ult., Mr. Robert Trarers (formerly an inhabitant of Cahawba) in the 54th year of his age.

The subscriber designing to leave the state, requires all persons who are indebted to him to come forward and make immediate payment. Thos. O. Meux

Miscellaneous Alabama Newspaper Abstracts --- Vol 1

Private Entertainment: The subscriber informs his friends, and the public generally, that he has charge of his father's house, two miles from Washington, Autauga County, on the road to Selma, where he will accommodate travelers at all times.... Wm. Huddleston

Notice: By virtue of a deed of trust, executed to me on the 6th day of June, 1826, by Gen. William Taylor, of the County of Dallas and State of Alabama, for the purpose of securing the United States of America, in the payment of a certain debt owed by him, I shall offer at public sale, to the highest bidder, on the 7th day of March, 1828, at the plantation of said Taylor, in Dallas County, State of Alabama, the following slaves, to wit: Cornelius, Andrew, Daniel, Martin, William, Henry, Luke, Maria, Judah, Rachel, Cely, Sarah, Suky, Louisa, Jane, Monroe, Madison, Amy, Ransom, Mary, Barscna, Lucy, Sally, Silsina, Richard, Jeffrey, Othello, Moses, Nancy, Betty, Sally, Jacob, Sue, Easter, Alabama, and a child of Sue's aged about 3 years.... Alexander Anderson

Ranaway from the subscriber, on Sunday the 30th Dec. last, a negro fellow, named John, about 25 years of age, dark complexion, 5' 8 or 9 inches high.... Henry Avery

Notice: All persons indebted to the late firm of M'Laughlin, Read, & Simpson, will please call and make payment to the subscriber.... Matthew M'Laughlin

Ad for Selma Jockey Club, Adam Taylor, Trea'r.; G. Shearer, Sec'ry

A liberal reward will be paid by the subscriber, living 7 miles below Cahawba, for the apprehension of the following described negroes, who ran away from him on the 3rd inst. Viz: John, a tall slim black fellow about 27 or 8 years of age; Cisily, John's wife, about 21 years old; her complexion not very black. Robin, a yellow fellow, tall and stout made; has a large foot and remarkable long great toes. He has a scar on his left arm just above the wrist about the size of a quarter dollar, and is about 20 years of age. They will no doubt make for North Carolina, as I am told John persuaded the others that he could take them there without any trouble. James M. Lenoir

Notice: All persons having any claims or demands against the Estate of Abner Cleveland, late of Wilcox County, deceased, are requested to render in the same for settlement.... Carter H. Cleveland, executor

Notice: All persons indebted to the estate of Ebenezar Miles, deceased, are hereby requested to come forward and make payment.... Elizabeth Miles, Adm'rx

MISCELLANEOUS ALABAMA NEWSPAPER ABSTRACTS --- VOL 1

Notice: Those who are indebted to the subscriber for medical services or otherwise, previous to his partnership with Dr. Hogan, are earnestly requested to make immediate settlement by note or cash. John H. Miller

<u>List of letters in the Post Office at Selma, on the 1st day of January, 1828:</u>

Samuel Adams, Rev. T. Alexander

John Brautly, John M. Bigham, Griffin Bender, William S. Ballard, Josiah E. Brown, James Barfield, Tyre Belvin, George Buchanan

Thompson Coventry, William Cole, Cephas L. Chapin, Robert L. Crawford, John Campbell, William Cooke, William L. Carney, Elizabeth Coleman, Thomas B. Carroll, Mary Clanton

Ransom Davis, John H. Daily, John Dunn

Bennet Elkins, Rebecca Earle

James Flanagan

Mary Gardner, George Goffe, Benjamin A. Glass

William Hines, James M. Holiness, Moses Higginbotham, William Huddleston

S.A. Jones, Abraham Jones, Sen. John B. Jones

Memory J.A. Keith

Thomas Lindsy, Roygaman Lloyd, Charles C. Langdon, James G. Lyggin, Samuel Love, James Lanksten

John McLeod, Samuel Murray, Ann E. Maxwell

John Nettles

Mary Porter, Joseph Pepper, Daniel Patridge, Reuben Price, William Peeples, Ezekiel Pruitt, Elias Parkman

Rev. Wilson Ruesum, Isaac Rich, David Russell

Abraham Sheperd, B.G. Sims, Reddick Sims, Roddy Smith, William Shoat, Dennis Shaw, Daniel W. Stokes, Pleasant Stokes

MISCELLANEOUS ALABAMA NEWSPAPER ABSTRACTS --- VOL 1

Sally Tate, Isaac Tignor, Lucy Tignor, Moses Tilton, Jesse Turner

Joseph Wood, W.D. Waddell, John Welch, Jesse Williams, William Warren, Henry Wilkison
J.B. Griffin, P.M.

Ranaway from the subscriber, residing in Coosawda, Autauga County, about the 23rd November last, a negro fellow, named Sanno, about 28 years old, yellow complexion, small statue, of a surly disposition. He is American born, but has been brought up in a French family. He speaks broken English and understands something of the French language.... Henry Allen

Notice: All persons having demands against the estate of Mary Grier, deceased, of Dallas County, State of Alabama, are hereby requested to present them for settlement.... Wm. P. Molett

All persons indebted to the estate of Thomas Gamage, deceased, will please make payment.... Lucretia Gamage, Ex'rx, Elijah Wilson, Ex'r

Notice: John Johnson, Administrator with the will annexed, of the estate of Robert Greer, Sen., deceased.... make final settlement of said estate.... Dallas County

ISSUE 1-31-1828

Married, in Butler County, on the 17th inst., by the Rev. John Purdue, Mr. Alexander Watson, recently of this county, to Miss Nancy P. Purdue, of Butler County.

Died, on Thursday last, Mr. John H. King, a respectable citizen of this county, at the advanced age of 65 years. Mr. King was a native of the State of North Carolina; from North Carolina he removed to Tennessee, and from thence to this county. Seventeen children are left to deplore his death.

Dallas County,: Armstrong Y. Blackburn, Executor, in right of his wife, who was sole executrix of the last will and testament of Hampton Bostick, late of Dallas County, and state aforesaid, now deceased, has made application to the Court for leave to sell the real estate that was of the late Hampton Bostick, now deceased, for the benefit of the heirs.... Nov. 12th 1827

ISSUE 2-7-1828

Doct. Evans respectfully informs the public, that he has located himself at Samuel H. Bogle's, on the Mulberry....

MISCELLANEOUS ALABAMA NEWSPAPER ABSTRACTS --- VOL 1

Died, in Mifflin County, Pennsylvania, on the 9th ult., Mrs. Jane, consort of Mr. G. Frow, and mother of the editor of this paper. Thus a husband has been bereaved of the tender partner of his bosom, six children, of an affectionate parent....

ISSUE 2-14-1828

Trust Sale: Whereas William B. Allen and Westley W. M'Guire, on the 8th October, 1824, executed a deed, and thereby conveyed to Samuel Pickens, Uriah G. Mitchell and Jesse Beene, all the right, interest and claim which they the said Allen and M'Guire had in and to the printing establishment of the new series of the *Cahawba Press*, in trust for the payment of the sum of $480 cash, and some other demands, mentioned in said deed, to the said Pickens, Mitchell and Beene; and the said Allen and M'Guire having failed to pay to the said Pickens, Mitchell and Beene any part of the aforesaid sum of $480, and some other demands, these are therefore to give notice that we will, on Monday the 10th day of March next, in the town of Cahawba..sell to the highest bidder for cash, the printing establishment of the new series of the *Cahawba Press*....

I hereby notify all persons having claims against the estate of James Harrod, late of Bibb County, deceased, to present them to me.... William H. Peeples, Executor

ISSUE 2-21-1828

Absconded from the Bell Tavern, in Selma, on the 1st inst., a negro man, named Orin. 28 or 30 years of age, about 5' 6 or 7 inches high, slim made.... He was purchased by the late _____ Roberson in Fayetteville, Tennessee.... his mother living there, it is supposed that he will try to get to that ?????. Isom Roberson

All persons indebted to Joseph McReynolds would do well to call at the store of J.W. Burke and left their notes.... James McReynolds, agent of Joseph McReynolds

Died, in New York, on the 10th ult., Adrian A. Kissam, a promising and highly respectable student of Rutgers' Medical College. His death was occasioned by the absorption of a deleterious matter from a slight cut received in one of his fingers, while engaged in prosecuting Anatomy.

Married, in Montevallo, on Thursday last, Mr. John Daugherty to Miss Olive Ann Echols, both of this place.

MISCELLANEOUS ALABAMA NEWSPAPER ABSTRACTS --- VOL 1

(Married) In Perry, Georgia, on the 7th inst., Maj. Michael Barnwell, a native of France, aged 70 years, to Mrs. Anne G???, a native of Switzerland, aged 75 years....

M.G. M'Keagg requests all persons indebted to him to make immediate payment.

A brown mare mule came to my plantation, on Pine Flat, 5 miles east of Selma, in July last. Benj. J. Tarver

Ranaway from the subscriber's plantation, on the south side of the Alabama River, 10 miles from Selma, on the night of the 18th inst., two negro fellows, named Pompey and Moses. Moses is about 22 years of age, 6' high, 184 pounds.... Pompey is 20 years of age, 5' 8" high, 160 pounds, very black and considerably knock knee'd.

ISSUE 2-28-1828

Notice: The public are cautioned against purchasing a note of hand, drawn in favor of Samuel W. Davidson, payable in Dec. last, forty three or four dollars, wherein Zacheus Woolley is principal.... Bibb Co., Adam Rhinehart

All persons having claimes against the estate of Abner Franklin, late of Dallas County, deceased, are hereby requested to present them.... Carter H. Cleveland, executor

Married, on Tuesday the 19th inst., by the Rev. James S. Guthere, Mr. Jacob G. Maull, of Montgomery County, to Miss Winney R. Cole, of this county.

(Married) On Thursday last, by the Rev. James C. Sharp, Mr. John S. Brown, of Roane County, E. Tennessee, to Miss Elizabeth H., only daughter of Benj. Tarver of this county.

(Married) On Sunday evening last, by the Rev. N. Haggard, Mr. John D. Haynes to Mrs. Nancy Bogle, both of this vicinity.

(Married) In Bibb County, on the 18th inst., by N.B. Coaker, Mr. Isaac Horne to Mrs. Leticia Loving.

(Married) In Montgomery County, on last evening, by Isaac Hudson, Mr. Wm. Mock, to Miss Ann Allen, all of said county.

Died, at his residence in this county, on Saturday evening last, Maj. David McCord, Receiver of Public Monies for the Cahawba District. His remains were interred in due form by the members of Halo Lodge and Selma Fraternal Lodge, on the Sunday following.

(Died) On Tuesday last, at the residence of his brother-in-law, Mr. John Shields, of this county, Mr. Robert Paulding, formerly of Huntsville.

INFORMATION WANTED: The subscriber is very desirous of knowing where Hugh M. Rose resides. Any person who will give this information in a letter, directed to Eatonton, Georgia, will confer an obligation which will be remember with gratitude. Printers throughout the U. States will do a favor to a widow and two Orphans', by giving one or more insertions to the above advertisement. Eatonton, Ga. John Kennon

ISSUE 3-13-1828

Married, in Perry County, on Thursday evening the 21st. ult., by the Rev. R. Holman, Mr. Joseph Wiley, late of North Carolina, to Mrs. Mary A. Johnson, only daughter of Mr. William Curry.

(Married) At the market-house, in Augusta, Ga., at 5 o'clock on Wednesday evening last, by J.W. Meredith, Mr. Bright Prickett to Miss Eliza Cole. The above pair were emigrating from North Carolina, and became first acquainted with each other "on the long road to Georgia."..... A subscription was instantly raised to pay the license fee, and our worthy Squire of the 22nd district, volunteered to officiate on the occasion without "fee, reward, or the hope thereof".... the happy pair took up their line of march, arm in arm, towards Tallahassee.... (*Aug. Chron.*) [condensed]

ISSUE 3-20-1828

Ad for the saw mills of Wm. R. Pickett, Autauga Co

Absconded from the Bell Tavern, on the night of the 15th inst., a negro man named George. He is about 23 years of age, stout made, and with prominent forehead, 5' and about 8 or 9 inches high, slow in motion and in speech.... he is the bona fide property of the estate of John Roberson deceased, who in his life time purchased him of the agent of Joseph McReynolds. Isom Roberson, Adm'r

Dallas County Circuit Court, October Term 1827: Temperance Rose vs William Rose, not an inhabitant of this state. Petition for Divorce.

MISCELLANEOUS ALABAMA NEWSPAPER ABSTRACTS --- VOL 1

ISSUE 3-27-1828

Perry County Circuit Court, November Term, 1827: Catharine Williams, by her next friend John Carr, vs Henry Williams, non resident. Bill for Divorce.

Trust Sale: I will, on Monday the 12th of May next, in the town of Cahawba, sell at public auction.... the following slaves, to wit: Wappin, Bill, Natt, Harma and her child, which were conveyed in trust to me by Robert Gantt, in his life time, to satisfy a demand which he owed John McGhee. Jesse Beene, trustee

The copartnership of Wm. Sloan & Co. is this day dissolved by mutual consent. Ashville, St. Clair County, March 10, 1828, Wm. Sloan, Hodges & Butler of Selma

Letters of Administration having been granted to the undersigned, by the judge of the County Court of Dallas County on the estate of John Roberson, deceased.... Isom Roberson, Adm'r, Catharine Roberson, Adm'x.

Ad for H. Heintz, Selma, Ala

Dr. Wiley respectfully informs his friends and the public, that he has located himself at Centreville, Bibb County, Ala.

Will be sold at public auction on the 8th May next, at the house of the undersigned on the Mulberry, the property belonging to the estate of John H. King, deceased. Benjamin King, Adm'r

Married, on Thursday last, by the Rev. Mr. Heard, Mr. Thomas Cook to Mrs. Sarah A. Bass, all of this county.

(Married) In Tuscaloosa, on Thursday evening, the 13th inst., by the Rev. Robert Davis, Mr. Henry Moffett, of Cahawba, to Miss Damaras Ewing.

(Married) On Thursday the 13th inst., Mr. Green T. McAfee to Miss Chalsia Ann Hall, both of St. Clair County.

(Married) On Tuesday evening the 18th inst., Mr. William Mathis to Miss Charlotte Hanley, both of Wilcox County.

(Married) In Connecticut lately, master David Turner, of Palermo, aged 17, to Miss Almira Brown, of Liberty, aged 14, after a courtship of five years. Certainly the little God was in one of his finest frolics when he aimed his darts at the breast of 12 and 9 years. He must have taken a sip of nectar too

Miscellaneous Alabama Newspaper Abstracts --- Vol 1

much.... (*N.Y. Enquirer*)

William H. Gillis can be referred to a source where he may hear something about a law suit he had pending in South Carolina, by application at the office of the "*Selma Courier.*" His attorney thinks he resides either in Dallas or one of the adjoining counties.

ISSUE 4-3-1828

Dallas Co. admin. notice estate of John O'Sullivan, dec.; L. Roberts, adm'r

Died in Greensborough, 21 ult. Absalom Alston, Innkeeper, aged about 60

ISSUE 4-10-1828

Died, on Monday, the 31st inst., in Pleasant Valley, Mr. Starkey Hill, at an advanced age. Lately, at the Falls of the Chatahcoohie, Mr. Zachariah Dewell, formerly at Cahawba.

(Died) At his residence in Montgomery County, on Friday last, William Ashley, Sen. Mr. Ashley emigrated to this state from North Carolina about 10 years ago.... He has left a large and respectable family of children to deplore his loss...

Absconded on the 5th inst., my negro man Milo. He is an African, short and stout made.... he is about 40 years old. Andw. Pickens

ISSUE 4-17-1828

A list of letters remaining in the Post Office at Selma, Alabama, on the 1st day of April, 1828.

Thomas Alexander, Jesse Adams, John Anderson

Samuel H. Bogle, William Burgess, James K. Buckley, Absalom T. Barnet, F.H. Badger, Alfred Buck, Daniel Boon, John Barney, Isaac L. Barnes, Wm. Biggle, James Baley, Jesse T. Butler, Reuben Brabham

Carter Cleveland, Sedadiah Cook, John Craig, David M. Candless, Miss F.E.D. Cheek, Nathan Chafin, Wm. H. Clark, Thos. D. Carroll, Mr. Campbell, Thompson Coventry

Gideon Denton, Bradley Deer, Wm. J. Dennis, Samuel Draper, A.G. Deweese

Miscellaneous Alabama Newspaper Abstracts --- Vol 1

Bennet Elkins, Lewis Edward, Thos. Edmondson, Litleton Edward, Edmund Ethridge, Sr.

Clayborn Feicman, Armel Fincher, Francis Ford

James M. Glen, Rich'd Graham, Mrs. M. Gillem, Jas. F. George

Bethel Holmes, Mr. Hutto, Mathew Huff, Tillmon Hitt, Samuel Hester, Henry A. Hagler, John Howie, Caswell Henderson

William Johnston, Lewis Johnston, Samuel Johnston

Benjamin Kirk, J.D. King

Benj. Levenworth, John Lucas, Sam'l S. Leach, David M. Lloyd, W.W. Lewis, Thos. Lindsey

David Miler, Carson McNeal, James McCoy, Jacob McCarty, John Murphey, Joseph Murry, Benj'n Mott, Henry Mickelbury, Charles McGraw

Wm. Norris

Robert Orr, John Ormand, Elias Ogdon

Wm. S. Phillips, Reuben Price, Andrew Porter, Rob't D. Paulling, Benj. Phillips

Samuel H. Rees, Cornelius Roberson, Virgil B. Roberts, John Roberson, Stoddard Russel

Sam'l W. Shelton, John Stewart, Mary Saffold, Byrd Saffold, Hugh Spence & Co., Solomon Stephens, John Shields, Alexr. Samplee, Abraham Shepherd, Josiah Skinner, Wm. N. Sigler

Benj. Tippett, Capt. J.A. Tucker

Rev. Joseph Walker, Franklin Walker, James Webb, Elijah Wilson

<u>List of letters in the Post Office at Cahawba, Alabama, the quarter ending March 31st, 1828.</u>

John Abercrombie, Wm. B. Allen, Alabama Chapter Atheneum of Alabama, John Avery, Am Akeson, John Ashley, George Andrews

MISCELLANEOUS ALABAMA NEWSPAPER ABSTRACTS --- VOL 1

Wm. Bower, Marinda Bryan, John T. Beckley, Abraham Bolan, Richard J. Bryan, Wm. K. Beck, Miss Martha L. Byrd, Mrs. Elizabeth Boles, L. Brunson, Martha Buster, R.H. Barbour, James Brown

Frederick Carn, S & Martha Chapman, Thos. Casey, M.D., Rob't. L. Crawford, James Crawford, Miss Nancy Crawford, Sasuel Carter, John Cunningham, Captain Chisolm, Mrs. Henrietta B. Curtis, John McAddam, Michael Camack, Hardy Crim, Lewis Cook, Isaac N. Campbell, Eddin Cotton, John Coalman, Isaac Coalman

John Durden, Thomas Davis

Sam'l B. Ewing

Samuel Flanegin, R.J. Farrall, Abner Franklin, Philip Faulk, Miss Sarah Faulk

Matt. Gayle, Rich'd W. Gayle, Lewis C. Gaines, Sidney M. Goode, Virgil H. Gardner, Wade H. Greening, Miss Rebecca Gilmer, Wm. Green, Wm. Grant

Wm. H. Heap, John Howard, Wm. G. Hyde, Johnson Hayman, Wm. Hamner, Winston Hall, John H. High, Matthew Hinson, John Hewes

James Jernett, James B. Ivy, Hezekiah Johnson, James Jennings, Thaderick Jones, Elisha Jarald

M.J. Kenon, Thos. D. King, John King, Samuel Kendel, Patrick Keogh

Wm. Morison, Wm. Moore, Charles Mundine, Susan D. Mayer, Lewis B. Moseley, Daniel McCormack, James Marr, John Myrick, James Moor, Abner Mobley, John McConok, Irea Meadows, James McElroy, Sen., Benjamin Mayers, Wm. McKee, James Moreson, Stephen McKinzey, Rachael Mitchell, Sarah Moseley, William May, Charles Matthews

Oliver Norred, S.H. Nelms

Alex Outlaw, John W. O'Neal, James Owens, William Odom

Enoch Phelps, Nancy Patterson, John B. Patrick, Sarah Jane Poosee, George Phillips

Josiah Read, John G. Rainer, Thos. G. Rainer, Sam'l H. Reece, Wm. F. Roper, George W. Rea, Thomas D. Rumph, William Roberts, Sam'l H. Reece, Benjamin Renoulds, Wm. Rutherford

MISCELLANEOUS ALABAMA NEWSPAPER ABSTRACTS --- VOL 1

Thomas Stamps, Samuel Stabler, Abraham Shepherd, Benjamin Sewel, Alexander Shaw, Jesse Sparks, Secretary of Alabama Chapter, J.C. Sharp, Ethelbert W. Sanders, James Saffold, John C. Smith, Elisha Stamps, William Soles, Joseph Soles, Froeson Simpson, David B. Smedley, Mrs. Sorrell

John L. Taylor, B. Tippett, Adam Taylor, Sanders & Trigg, Wm. Toler

John E. Vasser, Joseph Vann, Lemuel Vasser, Charles Voultz

Lucy S. Wright, John Williams, Wm. B.C. Walker, H. Walker, Wm. Whatley, Ivy Wyett, John W. Wheeler, Noah F. Williams, Page R. Windham, Zelphia Windham, Andrew Walker, David D. Wakeley, Erasmus Walker, Eaton P. Wilson, Annis Wyott, David White, Joseph Walker, Alpheus B. Wright, Thomas G. Wilson, P.M.

ISSUE 5-1-1828

The woman called my wife, left my premises on the 15th inst., alleging as an excuse for so doing, that I had corrected two of my negroes, which I consider I am privileged to do, when they disobey me. She returned home, however, on the 16th inst. and appeared very find [sic]. On the 19th I ascertained that she had a peace warrant issued against me; and conceiving that unless I expose her conduct, I might be injured. As we were never legally married, and her conduct having been reprehensible, I therefore forewarn all persons from trusting her on my account, as I am determined to pay none of her contracts.... F. Davis, Mulberry, April 23rd

The public are cautioned against purchasing a note, drawn by the subscriber in favor of John Smith, for two hundred and forty dollars, with credits endorsed on the back amounting to probably one hundred dollars. This note is now held by Wm. Higginbotham, and as I hold notes on said Higginbotham sufficient to cancel the same I will not lift said note from any other person than him, unless compelled by a due course of law. Franklin J. Walker

ISSUE 5-8-1828

Letters of Administration having been granted, to us, by the Judge of the County Court of Dallas County, on the estate of Starky Hill, deceased, all persons having claims against the said estate will present them within the time prescribed by law.... Wm. Hill, Wiley W. Hill Adm'rs

County Clerk's Office, Dallas County, 14th April, 1828: Robert C. Morrison, administrator on the estate of Allen Orr, deceased, having represented the estate of said deceased insolvent....

MISCELLANEOUS ALABAMA NEWSPAPER ABSTRACTS --- VOL 1

Ranaway from the subscriber, in Montgomery County, Ala., 12 miles south of Vernon, on the 6th of March last, a negro man named, Frederick, about 25 years of age, 5' 7 or 8 inches high, very stout, of very black complexion, has one or two front teeth out, thick lips, rather submissive in his manners, and quite artful in passing himself. I suppose he will make his way to Georgia, where he has as often as twice secreted himself for some time.... Fielding Sharp

Letters of Administration on the estate of William Richy, late of Perry County, deceased, were this day granted to the undersigned.... A.G. McCraw, Adm'r

Shelby County, (Orphans' Court in vacation) Ordered by the court, that a citation issue, directing all persons interested in the lands, tenements and hereditaments of the estate of Job Mason, deceased, to appear before the Orphans' Court of said county, on the first Monday in June next, to shew [sic] cause why all the lands, tenements and hereditaments, of said Testator, should not be sold, as will be sufficient to pay his debts or the residue thereof. Leonard Tarrant, Judge

Shelby County: Posted before Abraham Smith, by Henry Haclow, a small, sorrell mare.

Ranaway from the subscriber on the 17th January last, living near Selma, Dallas County, a negro boy named Jacob, about 19 years of age, yellow complected, and has one of his fore fingers off. Any persons delivering the above described negro to me, now living in Perry County, shall be paid.... Benjamin Young

ISSUE 5-22-1828

Robert G. Gordon & John W. Paul have formed a copartnership in the practice of Law. The office of the former is in Mobile, the latter in Cahawba.

NOTICE: The copartnership of Burke, Shackelford & Co. is this day dissolved by mutual consent. D.H. Burke, Jack Shackelford, V.R. Shackelford

ISSUE 6-5-1828

Married, in Mobile, on the evening of the 29th ult., by the Rev. Lambeth, Gen. William Taylor of this county, to Miss Eliza H. Mead, of that city.

I hereby caution the public against purchasing a note of hand, drawn by me in favor of Carter T. Hall, for about two hundred and twenty-five dollars, and dated between the 1st and 15th April, 1823.... Mulberry, June 5th

Miscellaneous Alabama Newspaper Abstracts --- Vol 1

Richard Hall

Committed to the jail of Dallas County, on the 4th day of June, a negro man, who says his name is Isaac, and that he belongs to Charles Thaxton. He is about 20 years old, lisps in talking, has a small scar on the right temple, and one on the left shoulder, is about 5' 6" high. S.E. Harrison, jailor

EAGLE HOTEL: Mrs. Elizabeth Alston takes this method of informing her friends and the public, that she has opened a House of Entertainment, at the above sign, in the town of Greensborough, Alabama, under the management of Mr. David Harding....

ISSUE 6-12-1828

Married, on Thursday last, by the Rev. J.S. Guthrie, Mr. John Moore to Miss Elenor Oliver, all of Cedar Creek.

The Rev. Mr. Alexander will preach the funeral sermon of the late William Trigg, at the house of Col. E.W. Saunders, on Sunday the 22nd instant.

INFORMATION WANTED: Any person who can give any information of a young man by the name of Patrick Berine, from the County of Leitrim, Jamestown, Ireland, will confer a great favor on his anxious sister, by addressing a few lines to Timothy Corcoran, Jackson, Louisiana.

Ranaway from the plantation of Mr. Henry Adams, living on Little Cedar Creek, Dallas County, about the 14th April last, a mulatto fellow named Harry, a carpenter, between 35 and 40 years old, about 6' 2 or 3 inches high, and thin visage, has a white or gray spot on the top of his head about the size of a dollar, speaks through his nose and is a good worker.... Jesse Turner, Cedar Creek

ISSUE 6-19-1828

Taken up by the subscriber living on the bend of Valley Creek in Perry County, on the 1st inst., a bright chesnut sorrel horse.... Isaac Suttles

I forewarn the public against trusting my wife Sarah Goodgame on my account. I do not intend paying any of her contracts. Bibb County, May 3rd, John Goodgame

ISSUE 6-26-1828

The painful duty of recording the death of James P. Bates, late sheriff of the

MISCELLANEOUS ALABAMA NEWSPAPER ABSTRACTS --- VOL 1

County of Mobile, devolves upon us. He died at his residence, about 3 miles from this city, on Wednesday last, in the 29th year of his age, after a short illness, and without any apprehension being entertained of his safety until a few moments before his decease. (*Mobile Register*, 14th inst.)

ISSUE 7-3-1828

Married, in New York, on Tuesday the 24th ult., by the Rev. M.D. Thomason, Mr. Russel Williams to Miss Upha Campbell, all of Pleasant Valley.

Died, recently, in new York, Mrs. Troup, consort of Col. G.M. Troup, late Governor of the State of Georgia.

<u>A list of letters remaining in the Post Office at Cahawba, the quarter ending 30th June, 1828:</u>

Lenord Abercrombie, Spencer Adams, Jr., John Allison, Joel T. Avery, C.A. Abercrombie, John Allison, Allen Avery

A.S. Black, Ephraim Butler, Abner Buckhalter, Rev. Wm. Blackstock, John B. Burke, George Boundes, Hugh D. Bozeman, Absalom Barnett, Griffin Bender

Rob't L. Crawford, Richard Clark, Sasuel Carter, Mrs. Patience Colly, Dr. Robert Collins, Thomas V. Carson

John Dunn, Abner C. Duese, Richard M. Davis, Ulysses B. Davis, Col. Samuel Dale, John Dennis

Robert English, Edmund Ethrige

John Fowler

Wm. Grant, Matt Gayle, Rufus Greening, Jacob Givhan, Mrs. Mason Gillom, His Excellency the Governor, Jas. S. Guthrie, Benjamin Grumbles, Daniel Grant, John Garnor, Grayfield Goosa

Thomas Hardin, John Halcome, Abner A. Hughes, James Harrison, Sam'l Hughes, Miss E. Oliver, C.B. Harrison, James Hatcher, Col. John Hale, Skiler G. Harris, Sam'l Hitchcock

John B. Jones, Jacob Jackson, James J. Jordan, Wm. Jones, Col. Harwood Jones, Jesse Jones

George King, B. King, Wm. C. Kent, Allen Killgore, James B. King

MISCELLANEOUS ALABAMA NEWSPAPER ABSTRACTS --- VOL 1

David Lee, Loved Lee, Allen Love, Daniel Ligon, Jesse Lamb, Joseph A.L. Lee, John W. Lynch

Isaac Moore, John McCamy, Charles L. Matthews, Anderson H. Moss, Wm. McCord, Jas. Moore, Miss Polly Moore, Mrs. Nancy McHenry, Mrs. Dicy Matthews, Hugh McPhail, Wesley McGuire, Dr. Thos. O. Meux, Riley Moody, Sam'l Moses, George Mozingor & Wife, James McElroy, James Martin, John Myrick

Willis Nunnelee

Wm. Odom, John W. O'Neal, Alex Outlaw, Wm. W. Olds

Alex Pope, E. Pickens, James Parker, Phillip Payne, Andrew Pickens, A.P. Pleton Adkins, Enoch Phelps, John W. Paul

John W. Rinaldi, Wm. Radford, James Rowsey, Riland Roberts, Mrs. Eliz'th Rutledge, Josiah Reed, James Reynolds, Noah Rodgers, Thomas Ross, George R. Rice, Wm. Roberson

Wm. Sims, Thomas J. Smith, David Smith, Needham Smith, James Sharp, Lroy Skinner, Isaac Simmons, William Scott, Benjamin Seawell, Charity Smith, Sam'l S. Simmons

John S. Tinsley, Mrs. Sarah Tate, Abram Trigg, Benjamin Tarver or Mrs. Gillum, Miss C. Thweatt, Sam'l H. Taylor, Williamson Tarver, Miss Martha Thweatt

J.C. Van Dyke

Joseph Walker, Mary Ann Walker, Moses Williams, Hannah Wrabon, Henry West, Benjamin Wallace, Fedrick Wittich, David White, Thos. H. Wiley, Thomas G. Wilson, P.M.

A list of letters remaining in the Post Office at Selma, Alabama, the quarter ending 30th June, 1828:

Elias Artiberry

Absolem T. Barnett, Moses Bradshaw, James C. Burkley, Nicholas Boyter, James Bailey, Griffin Bender, William Blythe, William Ballard, Abraham Banfield, Elizabeth Bowles, Reuben Braddum, George Burte

John Carter, James Crawford, Hampton Crawford, John Crawford, Clarke

MISCELLANEOUS ALABAMA NEWSPAPER ABSTRACTS --- VOL 1

Croker, Richard Covington, Abraham Card, James L. Clark, Isaac Carr, Rev. Charles Crow, Robert Crenshaw, Michael Caruman

John H. Daily, Samuel Davis, Frederick Day, James Dunn, Walton Drane, Chas. C.P. Duke, H. Davis

Wm. P. Echols, James Elliott

John Fanin, Wilhorn Flanigin, Elisha Fyke

Thos. B. Goldsby, James Griffin, Bright Gardner

Miss Caroline Henderson, Miss Caroline L. Henderson, Obediah Hulet, John Hunt, John A. Hopkins, George Hopper, Joshua Hughs, Mrs. Eliza Harris, Christopher Hinton, Thomas Harvill, William Holston, Allen Hemmingray, W.W. Hill, William Humphreys, Capt. Henry Haynes, Seborn Hillard, Joseph Hurd

A. Jones, John Jones, Enoch Joseph

Benajah King, Willis Kilcrease, A. Killingsworth

James Loocus, James Langford, James G. Liggin, Wm. R. Laughlin, B.F. Leavingsworth, Henry Looney

Isaac Melon, John B. Marshall, Thomas McCraw, Mrs. Jane McFarlin, James McDounal, Benj. McReynolds, John Moore, Allen McReynolds, Thomas Moore, Jacob McCarty, Thomas H. Moore, Elizabeth Manning, W.W. McGuire

Andrew A. Noble

James Orman

Rev. Robert Porter, Col. Joab Pinson, ?? Parker, Maryan Prewett, Thos. Jefferson Pugg, John Parry, George Phillips, Archibald Porter, A. Perry

Wilson Russun, Thomas or William Rutledge, Jesse D. Roundtree, John Ray, Leonard P. Ray, Mrs. Eliz'th Riddle, Temperance Rose, Cornelius Robinson, Phebe Richey, Reubin J. Rogers

Reddick Sims, Bird Saffold, John Stone, Samuel W. Shelton, Thomas Stone, William Smedley, A??il Sawyer, Pierce Stephens, William Schofield

Jeremiah A. Tucker, Thomas Taylor

MISCELLANEOUS ALABAMA NEWSPAPER ABSTRACTS --- VOL 1

Lemuel Vasser, Miss Martha Vaughn

James C. Winter, Mrs. Jas. C. Winter, Thomas Wright, William Wright, Oliver L. Wili?, Jonathan Woodbry, William H. Warren, James Wilton, Aron Warren, George Wilson, John D. Watson

Adam Zimmerman

James Melton left his wife and one child in Blount County, the last of August last. He started to Albermarle County, in Virginia, to move his brother to this country, and by a letter from her, I am informed he had not been there yet. He is a small man, sandy-haired; a shoe and boot maker, and says he learnt his trade with one Roberson, in Albemarle. I hereby forewarn all persons from marrying him, as he has already one wife. Whoever may hear or know anything of him is requested to write to me, and direct to Maryville, Blount County, Tennessee. annah [sic] Melton

ISSUE 7-10-1828

Married, on Thursday evening last, by the Rev. J.C. Sharp, Mr. Benjamin Ivy, of Pleasant Valley, to Mrs. Martha Burster, formerly of Madison County.

ISSUE 7-24-1828

Letters of Administration having been granted to the undersigned, of the estate of John Allen, late of Shelby County.... Sally B. Allen, Adm'rx.

Strayed from the plantation of John Morgan, on Bogue Chitto Creek, a bay mare.... application be made to me, near Portland, Dallas County, Ala. Portland, July 11th, Thomas Colbert

Strayed or stolen, from the subscriber, about the 15th of Feb. last, a sorrel horse.... Prairie Bluff, July 12th, A.M.B. Thomson

Information to William Haynes: I received a letter form Mobile, dated Nov. 10th, 1827, and postmarked March 6th, 1828, from Robert Haynes, enclosing another letter directed to William Haynes, with instructions to me to deliver it to him. I have made every possible inquiry after the said William Haynes without success. The letter contains cash, and must be of importance to him, who, on application to me, at Old Town Creek, can receive it. Peter Robertson

Bibb County Orphans' Court, March Sitting, 1828: This day came Nancy Brown, Executrix of the estate of John Brown, late of said county, deceased, and exhibited on oath, a statement of the situation of said estate, and representing the same as insolvent....

ISSUE 7-31-1828

Married, at Paterson (N.J.) on the 10th inst., by the Rev. Mr. Fisher, Russel Stebbins, of Mobile, to Miss Ann Eliza Davis, of the former place.

Died, suddenly on Saturday last, Robert Cicero son of James Morrison, of Pleasant Valley, in the 8th year of his age.

(Died) Near Ashville, St. Clair County, Ala., on the ? inst., Mr. Arnold Thomason, (merchant) formerly of Cahawba, brother of the Rev. M.D. Thomason of Pleasant Valley, in the 38th year of his age. His death is deeply deplored by a wife and six small children...

Beware of the Imposter: Absconded from this place, on Wednesday night, the 23rd inst., Benjamin H. Mordecai. Mordecai is a youth of about ?o years of age, nearly five feet high, thick and clumsy and rocks very much when he walks; features regular, black eyes and heavy eyelashes, has a small scar on one side of his forehead, in the edge of the hair; lisps a little in his speech.... Mordecai came here on foot, about a month or six weeks since, from Montgomery Alabama, where he had lived for some time. He is a native of Savannah, Georgia. I understand he made some stay in Milledgeville, previous to his being in Montgomery. He advertised himself here, as a watch maker, and repairer, contracted some small debts, besides his board with me, and ranaway without paying anything.... John Erwin

Dallas County Circuit Court, October Term, 1828: Temperance Rose vs William Rose: Petition for Divorce.

ISSUE 8-14-1828

Died suddenly at his mother's residence near Cahawba, on the morning of the 7th Mr. Lark F. Perry, a native of Franklin Co. N.C. in the 25th year of his age.

Died on Thursday last, at his residence in Wilcox Co., John Gayle, Sen.

Married on the 5th inst. at Old Town, in this county by Jarvis-----? Mr. Louis Tignor to Miss Ann Buckhalter.

ISSUE 8-21-1828

MISCELLANEOUS ALABAMA NEWSPAPER ABSTRACTS --- VOL 1

Warrenton, (Geo.), Aug. 6th: In this place, on Saturday last, young Philander Paris, a little boy, was killed by the accidental discharge of a pistol, in the hands of David Holder, an apprentice boy....

Married, on Sunday evening the 3rd inst., by the Rev. Mr. Mealy, Mr. James Farness, to Mrs.(?) Rebecca Forsyth.

Died, in Mobile, on the 6th inst., Willonghty Barton, attorney at law, formerly of Augusta, Georgia.

ISSUE 8-28-1828

Married, on Thursday the 15th inst., by Thomas Hogg, Mr. Moses W. Collins, to Miss Elizabeth Sample, all of Autauga County.

Ranaway from the subscriber on the 6th August last, a stout good looking, athletic built negro, named Lewis or Lewis King, 5' 8" high, or over, about 24 or 26 years of age.... skin black; mouth small, and lips thinner than negroes in general.... He formerly belonged to Mr. John King, of Conecuh County, Alabama, about 10 miles from Sparta.... James Innerally, Pennsacola

ISSUE 9-25-1828

Dallas County Orphans' Court, Aug. 30th, 1828: This day the Executrix of Nancy Rutherford, deceased, her accompts and vouchers of the executorship of said descendant's estate, for final settlement.

Dallas County Orphans' Court, Aug. 30th, 1828: This day the executors of Thomas B. Rutherford, deceased, have filed their accompts and vouchers of their executorship, on said descendant's estate, for final settlement...

Letters of Administration have been granted to the undersigned, on the estate of William Dunklin, late deceased, of Dallas county.... Hance H. Dunklin, Adm'r

I forewarn all persons from trading for a note of hand given to me in December, 1827, with Tillman Watley security, to Joseph W. Jones of Bibb county, for $15. Said note with a letter, in which it was inclosed, directed from that place to James Broadhead at Weaver's Store, Bibb County, were lost. James Weeks

LOST OR MISLAID: Lately, in Selma, a due bill drawn by John Connely, in favor of R. Hatch, for $9.93.... Henry Koontz

Miscellaneous Alabama Newspaper Abstracts --- Vol 1

Mr. Joseph M. Derry having prepared himself for the reception of Boarders & Travelers, at Cahawba, tenders the use of his house to his friends and the public generally.

Dallas County Orphans' Court, Sept. Term, 1828: This day came Gabriel Herrald and filed his petition in this Court, requesting the Executor of Baxter Smith deceased to make titles to a certain tract of land, & c.

ISSUE 10-2-1828

Married, on Monday the 22nd ult., in Autauga County, by the Hon. Alvin A. M'Whorter, Moseley Baker, of Montgomery, Editor of the *Alabama Journal*, to Miss Eliza W., only daughter of Col. Wm. R. Pickett, of Autauga County.

(Married) On Wednesday the 24th ult., by Judge Tarrant, James W. Smith, Clerk of the Circuit Court of Shelby county, to Miss Angelina Stamps, daughter of Mr. Elijah Stamps, all of Shelby County.

(Married) On Thursday last, by Thomas Harville, Mr. William Williams, of Perry County, to Miss Emeline Campbell, of Pleasant Valley.

(Married) On Sunday the 14th ult., by the Rev. Dr. West, Mr. Charles Brown, of Montevallo, to Miss Jane Farley, of Spring Creek, all of Shelby County.

(Married) On Thursday the 25th ult., Mr. Richard Walker to Miss ____ Lolly, all of Shelby County.

(Married) On the same day, by the Rev. Dr. West, Mr. Edward Mahan, of Bibb county, to Mrs. Sarah Crawson, of Shelby County.

(Married) On Thursday, the 17th ult., by the Rev. Dr. West, Mr. David Lendsy, of Bibb County, to Miss Susan Porter of Shelby County.

A list of letters in the Post Office at Selma....
Rev. T. Alexander, John Anderson, Capt. Thos. Arnold

Nicholas Boyter, John G. Butler, Micajah Busby, Elizabeth Bower, Thomas H. Brickley, John Brantley, Joseph D. Burch

John Culbertson, George Carr, James G. Couan, John Chandler

William Dulaney, Hance H. Dunklin, Paschal Davis, Timothy Duck

Louis Edwards, Elizabeth Elliot, Dr. Wm. P. Echoles, Littleton Edwards

MISCELLANEOUS ALABAMA NEWSPAPER ABSTRACTS --- VOL 1

Stephen Frederick

Miss Elizabeth Gantt, Dr. Edward Gantt, Henry F. Greer, Miss Mary Garner, Wm. W. Goodwin, Jesse Gardner, Richard Gibson, Miss Louisa Goffe, George Goffe, Virgil H. Gardner

Mathew Huff, William Humphrey, Edward Hanrick, William Henry, Thomas Hardin, Rev. Mr. Houghton, Mrs. Mary Harris, William E. Henry, William Harvill, Thomas Harvill, Wilham Hinson, Andrew Hyller

Benjamin Jones, Jefferson Jordan, Richard Jones

John D. King, Hon. Wm. R. King, Allen Kilgore, Robert Kilgore, Benajah King

Thomas Low, William S. Lane, B.F. Leavinworth, James C. Laurence

Hugh McIlwaine, John Mixson, Mrs. Polly Moore, Mrs. Mary Moore, Dr. John McNeill, Charles Moore, John Macksfield, John J. McMillen, Benj. H. Mordicai, Mrs. Ann Maxwell, Henry D. Morrison, John McLoud, William May, H. Mickelborough, David McMillan

William Norwood, Eli Nobles

Elijah Pearson, Mark Philips, James Porter, Andrew W. Porter, Thomas Patterson, William Patterson, Bird Prewit, Paper Maker, Asa Parker, Boling H. Perry

James Reynolds, James Rollins, Samuel Radford, Thomas Roland, Thomas Rutledge

William Sharp, Bird Saffold, Robert Stringfellow, Robert Sturdivant

Clayton Thompson, Lawson H. Thompson, John Thomas, John H. Thompson

Jacob Vanderslice

David White, Mrs. Mary S. White, Elisha M. White, Erasmus Walker, Franklin Walker, Eaton P. Willson, John Welch, Robert Warnock

ISSUE 10-9-1828

<u>A list of letters remaining in the Post Office at Cahawba, the quarter ending 30th September, 1828:</u>

MISCELLANEOUS ALABAMA NEWSPAPER ABSTRACTS --- VOL 1

Allen Avery, John Arnold, Miss E. Adkinson, Evan Austill, Stephen S. Andrews, Atheneum of Alabama

Jacob Barron, Walter O. Beckley, Thomas Bellengslea, care of J.I. Croheron, George Buchanan, John Brantley & A.M. Minter, Joseph J. Borden, P.J. Bowan, Shepherd Brazellon, James Brown, Mrs. Dorcas M. Burk, Benjamin F. Burk

John Campbell, John Cotton, Isaac Carr, Mrs. Sarah Canady, H. Cheeseborough, Samuel Cartor, William Cross, Edwin Curtis, Patrick Colly, Nathan Chafin, Michael Cammack

A.C. Deweecse(?) P.M. Pleasant Hill care of P.M. Cahawba, Randle Duckworth, Walter Drane, T.H. Duglass, Jr., Benjamine Davis, Bryson T. Doubrins, William Dennis, Robert Dobbins, Zachius Day, William Day, J. and J. Derden

John Ellis

Francis Ford, Lardner C. French, William French, Sen.

Rev. J.S. Guthrie, James A. Gardner, Barnabas Grice, William Grant, Matt Gayle, Clerk of the Circuit Court, Thomas Gardner, Joseph Gee

Joseph C. Hudaleston, Mrs. N. Henry, Rev. E. Hearan, Henry Hitchcock, Wm. Higginbotham, Isaac Harkins, Col. John Hall

Thomas Jackson, Miss E. Jenning, William Johnston

Hugh Kennedy, William B. King

Joseph Lenel

Lewis Moore, P. McAdams, Jeremiah Mitchell, John Milly, Col. C.L. Matthews, Thomas O. Miux, Alexander McGirty, William Moore, William McCrackin, Henry Moffet, Mrs. Ann McCuller, Joseph McGee, Alexander McCaskal, Henry McCaghran

Alex. Pope, Reg. of the Land Office, Henry Pulmer, Post Master Pine Hill D. Co., James Porter, Mrs. C. Pelham, Miss S.J. Pooser

Miss E. Rutherford, Ephram Rigly, Benj. Reynolds, John W. Renalde, Alfred Roberts, J.D. Roundtree

Miscellaneous Alabama Newspaper Abstracts --- Vol 1

Esther Skinner, Charit C. Smith, Jonathan T. Sims, Elijah Sherrer, James P. Smith, Thomas Stamps, Voluntine Shulz, Joseph Sorals, Reuben Satterwhitt, Samuel Stabler, Mrs. Chrisley Shulz, Doct. A. Saltmarsh

Mrs. Sarah Tate, Lewis Tigner, James Todd, John Tubb, Henry Taylor, Rev. T. Trowel

Joseph Walker, T. Watts, Sen., Elisha M. White, Gideon White, John H. Walker, Charles Wood, George Walker, Ivy Wyatt, Mrs. P. Watkins, Thomas Wiley, Rev. Z. Williams, Thomas H. Wiley
Andrew Youngblood

ISSUE 10-16-1828

Married, on Wednesday evening the 1st inst., by the Rev. Noah Haggard, Mr. Paschall Traylor, to Miss Jane Gardner, both of this county.

(Married) In Macon, Geo., on the 25th ult., by the Rev. Mr. Patterson, Doct. Thomas R. Lamar, formerly of Marion, Perry County, Ala., to Mrs. Nancy Fullwood.

(Married) On Tuesday the 30th of September last, in the town of Washington, Autauga County, by Ward H. Cox, Dr. William Burt, of that county, to Miss Carolin Mathews, of Georgia.

Died, in Centreville, on Monday the 7th inst., Mrs. Betsey, wife of Col. Alexander Hill, in the 46th year of her age, after twenty four days severe illness.

The partnership heretofore existing between Robson & Scott is this day dissolved by mutual consent. Grocery business.... Selma, Sept. 30th, Joseph Scott, George Robson

ISSUE 10-23-1828

Dallas County Orphans' Court, Oct. Term, 1828: This day the Administrator of the estate of Thomas Ewing, filed his accounts and vouchers of the estate aforesaid for final settlement.

Dallas County Orphans' Court, Oct. Term, 1828: Notice of settlement of the estate of Samuel Parsons, deceased...

Dallas County Orphans' Court, Oct. Term, 1828: Notice of final settlement of the estate of John Carmichael, deceased.

MISCELLANEOUS ALABAMA NEWSPAPER ABSTRACTS --- VOL 1

ISSUE 11-6-1828

Died, near Port Gibson, Mississippi, on the 14th Sept. last, Joseph Miller, in the 53rd year of his age, brother of Dr. John H. Miller, of this vicinity.

Died. Lately, at Milford, Massachusetts, Doct. Elias Parkman, father of Mr. Elias Parkman, of this village.

(Died) At Columbus, Ga., on the 9th inst., of a pulmonary consumption, Mr. James B. Crawford, aged about 30 years. Mr. Crawford was for many years a resident of Cahawba, Alabama, and for a shot time a citizen of Columbus.... He was buried with Masonic honors.

ISSUE 11-20-1828

Married, in Pleasant Valley, on the 15th inst., by the Rev. Thomas Alexander, Mr. Addison H. Sample, formerly of Liberty County, Ga., to Miss Milly, daughter of Robert C. Morrison, of this county.

Died, at his residence in this county, on Friday the 15th inst., Major William Marsten Cowles, in the 70th year of his age. Major Cowles was a native of Charles City County, Virginia, and although a very young man at that time, voluntarily put on the armour of his country, in defence of her violated rights. He was a member of a volunteer corps of cavalry, stationed at Charles City court house; was taken prisoner at that place, carried to Westover and put on board an English ship of war, then lying off that place, where he was detained two months, when he made his escape, carrying off six other prisoners; he landed at Ferry Point, from whence he proceeded to the Great Bridge, to the camp of General Gregory, reaching that place the day after the battle fought there; he thence returned home. Shortly after this period, Lord Cornwallis was besieged by the American forces under General Washington, at Little York. Major Cowles, in company with several gentlemen of his acquaintance, repaired to the scene of action & was present at the surrender of that place. In 1784, he emigrated to the state of Georgia, and settled in the County of Richmond, near Augusta. For many years after the peace with Great Britain, the Creek Indians continued to be troublesome to the settlements on the frontiers of Georgia, and in an expedition ordered out by the state for their chastisement, Major Cowles volunteered his service, and during the expedition, served in the capacity of Aid to Major General Twiggs. He continued to reside near Augusta, until 1818, when he removed to this state and located himself in this county....

Died, in Monroe County, Alabama, in Sept. last, G?? Watkins, a native of Sand Gate, Vermont, where his friends are suppose to reside.

MISCELLANEOUS ALABAMA NEWSPAPER ABSTRACTS --- VOL 1

ISSUE 11-27-1828

The co-partnership of Willis Brown & Co., of Centreville, Bibb County, is this day dissolved by mutual consent. Willis Brown, Hodge & Butler, of Selma

Married, on Thursday last, on Old Town Creek, by ----- Scott, Mr. John Day, to Miss Lucinda Calloway, all of that place.

(Married) At Claibore, on Thursday evening the 30th ult, by his Honor Judge Lipscomb, A. P. Bagby, to Miss Elizabeth, daughter of Capt. Simon Connell, all of that place.

Died, on the 19th inst, at his residence on Cedar Creek, in this county, Captain Lemuel Vassar, in his 64th year, after a lingering pulmonary disease of upwards of two years, which baffled medical skill. He was a native of Virginia and emigrated from that state to South Carolina upwards of 40 years ago --from thence he removed to this county, and settled where he died.

(Died) In Pleasant Valley, Monday 17th, Mrs. Lucinda Davis, consort of Mr. Benjamin Davis, 22 years old... laboring under a consumption for 2 years.

I expect to leave this county about the first of January next. Persons indebted to me will please call and settle by that time.... Cahawba, Nov. 27th, S.E. Harrison

ISSUE 12-4-1828

Married, at Paris, Kentucky, on Tuesday evening, the 4th ult., by the Rev. James Blythe, D.D., Thomas Witherspoon, lately of Williamsborogh, S.C. now of Greene County, Alabama, to Mrs. Sarah W. Lapsley, relict of the Rev. Joseph Lapsley, late of Bowling Greene, Kentucky, deceased.

(Married) On Tuesday evening, the 25th ult., by the Rev. Mr. Lee, Joseph Shannon to Miss Sarah Phillips, all of Autauga County.

(Married) On the 26th ult., by the Rev. Mr. Hare, Mr. Jesse Minor, of Autauga County, to Miss Sophia Wooter, of Bibb County.

(Married) On the 23rd ult., by Peter Ford, Mr. Charles Anaraon, to Miss _____ Crowson, all of Shelby County.

$150 Reward will be given for the apprehension and delivery to me of my negro man, Milo... he is well known and sometimes seen, or in the neighborhood of Mr. Benjamin Young (where he pretends to have a wife) who

Miscellaneous Alabama Newspaper Abstracts --- Vol 1

lives in Perry County, near Pitts' Ferry on Cahawba river.... Andw. Pickens

Letters of Administration having been granted to the undersigned by the Judge of the County Court of Perry County, on the estate of John Perry, deceased.... Britton Perry, Executor

ISSUE 12-11-1828

Died, at his residence, near Washington, Autauga County, on Monday morning the 1st inst., James Huddleston, in the 68th year of his age. He was a native of Maryland, a participator in the Revolution.... For the last ten years he has been afflicted with a paralytic affliction, that rendered him almost helpless....

(Died) On Saturday last, whilst in attendance at the land sales in Cahawba, John Oden, a respectable citizen of Bibb County and a member of the Baptist Church.

Will be hired at the store of Ezell & Gordon on Tuesday the 30th day of December instant from 18 to 25 of the negroes belonging to the estate of Baxter Smith, deceased.... and plantation to be rented.... Lewis Tyus, Ex'r

Will be sold to the highest bidder, on Saturday the 10th day of January next, at the late residence of Job Mason, deceased, in Shelby County, Alabama, all the residue of said deceased's estate, consisting of all the land, except the widow's dower, two lots in the town of Montevallo.... Edm'd King, Jack Shackelford Ex'rs

ISSUE 12-18-1828

Married, on Thursday evening last, at Harpersville, Shelby County, Mr. Theodrick Johnson, merchant, to Miss Mary, daughter of John Kidd, all of that place.

Letters of Administration upon the estate of John Gayle, Sen., deceased, were granted by the Judge of the County Court of Wilcox County to the undersigned on the 28th of October 1828. Matt Gayle, Jabez W. Heustis Administrators

ISSUE 12-25-1828

Ranaway from the subscriber, about the first of December, a negro man, named Charles. He is a little lame in his left leg, about 5' 10" high, 35 years of age, and is suppose to be in the neighborhood of Montevallo, as his family

MISCELLANEOUS ALABAMA NEWSPAPER ABSTRACTS --- VOL 1

lives there.... Selma, Dec. 18th, P.L. Weaver

Married, on Sunday evening the 21st inst., at Church Hill, Montgomery County, by the Rev. J.S. Guthrie, Mr. John Adams, Merchant, to Mrs. Elizabeth B. Harrison, all of that place.

Letters of Administration having been granted to the undersigned by the Judge of the County Court of Dallas County, on the estate of Daniel Ward, deceased.... Solomon Ward, Adm'r

Will be sold on the 22nd day of January next all the real and personal estate of James H. Huddleston, deceased of Autauga County consisting of that well known farm on the road leading from Washington to Vernon, containing 640 acres.... Jn. Huddleston, Thornton Rice Ex'rs

ISSUE 1-1-1829

Married, at Prairie Bluff, on the evening of the 3rd inst., by the Rev. J.A. Butler, Alex. Terryman, of Conecuh county, to Miss Martha, daughter of Capt. Bryan Marsh, of Wilcox county.

Died, suddenly, on Monday last, at his residence in this county, Mr. James Reynolds, aged about 45 years, a worthy citizen and the contractor for carrying the mail between this place and Montgomery. He has left a large family to lament his death.

ISSUE 1-8-1829

Married, on Thursday the 18th ult. by the Rev. William Harris, David N. Lloyd, of Perry County, to Miss Martha Goodwin, of Bibb County.

All persons having claims against the estate of the late William M. Cowles, are requested to present them.... Gilbert Shearer, John R. Cowles Ex'rs

Ranaway a short time since, a negro fellow, belonging to the estate of Lemuel Vasser, deceased, named Peter. He is about 50 years old, is of a light complexion, is near sighted and has a scar on the side of his head occasioned by a burn, he is about 5' 8" high.... It is probable he will make for South Carolina, or for Green or for Wilcox Counties in this state, as he has connections living in both.

$150 Reward: Ranaway from the subscriber, living near Exell's Store, in Autauga County, about the 30th June last, a negro man named, Jack, about 28 or 30 years of age, 5' 7 or 8 inches high, a little inclined to be yellow.... he

Miscellaneous Alabama Newspaper Abstracts --- Vol 1

can read and carries with him a Bible and hymn book. It is believed that he is in the neighborhood of Mr. Young Goodwin, near the Three Forks of the Mulberry in Bibb County, where he has a wife. Archilles Pope

ISSUE 1-15-1829

Notice is hereby given that A.G. McCraw has resigned his administratorship of the estate of William Ritchey, deceased; and that the Honorable Court of Perry County has appointed the subscriber in his stead.... Wm. Johnson, Adm'r

Perry County Orphans' Court, Jan. Term, 1829: This day came into open Court Daniel Moore and William W. Goodwin, administrators of the estate of John Goodwin, deceased, and made application for final settlement of said estate.

A list of letters remaining in the Post Office at Selma, on the 1st day of January, 1829:

Rev. Th. Alexander

Syor Belvin or Elkanah Belvin, Stephen Bishop, Joshua Barns, John Brantley, John Blewford Smith, James Brooks, William Burress

S. Carlon, Absolem Clark, William Cary, Miss Jane Campbell, James Campbell, Lawrence P. Carr, John Culbertson, George Carr, Hugh Coffee, Isac N. Campbell

David N. Dunlap, John Daffon, John Dundsons, Mary Dunaghy, Firman Dunham, John H. Daily, Isaac Denton

Arthur K. Elliot

William Fradly, William Flanigan, Isaac H. Fenimore

John Grimes, George Gardner, Stephen M. Gilmore, John Gray, William Gray, William Gibson, Dr. Edward Gantt

Stephen Hazle, Wm. Humphreys, John Howard, John Hamon, Saeborn J. Hillard, Wm. Hinds, Lewis J. Halloway, Caswell Henderson, Soen Holmes, John Hazard, Wm. Harris

John Irvaine

MISCELLANEOUS ALABAMA NEWSPAPER ABSTRACTS --- VOL 1

Jesse Jones

Gen. Th. D. King, Hamblin Kirkland

Thomas Leopard, Enoch Little, D.M. Lloyd, John Lucas

John Murry, Mr. M'Ginnis, Wm. R. Minter, James Mears, Gen. M. M'Langhlin, James M'Kinney, Luke Manning, Dennis M'Guire, James M'Reynolds, D. M'Leoad, H.T. Mickelborough, Bled Melton, Joseph Mitchell, David M'Cullough, Benj. H. Mordica

Wm. Olds

Col. Joab Pinson, Dr. G. Phillips, Wm. S. Phillips, Archibald Porter

Reuben Rambo or Matilda Rombo, Wm. Rutherford, Peter G. Reid, James Reynolds, Elizabeth Rutherford

M.D. Thominson, Daniel W. Stokes, Sheriff of Dallas Co., Reddick Sims, Wm. N. Sigler, James Sample, George J. Strong

J. Anderson Tarver, John Tompkins, Jeremiah Tucker

?. Vasser

E. Walker, Gen. T. Woodward, Olivar L. Wiley

Maj. Benj. Young, Osborn Youngblood

Married, on Tuesday evening last, by the Rev. J.C. Sharp, Mr. Bartlet Gamage to Miss Mary, daughter of Mr. William Sharp, all of Pleasant Valley.

Administrator's Sale: Agreeably to an order of the County Court of Dallas County, I will offer at public sale, on Saturday the 28th day of Feb. next, at the residence of James Bogle, deceased, a Bark Mill and all the tools of the Tanyard, of said deceased.... S.H. Bogle, Adm'r

A list of letters remaining in the Post Office at Perry Court House, January 1,1829:

P.P. Ashe, Thomas S. Ashe, William Armstrong, Mark J. Allen

Jeremiah S. Beeson, Lewis Brown, Gabriel Benson, William Brown, Doct. E. Benson

MISCELLANEOUS ALABAMA NEWSPAPER ABSTRACTS --- VOL 1

William Chestina, Miss Eunia Carter, William Cooksey, Thomas Cumings, George Crim

Mrs. Darling, Hasting Dial

John Elders, Lewis Edwards

James M. Fiske, William Ford

James Goggans, Thomas Gillespie

Wiley Henderson, John Hoggue, David Holo?n, James Haskins, William Harvell, J.J. Harrison, George Hopper, Hackworth & Keith, Noah Haggard, Henry Horn

Branch Jordan, John Jones

Allen Kilgore, William Kelly, William King, Col. Edwin King, Jesse Kelly

Temple Lea, Lemuel S. Leech, John Little, John Lockhart

Doct. James Meek, Alexander M'Ginty, William M'Lendon, Michael Mowdy, Thomas M'Connel, ??? Wm. M'Kee, Wilson M'Kinney, Elijah Miers, Selo?on Mim

Jesse B. Nave

J.K. Pool

Samuel Richardson, Thomas Reeder, James L. Ross, Robert G. Reid

Samuel Strudwick, David Smith, Wm. Stringfellow, Miss E. Shackelford, Thomas M. Smith, Wm. Saunders, Robert Sturdivant, Mrs. Thirza Sanders, Daniel Sears, G.N. Sanders, R.D. Shackelford, Sherrod Sanders

Richard Tubb, John Tubb, James Tubb, William Tate, Daniel Tubb, Mr. Turnbough

Samuel Utley

William Wallace, James Wallace, William Walters, Miss Catharine Webb, Coline Waters, Edmund Warrin, Robert Williams, George W?????, John Warren, Hiram Wilson

MISCELLANEOUS ALABAMA NEWSPAPER ABSTRACTS --- VOL 1

Thomas Young, Mrs. Mary Yeates

ISSUE 1-22-1829

Perry County estray notice: Taken up on the 7th Jan., 1829, by Adam Summons, in said county, an iron gray horse....

Perry County estray notice: Taken up on the 15th Jan, 1829, by William D. Harrington, of said county, a light bay horse....

Dallas County Orphans' Court, Jan. 1st. 1829: The executor of Willis Randle, deceased, having this day filed his accounts and vouchers of his executorship of said decedent's estate for final settlement.

Will be hired, for one year, on the 7th day of Feb. next, at the plantation of Lemuel Vasser, deceased, a prime negro boy, about 16 years old. Also, the plantation on which U.B. Davis has resided for several years, consisting of about 60 or 70 acres.... adjoining the farm of James Smiley.... Jno. E. Vasser, Guardian

To William Hill, Polly Hill, Wiley W. Hill, Betsey Hartley, wife of Joseph Hartley, Milley Arterbury, wife of Archilles Arterbury, Sally Sturdivant, wife of Ira Sturdivant, and Benjamin Hill: Take Notice that, according to an order of the Judge of the County Court, of Dallas, to us directed for that purpose, we, or a majority of us, will on the 23rd day of Feb. next, proceed to divide and distribute.... the real estate that was of Starkey Hill, now deceased. Geo. Phillips, Isaac Moore, Wm. Blevins, Samuel Morrow, Charles Walker, Comm'rs.

Information wanted, of a certain William Otterson, the son of John and Jane Otterson, of Washington City, D.C. The last time he was heard from was about 5 years ago and then was at Cumberland County, Va., on his way to Charleston, but there is reason to believe that he afterwards emigrated to Alabama.... information, by letter, addressed to the Rev. Mr. Balch, Georgetown, D.C., will be thankfully received.

Dallas County Orphans' Court, January 12, 1829: The administrators of the estate of Edward Woods, deceased.... filed their accounts & vouchers of their administratorship for final settlement.

Dallas Co. Orphans' Court. Nov. term 1828. This day the administrator of Joseph Noble, dec., filed his accounts and vouchers of his administratorship on said decedent's estate for final settlement.

MISCELLANEOUS ALABAMA NEWSPAPER ABSTRACTS --- VOL 1

ISSUE 2-5-1829

Married, on Thursday last, by the Rev. Mr. Holman, Robert W. Craig, to Mrs. Elizabeth Bryant, all of Perry County.

(Married) On the Mulberry, in this county, on Thursday evening last, by the Rev. Wm. Harris, Mr. Athelston Andrews, of Autauga County, to Miss Elizabeth Hall, daughter of Mr. Richard Hall, of the former place.

Co-Partnership: Peter Robertson having taken his brother William Robertson, into partnership, the business will hereafter be conducted under the firm of Peter & William Roberston. Old Town Creek, Feb. 1st.

John Ewing, Clock & watchmaker, having commenced business in the town of Selma, tenders his services to the public. He occupies part of the office of Albert G. Perry, and pledges himself to execute all orders in his line with promptitude, and on the most reasonable terms. Feb. 5

ISSUE 2-12-1829

Married, on Thursday the 29th ult., by the Rev. Mr. Hearn, Mr. Lerd Graham to Miss Mary Ann Smiley, daughter of Capt. John Smiley, all of Cedar Creek, in this county.

Dallas County Orphans' Court, Feb. Term 1828 [sic]. The administrator of the estate of Samuel Wallace, deceased, having applied for final settlement of said estate.

Letters of Administration having been granted to the undersigned by the County Court Dallas County, on the estate of James Reynolds, deceased... Pricella Reynolds, Adm'rx, Carter B. Harrison, Adm'r

The co-partnership of Hodges & Butler, is this day dissolved by mutual consent. Wm. F. Hodges, Edwin Butler

ISSUE 2-19-1829

Be cautious of two swindlers and rascals, James Owens and Elisha Owens, who have left Dallas County, Alabama, for debt, after defrauding every person they could.... Turner Ivy, of Dallas County, near Selma

ISSUE 3-5-1829

For Rent: The store house recently occupied by Benj. Smith, apply to

MISCELLANEOUS ALABAMA NEWSPAPER ABSTRACTS --- VOL 1

Parkman & Douglas, Selma, Feb. 26th.

Bibb County estray notice: taken up by Benjamin Griffin, a stray poney.... Bibb County estray notice: taken up by Minor Woolley, a sorrel horse....

Strayed or stolen, from the subscriber on the 7th inst., a bay horse.... I will reward any person who will deliver me said horses, at my residence, 3 miles above Portland, Ala., Wm. P. Molett

Notice: I forewarn all persons from trading for a note of hand, made by Langdon C. Carter, in favor of Ross & Crane, for some amount over one thousand dollars, signed Carter & M'Millan, as I do not intend to pay the same. A.B. M'Millan, Maplesville, Feb. 16th

ISSUE 3-12-1829

Married, on Thursday evening last, by Isaac Hudson, Mr. George Walker, of Dallas County, to Miss Eliza, second daughter of Major Wm. Browning, of Montgomery County.

Dallas County Orphans' Court, March Term, 1829: Robt. M'Gough, and John H. Armstrong, the executors of Robert M'Gough, Sen., deceased, having this day applied for a final settlement of said estate.

Dallas County Orphans' Court, March Term, 1829: This day the administrators of the estate of Samuel Houston, deceased, having applied for final settlement of the estate of said deceased.

Chancery, Clerk of the County Court, Dallas County: Hillory Lee vs Sabina Lee: Bill for Divorce. To Sabina Lee: Take notice, that I will, on Saturday before the first Monday in April next, proceed to take the depositions of William Fletcher and ___ Whatley, at the office of the Clerk of the County Court of Dallas County, to be submitted as testimony in the above case.... Hillory Lee

ISSUE 3-19-1829

The administratorship of the estate of Nancy M'Gill, late of Dallas County, having been transferred from Carter B. Harrison to the subscriber.... A. Taylor, Adm'r

$50 Reward: Ranaway from the subscriber, about the first of Dec., a negro man, named Charles, about 35 years old, 5' 10" high, a little lame in his left leg. He formerly belonged to Jesse Wilson of Big Cove, Madison County, and for the last ten years lived in the neighborhood of Wilson's Hill & Pleasant Vally. P.I. Weaver

Committed to the jail in the town of Canton, Wilcox County, Ala., on the 8th Feb., 1829, a negro boy, 14 or 15 years of age, who calls himself Daniel and says that he belongs to an Indian, near the Coosa River.... Canton, Feb. 9th, Nath'l. A. Jameson, Sheriff

The Judge of the Shelby Court, has appointed Mr. Martin M'Henry, Clerk of said Court, in the room of O.B. Havis, resigned.

Serious Affray: On Monday night last, an occurrence took place on the opposite side of the river (commonly called Kentuck) which ended rather fatally: A man by the name of William Henderson, but better known in this community, as Bill Henderson, was shot through the heart, and expired almost instantly, by a Mr. Hoy. Hoy kept a grocery near the bank of the river and some misunderstanding had previously existed between him and Henderson.... It is rumored that a brother of Henderson's (Bud) was shot the same evening in Greene County. (*Tusca. Chron.*)

SWINDLING: On Saturday the 31st ult., a genteely dressed young man, calling himself Jones, but whose real name turns out to be Levi, arrived in this place, and sold a negro fellow to the Rev. Robert Cunningham, of this neighborhood. On Sunday, (the next day) he left here; and on Monday, a Mr. Gilmer, from Mississippi, arrived in town, and claimed the negro in the possession of Mr. C. he having previously purchased him of the same man, the fellow ran off to Levi who brought him here, and again sold him. L was followed, and overtaken in Autauga County, in this state, and brought back Mr. Cunningham's money was returned to him, and Mr. Gilmer started on to Mississippi with the prisoner in custody....

MORE INDIAN MURDERS: Little Rock, (Ark.) Jan. 27th. The following is an extract of a letter to the Editor, from a respectable citizen of Miller County, dated 16th instant: "With deep concern, I have to inform you of more indian hostilities. A Mr. Whitesides has just returned from a trip to the Comanche country. His company, four in number, were all killed! Mr. Joel Dyer, of Hempstead County, was among the number"....

ISSUE 3-26-1829

TAKE CARE: Notice, is hereby given, that any person or persons found trespassing on the lands of the subscriber, by cutting timber of any kind whatever thereon, they will be prosecuted for such trespass.... C. Shearer, Selma, Dec. 11th

Miscellaneous Alabama Newspaper Abstracts --- Vol 1

Sheriff's Sale: Will be sold at public sale, on the first Monday in April next, in the town of Cahawba.... the following described negroes: Two negroes, Stephen & Dave, levied on as the property of George W. Gains, administrator of James S. Gains, deceased....

Died, lately, in Marion, Georgia, Mrs. Demaris, consort of Mr. Henry Moffitt, and daughter of the late Thomas Ewing, formerly of Cahawba.

Married, in Tuscaloosa, on Thursday last, by the Rev. Robert Cunningham, Mr. John B. Pas, merchant, to Miss Elizabeth Ann Ewing, all of that place.

(Married) On the 15th inst., by the Rev. Mr. Martin, Mr. Joseph Little, to Mrs. Polly Herad(?), both of Bibb County.

(Married) On the 19th inst., by the Rev. Mr. Martin, Mr. William Carey, to Miss Amy Barefield, both of Bibb County.

(Married) On the 15th inst., by Nathan Taber, Alexander Robeson, to Miss Jane Cook, both of Bibb County.

(Married) On the 19th inst., by Hugh Henry, Mr. John Chizm, to Miss Dawny Terry, both of Bibb County.

(Married) On the 9th inst., by Frederick James, Mr. Rabast Parker, to Miss _____ Lebury, both of Bibb County.

Will be sold at public auction.... in the town of Cahawba.... four likely negroes; levied on as the property of John Gayle, deceased, to satisfy two executions, one in favor of Edmund Randle, and one in favor of William D. Gaynes use of Jacob Jackson....

Will be sold in the town of Cahawba.... a negro boy named Rafe, levied on as the property of Robert English and William S. Ballard, to satisfy an execution against them, in favor of John J. Crocheron.

Will be sold, on the first Monday in April next.... in the town of Cahawba, the following slave: Sarah and her child, a boy named George, levied on as the property of William Higinbotham, to satisfy sundry executions against him- say one in favor of Joseph Deruy, two in favor of Wyckoff, Pickens & Co. and two in favor of Henry Overton....

Perry County, March 1829: Taken up, by Randal Bradford, on the 21st of Feb. last a chestnut sorrel horse. Taken up by Abner Wynn, of said county, on the 26th of Feb. last, a bay mare.... Taken up by Isaac Pool, in said

MISCELLANEOUS ALABAMA NEWSPAPER ABSTRACTS --- VOL 1

county on the 21st of Feb. last, a bright bay horse....

Workmen Wanted: The subscriber wishes to employ two journey men bricklayer. A. Worley, Selma

Perry County Orphans' Court, March Term 1829: This day came into open court Thomas Billingsley and Isaac Abercrombie executors of the last will and testament of Isaac Abercrombie, deceased, and made application to make a final settlement of their administration accounts with this court.

Sheriff Sale: Land levied on as the property of Alexander S. Outlaw.

ISSUE 4-2-1829

Married, on the 31st ult., at the Asbury Missionary Institution, near Fort Mitchell, Creek Nation, by the Rev. Mr. Hill, Mr. James Hill of the U.S. Army, to Miss Amanda Doyle, a Creek pupil of the Institution. This establishment is under the care of Mr. & Mrs. Hill.... (*Aug. Chronicle*) (lengthy description of wedding given.)

A list of letters in the Post Office at Selma, Ala., on the 1st day of April, 1829:

Abraham Adams, Lemuel Y. Allen

William Blalock, Beene & Walker, James Brantley, Bartlett Busby, James Brooks, Miss Mary Burns, William Bell, John Burnett, William Branch, Dr. Robert Beattie

Joel Chandler, Mrs. Roranah Cook, Joh Crawford, John H. Callen, John Culbertson, Hugh Coffee, C. Culbertson, Abner Cody, Charles Crow, David Covington, James Cannte, Elidia Crawford, James Campbell, John Cambell

Nancy Day, F. Davis

Thomas Elmonson

James Flanagan, A?nil Fincher, Shubael Foot

Dr. Uriah Grigsby, Thomas N. Gardner, Jacob Givhan, Dr. E. Gannt, Barnes Griffin, Jesse Garrett, Thomas G. Gardner

John Hope, John J. Meridith, Mason R. Harrison, Kindud Holston, David A. Hendon

Miscellaneous Alabama Newspaper Abstracts --- Vol 1

Thomas M. Jones, John C. Jones, William B. Johnson

John D. King, John Keiber, Hamblin Kirkland

Mrs. N.M. Ladlon, Enoch Little, Thomas Low, Micajah Lyles, John Lauson

David M'Gea, James Miller, Sen., Hugh McFail, A.P. M'Curdy, Isaac Morris, John J. M'Milland, Robert C. Morrison, Mrs. M. M'Leod

Nathan Nolly

Mrs. Nancy Ormand, James Owens, Captain Wm. Olds

Bowlen Perry, Elijah Pierson, Mrs. Elidia Pelham, Bird Pruitt, William S. Phillips, Norman Pettibone, Asa Parker, Doct. Philips, Andrew Pickens, Thomas Patterson, Thos. Jefferson P?gg, Britton Perry

Wilson Russum(?), Daniel Rather, Gabriel Ray, Daniel Robison

John Scarbro, Rev. J.C. Sharp, John Si?on, Isaac Stevens, John Shields, Hugh Spence, Thomas Stone, James S. Salters, Seeldon Swift, Anthony Smith, Robert Sparman, Samuel S. Simmons, James Sample

Maj. Gen. W. Taylor, Adam Taylor, Benjamin Tippett

James Varnell

Fredric Whitlock, Eaton P. Wilson, Gen. Woodward, John J. Walice, James N. White, William Watson, Erasmus Walker, James S. Wynn, James S. Wallace, William Williams, William Wiley

Notice of lost Certificate, Will. Taylor
Notice of lost Certificate, Jacob Denton

Committed to jail on the 22nd inst., a negro man about 21 or 22 years of age, 5' 2 or 3 inches high, very dark.... he calls his name Henry and says he belongs to James Hogan, of Tuscaloosa....

ISSUE 4-16-1829

Married, on Thursday last, by the Rev. Thomas Alexander, Doct. Taomas W. Gill, to Miss Nancy, daughter of James Craig, all of this county.

(Married) On the same evening, by the Rev. James C. Sharp, Mr. Osborn

MISCELLANEOUS ALABAMA NEWSPAPER ABSTRACTS --- VOL 1

Brewer, to Miss Emeline Hill, all of this county.

Died, in Cahawba, on Tuesday evening last, Doctor Thomas Lesly, aged about 30 years, formerly of Abbeville Court House, South Carolina. Dr. Lesly was a graduate of the New York University....

Ranaway from the subscriber on the 11th inst. a negro man named Daniel, 25 or 30 years old, about 6' high, complexion black, small and peaked, forehead high, of an active form, has some African marks on his temples, has a small scar on his right knee that looks like a burn, and speaks broken.... delivered to me near Portland, Alabama. April 16th, William P. Molett

ISSUE 4-23-1829

ASSASSINATION: On the 6th inst., Maj. James Taylor, a highly respectable citizen of St. Clair County, was inhumanly murdered on the Sand Mountain, about 6 miles from his residence, on his way to Gunter's Landing. It appears that he was shot, and his head and skull literally broken to pieces. When the body was found, it presented the most awful and appalling spectacle the imagination can conceive. His pockets were robbed of about 120 dollars in United States paper and a valuable gold watch. A man named Shade Biddie, who is known to have entertained ill-will towards the deceased, and who has frequently threatened his life, has been committed to jail on a charge of perpetrating the act. We also learn that Castile Lewis, who is somewhat notorious in this place, is suspected to have participated in the deed, and that the sheriff is in pursuit of him.

Died, at Darlington Court House, S.C., on the 24th ult., His Honor Judge Gaillard. He had been deprived of the use of his limbs by a paralytic stroke, and had been for some time unable to move but with great exertion. We are told he was about 62 years of age. S.C. will remember him in her history as one of her first judges.

ISSUE 4-30-1829

Died, yesterday morning, at his residence at Pleasant Valley, Mr. Alexander Porter, Sen., a soldier of the Revolutionary War, aged 90 years.

ISSUE 5-7-1829

Shelby County Orphans' Court, April Term, 1829: Thomas M. Adkins, administrator in right of his wife, Mary M. Porter, administratrix of Michael A. Porter, deceased, and made application to the court to settle the administration of said estate.

Miscellaneous Alabama Newspaper Abstracts --- Vol 1

Dallas County Orphans' Court, April Term, 1829: Benajah King, administrator of John H. King, deceased, this day applied for final settlement of said decedent's estate....

The undersigned have connected themselves in the practice of the law.... J. Gayle, T. Nixon Van Dyke

Dallas County Orphans' Court, Special Term, 1829: Robert Moseley, administrator of the estate of Elijah Moseley, deceased, reports said estate insolvent....

Dallas County Orphans' Court, Special Term, April 1829: The administratrix of the estate of John Roberson, deceased, having represented said estate insolvent....

Bibb County: James Reid, administrator of the estate of William S. Brown, present his accounts for final settlement of said estate....

ISSUE 5-14-1829

Committed to the jail of Wilcox County, a negro girl who says her name is Drucilla, and belongs to Mrs. Rakestraw of Dallas County....

Married, on Thursday last, by the Rev. Mr. Campbell, Doct. Benjamin W. Saxon, to Miss Mary C., daughter of the Rev. Eli Perry, all of Autauga County.
(Married) In Fall River, Massachusetts, on the 20th ult., Mr. Andrew ?earing, to Miss ???? Cowan.

Will be sold, on the first Monday in June next.... in the town of Cahawba, the following negroes: Orin, Lucy and her child, levied on as the property of John Roberson, deceased, to satisfy sundry executions against said Roberson's estate, one in favor of William Huddleston, one in favor of John Simpson and one in favor of Nathan Franklin....

Will be sold, on the first Monday in June next, in the town of Cahawba...the following described property: One negro woman named Mary, levied on as the property of Council M'Cullin, to satisfy an execution against him, in favor of George Roy??ter.

ISSUE 5-21-1829

Married, at Tuscaloosa, on Wednesday evening the 13th inst., by the Rev. Mr. Judd, John A. Tarver, of this county, to Miss Mary Frances, daughter of

MISCELLANEOUS ALABAMA NEWSPAPER ABSTRACTS --- VOL 1

the honorable Hume R. Field, of the former place.

Committed to the jail of Dallas County, a negro man, about 27 years old, 5' 6" high, dark complexion, a scar on the left side of his head, the two fore fingers of the right hand cut off at the second joint, who says he belongs to Shadrack Martin, of Perry County.. Jesse Cumberlander, Jailor of Dallas Co.

Ranaway from the subscriber on the 11th of April last, a negro man, named Jordan, about 24 years of age, and about 5' 10" high, rather a yellow complexion, talks rather slow when spoken to.... To any person apprehending said negro, and delivering him to me, near Vernon, Autauga Co. .... I will give a liberal reward. John Jackson

Perry County estray notice: Taken up by Ambrose Brisner.... a strawberry roan horse....

Wanted Immediately: Two or three laborers.... A. Worley, Selma, May 14th

Ad for James W. Dolen, tailor, Selma, May 11th

ISSUE 6-4-1829

Married, on Mulberry, on Thursday last, by the Rev. T. Alexander, Mr. Peter R. Wyckoff, merchant, of this town, of the firm of Wyckoff, Pickens & Co., to Miss Mary, daughter of the late Jasen Gardner, of the former place.

Married, in Greensborough, Ala., on Tuesday evening the 26th ult., by the Rev. James Hillhouse, Mr. Robert H. Kerr to Miss Maria M. Lawson, all of that place.

Ad for Simpson & Jones. Spring & summer goods and groceries

ISSUE 6-11-1829

Another of the revolutionary worthies gone! John Jay, of New York, died in the 84th year of his age.

ISSUE 6-18-1829

Married, on the 27th ult., by the Rev. Mr. Converse, the honorable George M'Duffie, to Miss Mary Rebecca Singleton, daughter of Richard Singleton, of Sumpter District, S.C.

Dallas County estray notice: Taken up by Samuel S. Shaddock, two horse....

MISCELLANEOUS ALABAMA NEWSPAPER ABSTRACTS --- VOL 1

Dallas County estray notice: Taken up by Jordan Ladd, a Gray horse

Olius Norman, taylor, respectfully informs his friends & the public that he has removed from Selma to Cahawba into the shop recently occupied by Mr. J. Green.

ISSUE 6-25-1829

The funeral sermon of the late Wilham M. Cowles will be preached on Sunday the 28th inst., by the Rev. Mr. Sharpe, at the late residence of the deceased.

The Rev. Wm. Harris will preach the funeral sermon of the late William Bozwell, on Friday the 26th day of June next, at the house of Col. E.W. Saunders.

Died, on the 17th inst., Dr. John Hunter of Greensboro formerly of Pendleton, S.C.

ISSUE 7-2-1829

Married, in New York, on the 18th May last, by the Rev. Mr. Ware, Mr. George W. Parsons, formerly of this town, of the late firm of Parsons & Taylor, to Miss Eliza G., daughter of Hugh M'Intire, of the former place.

(Married) On Tuesday evening last, at Portland, in this county, by the Hon. Reuben Saffold, Mr. Henderson Wade, of Cedar Creek, to Mrs. Eliza Flournoy, formerly of Georgia.

(Married) On Tuesday evening the 9th ult., by the Rev. S. Dulany, Mr. Thos. Waters to Miss Mary L., daughter of John Womack, of Butler County.

(Married) In Washington, Autauga County, on Wednesday the 10th ult., by Judge A. A. M'Wharter, William D. Pickett, Attorney at Law, to Miss Eliza G. Whitman, of Providence, Rhode Island.

Died, in Hamilton, Butler County, Ohio, on Thursday the 17th ult., Captain John Cleves Symmes, extensively known as the author of the theory of Open Poles and Concentric Spheres. Capt. Symmes was a native of New Jersey but emigrated at an early age to the western country.

ISSUE 7-16-1829

Married, at Harrisburg, Pennsylvania, on the 16th June last, by the Rev.

MISCELLANEOUS ALABAMA NEWSPAPER ABSTRACTS --- VOL 1

Keller, Mr. Samuel W. Frazer, merchant of Prairie Bluff, Wilcox County, Alabama, to Miss Eliza Seltzer, of the former place.

(Married) On Tuesday the 7th instant, by the Rev. Mr. Kennon, Col. Martin A. Lea, of Perry County, to Miss A. Kennon, of Tuscaloosa County.

(Married) In Washington, Autauga County, by Henly Brown, Mr. John Price to Miss Sarah Ann Turner.

(Married) In the same place, on the 2nd instant, by the Hon. A.A. M'Whorter, Henly Brown to Miss Charity M. House.

Ad. Leather Shoes & C. For sale at my tan yard, about 2 miles from Cahawba. Henry Ross.

ISSUE 7-30-1829

Married, at Berkeley, Charles City County, Virginia, on the 8th inst., Col. Andrew Pickens, of this vicinity, to Miss Mary W. Nelson.

(Married) On Tuesday last, by the Rev. T. Alexander, Joseph Pickens, merchant of this town, to Miss Caroline J. Henderson, of Pleasant Valley.

(Married) On Thursday evening last, Mr. James Grant, of Autauga County, to Miss Abigail Ann Shaddock, of this county.

Ad. Cotton Gin Manufactory. William Thomas continues business at Montevallo, Shelby Co. Alabama....

ISSUE 8-13-1829

$20 Reward: Broke jail in the County of Shelby, on the night of the 6th August, David M'Daniel, charged with the murder of Wiley Stocks.... The description of M'Daniel is as follows: 5'10" high, spare made, light complected, and thin visage: rather inclined to be cross-eyed, with a small scar on some part of his face not recollected. He is between 35 and 40 years of age; talks slow and long, and is remarkably fond of drinking whiskey.

Dallas County Orphans' Court, Aug. Term, 1829: Caleb Tate, administrator of the estate of William Woods, deceased, filed his accounts and vouchers of his administration, and applies for final settlement of said estate.

Dallas County Orphans' Court, Aug. Term, 1829: Caleb Tate and George Phillips, executors of the estate of Bailey M. Woods, late of said county

MISCELLANEOUS ALABAMA NEWSPAPER ABSTRACTS --- VOL 1

deceased,...filed for a final settlement of said decedent's estate.

Married, on Thursday last, by John B. Jones, Mr. Fielding Reynolds, Jur., to Miss Eliza Perry, all of this county.

ISSUE 8-20-1829

Married, on Thursday the 6th inst., by the Rev. James Hillhouse, Mr. John Lockhart, merchant of Marion, to Miss Emily R. Braime, second daughter of the Hon. George Washington Braime, of Perry County.

Sheriff's Sale: Will be sold in the town of Cahawba, on the first Monday of Sept. next.... a negro woman and her child, levied on as the property of Arthur Collins, to satisfy an execution against him in favor of George W. Harris.

ISSUE 9-3-1829

Broke jail about the 1st inst., where he was committed, a negro man slave named Bob, belonging to Dr. David Moore, near Huntsville. It is probable he will attempt to pass as a free man, as he has either traded for or stolen the free papers of a negro man in the neighborhood by the name of Hiram Cash, and will attempt to pass by that name. The said Bob is an artful, sensible negro, pretends to be pious, and has been a preacher for the last five or six years among the blacks: he is supposed to be about 25 years old, well made rather under the middle size, and although not a mulatto, yet he is rather of a yellow complexion for a negro; no particular marks recollected, though it is supposed there will be found on close examination some scars from a cut on the throat or neck. The transcript of free papers which he has with him given below, will detect him: The State of Alabama, Butler County, Court of Ordinary, Feb. 11, 1822, The mulatto man, Hiram Cash, coming into court with his employer John Booth, presenting a certificate touching his freedom, the same being legally attested by the proper authority of the state of Georgia, was ordered to be entered of record in this court, and affidavit being made by said Booth in support of his freedom, was allowed of and ordered to be entered of record as aforesaid.

Ranaway from the subscriber, residing three miles below Washington, Autauga County, on the road leading to Graves' Ferry, a mulatto man named Washington, about twenty one years of age, 5' 6 or 7 inches high.... Theodore May

Ad. Tailoring. The partnership heretofore existing under the firm of 'Doland & Plattenburgh', having been dissolved, the above business will be carried on

MISCELLANEOUS ALABAMA NEWSPAPER ABSTRACTS --- VOL 1

by the subscriber alone, at the old stand.... Salem, Wesley Plattenburgh

ISSUE 12-31-1829

The funeral sermon of the late Gabriel Harrell, deceased, will be preached at his late residence on Cahawba river, on the first Sabbath in January next, by the Rev. Mr. Moore.

Letters of Administration having been granted to the undersigned, at the November Term, 1829, of the Orphans' Court of Dallas County, on the estate of Gabriel Harrell, late of said county, deceased... Josiah Harrell, Adm'r

Letters of Administration were granted to the subscriber...by the Orphans' Court of Dallas County, on the estate of James Hayes, late of said county deceased... Richard H. Hays, Adm'r

Dallas County, Orphans' Court, Nov. Term, 1829, The administratrix of the estate of Elijah Mosely, late of said county, deceased, having this term filed the accounts and vouchers of her administration for final settlement...

Ad for public boarding house. Cahawba. Wm. Curtis
Ad for Booth & Morgan. Fashionable clothing & tailoring.... John Booth, Salem, John S. Morgan

Commissioners sale: Will be sold in Cahawba, the described real estate of Thomas Ewing, dec., Thomas Morong, Alanson Saltmarsh, William Hendrich, comms.

Ad. A plantation in Autauga Co. Ala. for sale for no other cause but to pay his debts.... William Harris

Lewis B. Mosely, admin. of the estate of Lewis Mosely, late of Dallas Co....

THE SELMA FREE PRESS

ISSUE 2-6-1834

Married, in Wilcox County, on the 23rd ult., by John Bonner, Major John G. Abrams, of Portland, to Miss Mary Ann, daughter of Mr. John Eubank.

In Mobile, on the 27th ult., by the Rev. Mr. Johnson, Mr. John Pollard, proprietor of the *Mobile Mercantile Advertiser*, to Miss Alice Stanton, of the city of New York.

Miscellaneous Alabama Newspaper Abstracts --- Vol 1

Married, at Columbia, Tennessee, on Thursday the 12th January, by the Rev. Mr. Labarre, Dr. William M'Neill to Miss Mary Crockett, daughter of the Hon. David Crockett, Member of Congress from Tennessee.

Died, in this town, on Saturday night last, Mr. John O. Grigg, after a lingering illness, aged about 23 years. Mr. Grigg was a native of Virginia, and had resided in this place about two years.... He was a member of the Selma Debating Society.... to wear black crape on the left arm for thirty days....

Departed this life, at the residence of her brother, John C. Perry, of this county, on the 19th ult., Mrs. Louisa H. Perry Wiley, in the 27th year of her age, wife of Mr. Thomas H. Wiley.

Departed this life, on the evening of the 28th ult., at his residence in Perry County, Temple Lea, in the 60th year of his age. Upwards forty years member of the Baptist Church.

Strayed or stolen from the subscriber, living in Portland, Alabama, a bright sorel horse.... Formerly belonged to Mr. F. Bohannon. Geo. W. Wright

Sheriff's sale: Will be sold in the town of Selma.... three square bales of cotton, levied on as the property of Phelps Haynes, to satisfy an execution in my hands in favor of James W. Burke, issue from the office of the clerk of the Circuit Court of Perry County. Wm. N. Burke, sheriff

Notice: Robert Maxwell having disposed of his interest in the firm of Maxwell & Walker, to Col. Robert Dunlap, the business will be hereafter conducted under the firm of Dunlap & Walker. They have recently received an additional supply of boots, shoes, hats, & caps.

Ad for the Rail-Road Hotel, eighty rooms above stairs.... Courtland.... Robert A. Taylor
Ad for G. & S.S. Dunn, store in Vienna
Ad for Gilbert Shearer, Selma
Ad for Johnson & Norris, Selma
Ad for Douglas & Woods, Selma

Sheriff's Sale: Will be sold before the court house door in the town of Cahawba.... the following described land, the S.E. 1/2 of the S.W. 1/4 of Section 15, township 15, Range 7, lying and being in the County of Dallas. Levied on as the property of John P. Blann, to satisfy three orders of sale, issued from the clerk's office of the Circuit Court of Dallas County, one in favor of James M. Lenoir, executor &c., one in favor S.J. Sorell & Brother, and one in favor of Benj. R. Hogan. At the same time & place, a house

MISCELLANEOUS ALABAMA NEWSPAPER ABSTRACTS --- VOL 1

formerly occupied by Horatio G. Perry as a law office & a lot of ground.

Ranaway from the subscriber in December last, a negro man named John. He is over 6' high, stout built, between 30 and 35 years of age, and of yellow complexion; whilst walking a slight lameness is perceivable, occasioned by corns on his toes. Richard Hall, Dallas County

Letters of Administration on the estate of William G. Gill, deceased, having been granted to the undersigned.... Thos. W. Gill, Admr

Ad for Charles G. Edwards, law office in Cahawba
Ad for Wm. S. Phillips, law office in Cahawba
Ad for Robt. E.B. Baylor & Geo. W. Gayle having associated themselves in the practice of the Law, office in Cahawba

Absconded from my plantation, about the first of May last, a negro fellow named Abraham, about 35 or 38 years of age. He is about 5' 10 or 11 inches high, stout made, and very black.... He was raised by the late Major Wm. Cowles, of this county, and may represent himself as belonging to one of his sons.... His father and mother are owned by Major Thomas M. Cowles, of Montgomery County.... G. Shearer

The subscriber has just opened a House of Entertainment at Vienna, in Dallas County, on the Stage road leading from Montgomery to Selma, 5 miles below Statesville, and 12 miles above Selma.... Accommodate Travellers & Boarders.... Josiah G. Dunn

Ad for T.P. Ferguson, Selma
Ad for land for sale, Selma, Henry Koontz
Ad for Drayage & Storage, Selma, James Adams
Ad for Dr. Reed at Prairie Bluff, Wilcox Co. Ala. Has on stock the following articles....

$100 Reward, will be given for the apprehension of a negro man named Sam, stolen from the subscriber, on Monday night the 20th inst. Said negro is from 30 to 35 years old; 5'8" high; of a tolerable light yellow complexion.... He is a good shoemaker, and a tolerable blacksmith.... Autauga County, William Ratcliff

Dallas County Orphans' Court, January Term 1834: Thomas W. Gill vs The Heirs of William G. Gill, dec'd: Petition to sell land.... the defendants, Elizabeth Taylor, John Gill, ____ Wallace and Jane his wife, and the unknown heirs of James Gill, deceased, live beyond the limits of this state.

Miscellaneous Alabama Newspaper Abstracts --- Vol 1

Dallas County Orphans' Court: Thomas D. Rumph administrator of Joshua Rumph, deceased, applied for a final settlement of estate....

Notice: Will be rented, for the present year, on the premises, the Plantation belonging to the estate of Patrick Keogh, deceased.... and eight negroes. Leo Abercrombie, Adm'r

ISSUE 8-8-1835

Died, in this place on Monday evening last, after an illness of three weeks, Mr. Daniel W. Garret, in the 25th year of his age. He was from Greene, Chenango County, state of New York, but for the last ten months a resident of this place.... died 3 inst. At a meeting of the young men of Selma....

Died, at the residence of her son, Mr. Samuel M. Hill, of this county, on Thursday evening the 30th ult., Mrs. Martha Hill, aged about 55 years. Mrs. Hill was a native of Fairfield District S.C., but for the last five years a resident of this county....

(Died) At the residence of his father, near Cahawba, on the 30th ult., Jefferson George son of Matt. Gayle, aged 9 months and 15 days.

(Died) In Tuscaloosa, on the 30th ult., of the tetanus, or lock-jaw, Mrs. Sarah A. Gayle, wife of his excellency the Hon. John Gayle, in the 32nd year of her age.

Notice is hereby given, that I have applied.... for the benefit of the laws enacted for the relief of insolvent debtors.... George Christopher

Stolen from the subscriber on the night of the 25th ult., a bright bay mare.... Benj. McGee, Near Oak Ridge Post Office, Perry Co.

Dallas County, July Term, ... will be sold to the highest bidder, all the real estate of Elizabeth Bryant, deceased....

$20 Reward, Absconded from my plantation, 6 miles north of Selma, a negro man named Burill, of a yellowish complexion, spare made, 6' high, weighs about 160, about 23 years old.... Lewis J. Moore

Dallas County: Letters of Administration granted to the undersigned.... upon the estate of James B. Pond, late of Dallas County, deceased....

MISCELLANEOUS ALABAMA NEWSPAPER ABSTRACTS --- VOL 1

ISSUE 8-22-1835

The subscriber, living in Butler County, Ala., has lost 15 slaves whom he has just reason to believe have been stolen and probably will be attempted to be taken to Texas. The names of said slaves are, Lary, Nancy, Piley, Lizzy, Jessey, Salor, Joshua, and Nan, and their children... H.P. Walker

Married, on Wednesday last, (at the residence of Thomas Gibson) by the Rev. Joseph D. Lee, Mr. Robert A. Cain, formerly of York District, S.C. to Miss Nancy S. Campbell, formerly of Wilson County, Tenn., all of this county.

(Married) On the evening of the 12th inst. at Montevallo, Shelby County, by the Rev. Joab Lawler, Mr. George G. Shortridge, of Montgomery, to Miss Elizabeth, daughter of Edmund King.

Departed this life, on Monday last, Mr. Stephen W. Maples, in the 39th year of his age, a resident of this place for the last 6 or 7 years.

Died, on Wednesday last, Martha Prior, daughter of Thomas N. Gardner, aged 4 years and 10 months.

The Rev. S.M. Nelson, will preach funeral sermon of Mr. Daniel W. Garret, at Cumberland Presbyterian Church in Selma, on 1st Sabbath in Sept next.

A few hundred pounds very superior Cincinnati hams, for sale by P.J. & D. Weaver, Selma, Aug. 22, 1835.

ISSUE 8-29-1835

Died, in Montgomery, on Friday 21st inst., Martha J., daughter of Mrs. Priscilla Reynolds of this vicinity, an interesting and promising child, aged 10 years and 4 days. Her remains were brought from Montgomery and interred in the grave yard near this place on Sunday morning last.

(Died) In this place, at the residence of her daughter, Mrs. Maples, on Wednesday night last, Mrs. Ann Williams, at the advanced age of about 70 years.

(Died) At her mother's residence (Mrs. Williams in Perry County) on Saturday last, Mrs. Nancy Dukes, wife of Mr. Charles Dukes of this vicinity, in the 20th year of her age.

(Died) In Wilcox County, on Monday last, John Jenkins, Attorney at Law, a young gentleman of considerable promise.

MISCELLANEOUS ALABAMA NEWSPAPER ABSTRACTS --- VOL 1

ISSUE 9-5-1835

Fatal Encounter: A misunderstanding having originated between Mr. Britton Simms and a Mr. Marr, at Cahawba, on Sunday last, an encounter ensued, which resulted in the death of the former by a pistol shot.

Married, in this place, on Wednesday evening last, by the Rev. Mr. Reeves, Mr. Andrew Walker to Miss Sarah Hughes, daughter of Mr. Joseph Hughes.

Died, on the 10th ult., Grey, infant daughter of Samuel F. Jones, of this county, aged one year and seven days.

ISSUE 9-12-1835

Died, on the 1st inst., Lucy Esporian, daughter of Mr. William McElroy of this county, aged 7 years, 2 months and 1 day.

(Died) On the 29th ult., Mr. Joseph Baker of this county in the 42nd year of his age.

(Died) At Blount Springs, the 29th ult., after a long and protracted illness, Miss Aletha A.M. Hill of this county.

(Died) On Sunday last, Edward, son of Capt. Thos. White of this county, in the fifth year of his age.

Eloped from my plantation on Sunday night, the 23rd ult., Jim and his wife Peggy. Jim is about 30 years old, of low statue, and raw boned.... Peggy is also of low statue, heavy built, and about the same age.... Monticello, Pike Co. Alabama, Sept. 4th, Wm. W.M. Graham

Dallas County Orphans' Court: Letters of Administration granted to the undersigned upon the estate of Britton Simms, deceased.... Juda Simms, Adm'x, Jona Simms, Adm'r

ISSUE 9-19-1835

Suicide: A friend has permitted us to extract from a letter he has received from Mobile, dated the 11th inst., the following particulars of a most distressing suicide.... John Elliott (the lawyer) committed suicide on the night before last, by cutting his throat! Medical aid was speedily rendered him, and strong hopes were entertained for his recovery; but last night in a fit of delirium, he tore open the wound and expired instantly.... I was called upon to sit up with the corpse, which I did, and spent a very unpleasant night of it;

MISCELLANEOUS ALABAMA NEWSPAPER ABSTRACTS --- VOL 1

for the deep and death like silence that pervaded the room I was in (with the corpse) was not infrequently broken by the piercing cries of his disconsolate widow. She has sustained an irreparable loss, and has seven small children to provide for.

Died, on Saturday last, Mrs. Mexico Ferguson, wife of Mr. Thos. P. Ferguson, in the 25th year of her age.... husband, four children....

(Died) On Thursday last, Mrs. Judah Maria Brantley, in the 2?th year of her age, wife of Harris Brantley, of this county.

(Died) On Thursday last, James, youngest son of Mr. James W. Burke of this town.

(Died) In this county, on the 13th inst., George Edward Bowie Smith, eldest son of Capt. William S. Smith, Jur., aged 8 years and nearly 3 months.

(Died) At the residence of Dr. A. Saltmarsh, near Cahawba, on Thursday last, Mr. Horace Ward, aged 23 years.

Died, at his residence in Pleasant Valley, on the evening of the 15th inst., after a short but painful illness, Dr. George Phillips. The subject of this notice was of Irish parentage, and was born the 1st of May, 1769, near the town of Charlotte, North Carolina. In consequence of the failure of the Government to redeem the paper currency, issued by authority of the Continental Congress, his father was reduced so low in a pecuniary point of view, as not to be able to afford him the advantages of an ordinary education, but when he had nearly attained the age of manhood, his love of letters was such that an elder brother (now no more) kindly helped him to acquire a knowledge of the more useful branches of English literature.... He commenced his professional career in Green County, Ga., and from thence removed to Oglethorpe, were he resided many years. In the early settlement of the country, he emigrated to this state. He was a member of the convention that framed our State Constitution...He left a wife and eight children... Died from a violent attack of congestive fever....

Died, at his residence, near Cahawba, at 8 o'clock on Sunday evening the 13th instant, after a short but severe illness, Col. Thomas Morong, of the firm of Thomas Morong & Co. This valuable citizen has departed in the prime of life, leaving a widow and four small children...

ISSUE 9-26-1835

Married, on Wednesday evening last, by the Rev. ?. S. Graves, Mr. Thomas

Miscellaneous Alabama Newspaper Abstracts --- Vol 1

L. Waddill of this town, to Miss Frances Reynolds of this vicinity.

(Married) On Thursday evening last, by the Rev. Wm. Harris, Mr. Ace Dean to Miss Sarah, daughter of Mr. Uriah West, all of this county.

Died, in this town, on Sunday last, Mr. Jacob V. Wills, merchant of the house of Messrs. Tredwill & Wills, aged about 33....departed this life on Sunday, the 21st inst., in the 33rd year of his age...short illness of six days.

Died, in Cahawba, on Monday last, Mr. Elias W. Norwood, Merchant, of the house of Messrs. McLaughlin & Norwood, aged about 25 years.

Obituary: The subject of this short memoir, Mrs. J.M. Brantley, consort of Mr. Harris Brantley, was the daughter of William Sharp and Mary Sharp, and was born in the state of Georgia, on the 6th December, 1806.... Methodist Episcopal Church.... 3 years past every symptom of a confirmed consumption. On 28th August Mr. Brantley set out from the Springs with a---of taking her on a visit to her father's on the Tallapaosa.... Remains to Methodist Church. Left affectionate husband and fond parents.

ISSUE 10-3-1835

Married, at the residence of Col. Wm. R. King, of this county, on Tuesday evening last, by the Rev. S.M. Nelson, Dr. Benjamin R. Hogan of Cahawba, to Miss Louisa K. Kornegay.

(Married) In Knox County, Tenn., on the 17th ult., by the Rev. Thomas H. Nelson, Mr. Andrew Yost of this county, to Miss Margaret M'Kinley of the former place.

Died, on Saturday the 26th ult., Miss Sarah, third daughter of James Craig, of this county, after a painful illness of two weeks....

ISSUE 10-10-1835

Died, suddenly, on Sunday last, Ann, eldest daughter of R.H. Croswell, of this town.

Died, at the residence of his father, in this (Dallas) County, on the 20th ult., Mr. Charles Olds, in the 24th year of his age, after an illness of several months. The subject of this short memoir, was born March 28th, 1812....

Died, at the residence of his father, in this county, on the evening of the 3rd inst., Mr. Thomas Craig, in the 21st year of his age, after a long and painful

MISCELLANEOUS ALABAMA NEWSPAPER ABSTRACTS --- VOL 1

illness....

ISSUE 10-17-1835

Died, at Col. Pinson's in Pleasant Valley, on the 6th inst., Mr. James Cooper, a resident of Caswell County, North Carolina.

Ranaway from the subscriber, residing near Valley Creek Academy, Dallas County, Alabama, on the night of the 16th Oct. inst., two negroes of the following description, Viz: William, a very black man, about 5'4" high, has a blemish in the right eye, has a scar on his shoulder occasioned by a burn, and aged 25 years. Shadrick: a yellow complected, likely fellow, bold and impudent look, about 5'10" high, 26 years old, wears his hair roached.... Caleb Tate

Ranaway from the subscriber on the 28th July last, a negro man named Stephen, about 22 years old, of dark complexion, 5' 4 or 5 inches high.... Stephen was brought from Virginia last winter by Wm. Batts. Lowndes Co. Ala., Oct. 16, 1835, Wm. P. Fisher

ISSUE 10-24-1835

Died, on Monday last, Robert, son of R.H. Croswell, of this town, aged two years and nine months.

Died, near Cahawba, on the 2nd instant, Richard S. Clinron, Attorney at Law, ...affectionate wife.

Died, at the residence of his son, James A. Tait, in Wilcox County, on the 7th inst., the Hon. Charles Tait, in the 68th year of his age. Judge Tait was born in Louisa County, Virginia, but removed at a very early age to Georgia.... he there presided several years as Judge of the Superior Court.... He removed to Alabama in 1819.... left an only son and a disconsolate widow....

Letters testamentary were granted to the undersigned, on the 12th Oct. inst., by the Orphans' Court of Dallas County, on the last will and testament of George Phillips, deceased.... Mary Phillips, Ex'rx, Wm. S. Phillips & Geo. C. Philips, Ex'rs

Letters of Administration having been granted to the undersigned, by the Hon. the Orphans' Court of Dallas County, on the estate of Kinchen F. McKinnie, late of Dallas County, deceased.... Gilbert McKinnie, Adm'r.

Letters of Administration having been granted the undersigned, by the

MISCELLANEOUS ALABAMA NEWSPAPER ABSTRACTS --- VOL 1

Orphans' Court of Dallas County, on the last will and testament of Lardner C. French, late of said county, deceased.... Ann Eliza French, Ex'rx, Cadar Hawthorn, Ex'r

A list of letters remaining in the Post Office at Cahawba, at the end of the quarter ending the last of September, 1835:

Abraham W. Arnold, Solomon Adams, H.W. Arnold

J.J. Blue, Richard Baxter, John Bozeman, Simpson & Berry, Samuel Bugg, John Balker, James A. Butler, Abraham Bhland, Joseph Babcock, Buddy Bohannon,

Edwin Curtis, R.H. Croswell, J.B. Clarh, Ezra Cleveland, James Clark, C.H. Cleveland, John R. Colwell, Daniel Conner, Miss Sarah Ann Childers, James M. Calhoon, William Craft, Edward Clement

Moses Davis, Manuel Dickard, John Davis, Mrs. Susan Dun, Stephen B. Davis

Vergil Eiland, William Edwards, Rev. Thomas J. Elliott, Mrs. Mary E. Elliott

Duke Goodman, Archibald Glen, L.C. Graham, Jacob Gary, George H. Godfrey, Miss Martha Hart O'Gilvie, Alexander Graham

Pascal Hardin, John Huneycutt, Ricqard B. Harrison, Stephen Harbersham, Jefferson Hogg, William Hardin, David Harky, Dr. P.W. Herbert, Dr. J.W. Heustis

H.G. Johnson, W. Jordon, Wm. C. Jones, Nelson B. Jones, Miss Matilda Jones, Thomas Jordon

Payton Kenneda, P.E. Kondrid, James King

Francis S. Lyon, Aaron Livingston, Maj. Paul S.H. Lee, Elizabeth Lovly, John C. Loy, John M. Lewis, William Lively

Mrs. Martha McDaniel, Abraham Mathews, Peter W. Markes, Gilbert McKinnie, Samuel G. Moses, James McGee, Ira Meador, Alexander McLeoud, Edward Murphy, Jame McCall, Thos. Morong & Co., John S. Morgan, Robert Mays, Sheriff of Dallas County

Samuel Oliver, David or Henry Overton

Miscellaneous Alabama Newspaper Abstracts --- Vol 1

Auston Pemberson, William Parson, Pally Burnds, Ann Pouncey, Henry D. Parkins, Robert A. Philpot

Linsey Rasco, E.T. Reese, Isaac Rich

John Shuney, C. Saltmarsh, A. Saltmarsh, James Spears, James P. Smith, John Skeen, Thomas P.G. Stephens, Robert H. Smith, R.A. Thompson, S. Tulson, Charles B. Tome?

Charles Valts

John Willis, G.J.S. Walker, Peter Williamson, N. Walker, William Woodall, Joseph Woods, John Walker, Evan W. Warre

ISSUE 10-31-1835

Married, on the 22nd instant, by the Rev. Levi Parkes, Jeremiah Dunaway, of this vicinity, to Miss Asenath Ann Ogelvie of Perry County.

(Married) At Pittsburg, Pa. on the 8th inst., by the Rev. Dr. Upfold, A.H. Gazzam, of Mobile, to Miss Letitia Jackson of the former place.

Died, in Wilcox County, on the 4th inst., Augusta, only daughter of Col. J.W. Bridges, aged about seven years.

ISSUE 11-7-1835

Married, on the 28th ult., by the Rev. Levi Parkes, Mr. Allen Coleman to Miss Julia Mathews, all of this county.

Died, in Cahawba, on Friday the 30th ult., Mr. David Adams, Innkeeper, a highly respectable citizen.

ISSUE 11-14-1835

Married, on Thursday evening the 28th ult., by the Rev. Mr. Ware, Mr. James G. Cowan to Miss Mary Moore, both of Cedar Creek in this county.

Died, this morning at 7 o'clock, at his residence, four miles from Selma, Alabama, Major John Smith Brown, aged 28 years 2 months and 17 days, son of Maj. Thomas Brown of Roane County, E. Tenn. He emigrated to Dallas County about seven years ago.... He has left an affectionate and kind wife, three small children, parents and friends....

MISCELLANEOUS ALABAMA NEWSPAPER ABSTRACTS --- VOL 1

Left the subscriber, who lives in Selma, Alabama, two negro men: Moses, on the 21st of this month, of a brown color, 25 or 30 years of age, about 5'6" high.... Ben, of brown color, down look, has a lisping impediment of speech occasioned by two extra eye teeth projecting in the roof of his mouth, weighs 130 or 135 lbs., about 5' high, and 20 years of age.... K. Harrison, Selma, Oct. 31, 1835

Stolen or absconded on the 4th inst., from the subscriber in Autauga County, a negro woman named Susannah, but commonly called Cresey, about 25 years old, of yellowish complexion, about 5'8" high and has remarkably small hands and feet for a negro. Circumstances have been developed which induces the belief that she was stolen by a white man named W. Dixon, who is about 5'11" high, stoop shouldered, down look when spoken to, marked with the small pox, one of his front upper jaw teeth out, and is an Irishman by birth. James H. Gorman

ISSUE 11-21-1835

Married, on Sunday evening last, by the Rev. Dr. Manley, Harris Brantley, to Miss Martha Wilson, all of this county. (see issue 9-26-1835).

(Married) On Wednesday last, Mr. Philip Milhous, to Miss Eliza Goodwin, both of this county.

ISSUE 11-28-1835

Died, in Greensborough, Ala., on the 17th inst., the Rev. James Hillhouse, an eminent clergyman of the Presbyterian Church.

ISSUE 12-5-1835

Departed this life, on the 30th ult., Gen. Matthew McLaughlin, in the 50th year of his age. The deceased was a native of Maryland, from whence he emigrated to this place in 1818, where he was engaged in the mercantile business from that time until within a few years, when he was afflicted with a paralytic stroke....

Died, on the 27th. ult., Mr. John Taylor, an aged and respected citizen of this county.

(Died) At Columbus, Mississippi, on Monday last, Mr. John Gillam, of this county, aged about 23 years.

Dallas County Sheriff's Sale: Levied on as the property of William A.

Miscellaneous Alabama Newspaper Abstracts --- Vol 1

Roberson, to satisfy sundry executions in my hands against him. W.T. Minter, Sheriff

Sheriff's Sale, town of Cahawba: Levied on as the property of Washington J. Outlaw to satisfy sundry executions in favor of James A. McElroy.

Sheriff's Sale, town of Cahawba: Lot # 39 in the town of Selma...levied on as the property of John C. Wells, to satisfy sundry executions in my hands. W.T. Minter, Sheriff

ISSUE 12-12-1835

Married, on the 31st inst., by the Rev. J.C. Ware, Mr. Robert M. Armstrong to Miss Jane, daughter of Hugh Kenedy, both of this county.

ISSUE 12-19-1835

Married, on Sunday evening last, by the Rev. Peyton S. Graves, Mr. Peyton S. Alexander, of Lowndes County, to Miss Mary P., daughter of Robert R. Minter, of this county.

Died, at his residence in Autauga County, of bilious pleurisy, Mr. Matthew B. Rice, aged about 33 years, a highly respectable citizen, who has left a young family to lament their loss.

ISSUE 12-26-1835

Will be sold in the town of Cahawba, on the first Monday of Feb. next, the South West quarter of Section 20, township 13 of range 11; levied on as the property of Jacob Bowen, to satisfy an execution in my hands against him in favor of Matthew Patton.

Will be sold at the court house door in Cahawba...a part of Lot # 3...levied on as the property of William Taylor....

On Tuesday last, James Cannte and Thomas W. Cash, of this place, proceeded to the neighborhood of Chelatche creek in this county, where Mr. Cannte procured a process from A.C. Mobley, for the arrest of Thomas Curtis, whom he charged as a fugitive from the laws of North Carolina, having been charged in that state, some 10 or 12 years since, with the murder of Thomas Cash, an officer of justice in Anson County, while serving a civil process on him. Under the state of facts, they proceeded to the plantation of Mr. John Pegues, where Curtis was employed in the capacity of an overseer, and presented the process charging him with the facts above stated. Curtis made

MISCELLANEOUS ALABAMA NEWSPAPER ABSTRACTS --- VOL 1

no resistance....

Married, on Thursday evening last, by the Rev. S.M. Nelson, Mr. Alexander Bolware, of Montgomery, to Miss Mary Reynolds of this vicinity.

ISSUE 1-2-1836

List of letters remaining on hand at the Post Office, Selma, December 30, 1835:

Elias Arterbury, Sarah Akin, Elijah Abston, Absolom Antery, Wm. Anderson

Whitfield Bryon, C.T. Bassett, Sanford Brant, Capt. Waddy Bacon, Stange Bradley, Jesse Bowers, Wm. E. Bird, Maj. Thos. Brown, Thos. Blarson, Wm. Bedingfield, Harris Brantley, Isaac D. Baker, Joel J. Butler, G.M. Bostwick, German Burres, James A. Beal

James Cannte, David Catheart, James M. Calhoun, C.H. Cleveland, James C. Cole, Charles H. Cox, Wilson Crocher, James W. Crosby, Milo C. Curry, John Crawford, Geo. C. Card, William Card, Nancy Childers, Thos. W. Cash, Nelson Childress, Archibald C. Currie, Agnes Callon, Henry Crittenden, James L. Claughton, Daniel M. Crosland, Mrs. Rosiama Cowan, John Carliles, Jane Cole, Thomas Crawford, Featherston Cross, Rev. Charles Crow

James Douglas, Person Davis, Jane T. Dreman, Samuel Dorroh, Charles C. Dukes, G.B. Douthet, H.C. Demean, Dokeman & Purpli, William F. Dubose, P.H. Delane

J. & D. Elmonston

Mrs. Mary Fike, Seth B. Ford, Thos. S. Fellows, John Frost, Burrell J. Fort, Eliza Fincher, Eliza Franklin, Louisa Ferguson, H. Fowler, James W. Fair, Wm. E. Fuller

Wm. Grimes, Wm. E. Gorman, Uriah Grigsby, Young Goodwin, David C. Gary, John C. Gildersleeve, Thomas Gibson, M.L. Grisham, T.B. Goldsby, Mary M. Grice, Rebecca Goodwin, Linsey B. Grice, Peyton S. Graves, Henry Gilmore, Thomas Gardner

Thomas P. Harvey, Thomas A. Heard, Wm. Y. Hooper, Robert Henry, John B. Hussey, Hooper & Newman, Rev. James B. Hill, Thomas Harvel, Henry P. Haynes, Jur., Noah Haggard, Munsoul Hyde, Thomas Haynes, Col. Jehu Hale, Archey Harris, Heiaene Hill, Elder Hosea Holcomb, Mary Hinson, Alfred Hatch

MISCELLANEOUS ALABAMA NEWSPAPER ABSTRACTS --- VOL 1

Turner Ivey

John B. Jones, Henry B. Jones, A. James, Wm. B. Johnson, Clement T. Jordan, John B. Jones, Robert Jones

Geo. Keaese, Peyton Kennedy, Kenith Kinzie, James W. Kelly, Geo. D. King

Frederick Lewis, Elizabeth Lucas, Sidney Lomax, Amos A. Loyd, Stephen Letcher, Thomas Lampley, Jackson Loper, Charles Leopard, Annanias Looton, James H. Laferne

Philip Millhous, David Meridith, Elizabeth M. Moore, Margaret E. Moore, A.G. McCraw, John McLarty, Miss Joanna Minter, A.M. Mahon, Thomas Melton, William McDaniel, Sarah Maples, Samuel Martin, James Morris, Rev. A.P. Manley, Dennis Morris, Drewry Muse, Thomas McGill, Jonas McCullough, Alfred McNaire, McCleod & Marshall, David McMillan, Col. W.T. Minter, John Miller, W.J. Matteson

Jos. M. Newman, Samuel New, A.M. Norris, Alexander Nace, Danl H. Norwood

James Pool, Catharine Pelham, Thomas Peterson, Benjamin Pearson, A. Prinderson, Ephraim Pool, Primm & Jones, Dr. McKindree Porter, John Paulding, Benjamin Pearson, Dr. Robt. C. Phillips, Mark Perry, Alexander Porter, J. Phealden, Phillips & Edwards, Wm. S. Prior

Joseph Rush, John Russel, John G. Roberts, Thomas Riddle, Col. Wm. Rutherford, Benj. T. Russel, Mr. Rion, George Randall

Samuel Sheldon, Sarah C. Stinson, Wm. C. Stedman, Joseph Shields, Elisha W. Simms, Edward Smith, Thomas M. Street, John Swift, Emily Saunders, Rebecca A. Sullivan, Washington A. Sledge, John Starr, John Stoner, John Simpson, Daniel Scott, Richard Smith, James Skelton, Thomas Saunders, Bryan P. Sparrow, Anthony Smith

A. Taylor, Robt. E. Thompson, Benj. Tarver, Leroy Thompson, John L. Tippett, B. Thomas, Editor Thompson, Thos. Thompson, David Thompson

Dr. J.E. Vasser, Wm. A. Vallient, Philip Vogeline, Charles Vanderford

W. B. Wood, Thos. L. Waddle, J.T. Watkins, Charles Webster, Martha L. Williams, James Webb, Sarah Webb, Ann Williams, John L. Wilkins, Jur., Thos. D. Williams, Wm. R. Williams, L.J. Wilson, William Weaver, Mr. Williamson, Jesse Woodward, Jacob T. Watkins, John C. Wear, Jesse West,

MISCELLANEOUS ALABAMA NEWSPAPER ABSTRACTS --- VOL 1

Charles Walker, Asa Wyatt, Alexander Walker, John H. Watters, J.W.B. Wright

Andrew Yost, Marcus D. Yale

Wm. Tredwell, P.M.

ISSUE 1-9-1836

Married, on Thursday evening last, by Rev. S.M. Nelson, Mr. James E. Hatcher to Miss Ann E. Morris, formerly of Charleston, S.C., all of this county.

(Married) In New Orleans, on the 20th ult., by the Rev. Mr. Mullen, Mr. William E. Turner, to Mrs. Maria A. Kelly, widow of the late Judge Wm. Kelly, of this state.

Died, on Thursday the 1st inst., Captain William Lee, an old and respectable citizen of this county.

(Died) On the 31st ult., Edward Everet, son of Henry West, of this county, in the 7th year of his age.

Sheriffs Sale: In Cahawba. Levied as property of Samuel Flanikin.

ISSUE 1-16-1836

Married, on the 9th inst., by the Rev. Mr. Ware, Mr. John Smith to Mrs. Dorathy B. Moore, all of Lowndes County.

(Married) On Thursday last, by the Rev. T. Alexander, Mr. John K. Gilmer to Miss Elizabeth, daughter of Robert Morrison, all of this county.

To Mechanics: The subscriber wishes to employ two or three good workmen as Gin Makers, immediately. Apply at Hamilton, Autauga County, to Wm. H. Benson.

Strayed from the subscriber on the 10th inst., a Bay Mare.... Selma, Jan. 16th, 1836, Thos. H. Adams

Ranaway from the plantation of the subscriber on Cedar Creek, Dallas County, on the 31st ult., a dark mulatto man named John.... aged about 25 years.... can read and write and is a very intelligent fellow, though his appearance does not indicate intelligence. As he was brought from North

MISCELLANEOUS ALABAMA NEWSPAPER ABSTRACTS --- VOL 1

Carolina he will probably try to get back to that state.... Flemming Freeman

Mr. Frow: Regard for my reputation, which has been basely assailed by a man who has left the country in disgrace, compels me to request you to give the following (which carries sufficient explanation on its face) insertion in your paper: Josephus Fulford, Dallas County, Jan. 8th, 1836; The State of Alabama, Dallas County: Personally appeared before me, Joshua Watson, a Justice of the Peace in and for the county aforesaid, Jerome Dudley, who being duly sworn, deposeth, and on his oath says, that Thomas Tolson came to him on the 6th inst., and told him that he had good evidence to prove that he (this deponent) and Josephus Fulford had set fire to his (the said Tolson's) fodder house and corn crib, and that unless he would go before a Justice of the Peace, and confess on oath that he had done this act, being hired by the said Fulford so to do, and that the said Fulford went with him, and himself assisted in putting fire to the said fodder house and corn crib, that he the said Tolson would prosecute him, and that he would be hung. But if he (this deponent) would make the said confession on his oath aforesaid, he should not be prosecuted. Whereupon this deponent, under fear of the said threat, and induced by the said promise, did, on the 6th instant go before David Reeves, a Justice of the Peace, and make oath, as is above stated he was solicited and induced to do by the said Tolson. And this deponent now further saith, that the said oath which he took before the said Reeves, is false and utterly without foundation in truth, and that so far as he knows or believes, the said Fulford is innocent of the said act of burning in every respect whatever. (signed) Jerome B. Dudley

ISSUE 1-23-1836

Married, on Thursday evening the 14th inst., by the Rev. David B. Smedley, Mr. Bynum Jones, to Miss Mary Mayes, all of this county.

(Married) On Tuesday last, by the Rev. Robert Nall, Dr. Abel Lancaster, of Perry County, to Miss Leonora, daughter of John Crawford, of this county.

(Married) In Tuscaloosa, on the same evening, by the Rev. Mr. Mathews, Doct. Paul H. Lewis, of this county, to Miss Elizabeth Ann, daughter of the Hon. Eli Rhortridge.

(Married) In the Sheriff's office at Cahawba, on the 19th instant, by George G. Brooks, Mr. Daniel Day, to Miss Mary Lee, both of Perry County.

ISSUE 1-30-1836

Ranaway from the subscribers on the night of the 17th inst., three Negroes, names and description as follows: Alfred, about 5' 10" high, light complexion, 22 years of age.... Margaret, 18 years of age, light complexion, heavy eyebrows, ordinary size.... Sophy, about 24 years of age, dark complexion, near 6', small in the waist for her size, full face and small eyes.... was purchased from a trader by the name of Ponder, residing in Florida. Ponder brought her from Virginia not long since. Alfred and Margaret were purchased in Virginia about 12 months since.... Dallas County, Buddy Bohannon, Philip Milhous

Absconded from the subscriber on the 29th June last, a negro man named John, who says his name is John Carter; he is 5' 6 or 7 inches high, weighs 160 or 170 lbs., is of rather yellowish color, has a spot of white hair on the top of his head, upon close examination one of his hands and arms will be seen to be larger than the other, which was caused by having been shot in the shoulder, and has several scars on his thighs by the bite of dogs. He was brought from Newbern, N.C. by Messrs. Franklin & Gildersleeve, and may possibly try to get back there or to Columbia, S.C., where he was raised.... Perry County, Ala., Jan. 30, 1836, John Welch

Dallas County: Taken up by Jesse Roark.... a sorrel Mare....

Copartnership: M.G. Woods having given A.M. Goodwin an interest in his business....

ISSUE 2-6-1836

Married, on the 27th ult., by the Rev. Mr. Ware, Mr. James M. Campbell, of Dallas County, to Miss Maria J. Moore, daughter of Mr. John Moore of Lowndes County.

(Married) On Thursday evening last, by A. Fair, Mr. James H. Armstrong to Miss Jane Howie, all of this county.

(Married) In Mobile, on the 28th ult., by the Rev. Mr. Hamilton, James Van Ness, of Columbus, Georgia, to Miss Caroline P.J. Leslie, daughter of the late James Leslie, of Abbeville District, South Carolina.

Died, in this town, on Thursday last, Mr. Jason Plant.

ISSUE 2-13-1836

Died, recently, in Lowndes County, Mississippi, Mr. Jackson Boon, son of Mr. Danl. Boon, formerly of this county.

MISCELLANEOUS ALABAMA NEWSPAPER ABSTRACTS --- VOL 1

ISSUE 3-19-1836

Died, at Cahawba, on the 11th inst., Mrs. Jane Paul, at an advanced age, consort of Mr. Archibald Paul.

Ranaway from my plantation near Woodville, Perry County, my negro man George, about 30 years of age, 5' 7 or 8 inches high, well made, with heavy beard and tolerable stout whiskers. I got the negro from John Duncan, near Portland, and I presume he will endeavor to get back to that neighborhood, as he has a wife at Col. Baykin's. Woodville, March 19, 1836, Starling Gorman

On the evening of Wednesday, the 9th inst. my negro boy Reuben, run away. He is a yellow boy, about 5'9" high, stout built, about 28 years old, wears small gold ear rings in his ears, has at present a burn on the under side of one of his arms, which will not probably heal for some time.... Mobile, March 19, 1836, Thomas Reid

ISSUE 3-26-1836

Married, on the 17th inst., Mr. James Miler, Jun., to Miss Matilda Mitchell, both of this county.

Died, at the residence of her brother James G. Cowan, in Dallas County, on Thursday, 17th inst., Miss Maldonata Cowan, daughter of the late John Cowan, in the 25th year of her age. She was a native of Tennessee, had resided in Alabama about three years, and sunk under a lingering pulmonary afflection, lamented by a family of dear relations.... attached to the Cumberland Presbyterian Church....

Ad for D.W. Sterrett, attorney at law, having located himself at Barboursville, in Wilcox County

Notice: All persons are hereby cautioned against trading for a note executed by me and made payable to Charles A. Abercrombie.... Sligo, Dallas Co. March 26, 1836, Andrew Mayes

Ranaway from the subscriber about the first day of October last, a negro man named Ransom, of dark copper complexion, 30 or 35 years of age, well made, 6' 2 or 3 inches high...Ransom formerly belonged to the estate of John Taylor, and is perhaps now lurking about Judge Wm. Smith's or Mr. Meredith Calhoun's plantations in Dallas or Autauga County. Athens, Dallas County, March 26, 1836, B.F. Adams

Miscellaneous Alabama Newspaper Abstracts --- Vol 1

ISSUE 4-2-1836

Married, on Thursday last, by the Rev. Mr. Harkey, Mr. Jesse M. Lewis, to Miss Orpha Adams, both of this town.

Died, on Saturday the 26th ult., at the residence of her son, Carter H. Cleveland, Mrs. Frances Cleveland, in the 80th year of her age.

(Died) On Tuesday last, Mr. Jacob Silvers, aged about 35 years. He was a native of Pennsylvania, and had resided for the last seven or eight years in this town.

Sheriff's Sale: I will sell at the front door of the court house in Cahawba....all the right which Timothy Duck has in the south west quarter of section 25, township 17, range 10, to satisfy an execution from the Circuit Court of Dallas County in favor of Jesse Beene, against said Duck.

ISSUE 4-9-1836

Died, in the vicinity of this place on Tuesday the 29th ult., Mrs. Selina Louisa Pickens, wife of Col. Samuel Pickens, leaving an infant son only five days old. ....(*Greensborough Beacan*)

Beware of an imposter! The public are hereby cautioned against a certain man calling himself Richard Simmons, who absconded from the neighborhood of Pleasant Hill, Dallas County, Ala., on the 17th March last, from the employment of Judge Reuben Safford, as overseer, having swindled nearly all the good people of the neighborhood, and leaving a young wife whom he married in December last. He, in all probability, will make his way for S. Carolina, from whence he came.... He is low in stature, being about 5' 6 or 7 inches in height, dark complexion, small twinkling black eyes, large mouth, black hair.... Richard Blalock, Green Underwood, R.E. Bohannon, A.C. Deweese, Wm. H. Bonneau, Wm. Gooding, A.W. Arnold, Reuben Safford, John Windsor, Ezra Cleveland, Jno. E. Vasser, Little Berry Vasser, Thomas Watts. April 9, 1836.

A list of letters remaining in the Post Office at Selma, April 1st, 1836:

Elijah Abston, Miss C. Armstrong, Benjamin Ashworth, Col. James Austin, Thomas Adams, William Anderson, Stephen Allen

William Barther, Mrs. Elizabeth H. Brown, Archibald C. Bunn, W.W. Bass, Miss J.L. Bynd, William Bell, Alexander Brand, Uriah Bass, Reuben Brabham, George Bryan, N. Beddingfield, W.G. Byran

MISCELLANEOUS ALABAMA NEWSPAPER ABSTRACTS --- VOL 1

Dale Child, W. Colwell, Michael Cook, Jun., Wm. Cuberhouse, D. Cumberland, A.G. Carter, Mrs. M. Chandler, Francis Coldman, W. Callens, John Crumpton, Mrs. Jane Clark, W. Cochran, Mrs. H. Carmichal, George W. Carpenter, Miss M. Clay, W. Conoly, J. Carrell, Jun., J. Clark, H. Campbell. W. Collins, B. Clark, Miss E.G. Chalmers, Miss E.A. Crumpton, Mrs. S. Crow, J.A. Clark, J. Colwell, Gray A. Chandler, W. Charlotte, Mrs. M.E. Chandler

J. Drennon, J. Dunn, M. Dennis, J.W. Davis, A. Davis, W. Dawson, D.T. Dupree, J. Dreman, J. Dudly, H. Davis

W. Edgerton, H. Emerson, J. Edves, J. Ezrack, Mr. Edwards, F. Edomonds, W. Echols, Miss J.D. Elmonston, R. English

Miss H. Furguson, D. Files, Thomas J. Frow, Leander K. Filinvi, R. Felton, Mrs. L. Furgson, Miss E. Franklin, T.E. Field, Major A. Fuller, F. Ford

Jesse Gardner, James Goman, P.V. Gamage, C.A. Gaylore, A. Glass, J. Greger, J. Gilmer, Mrs. Martha Givban, W.P. Givhan, P.S. Graves, J. Gibson, Miss Martha L. Gurry, Young Goodwin, C.T. Gorman, J. Goodger, E. Gant, J. F. George, D.C. Gary, J. Grant, Thomas Gibson

R.W. Habersham, J. K. Heice, George Hopper, Mrs. M. Hays, J.B. Harris, Mrs. M. Honsom, Mrs. Nancy Hatcher, A.W. Hays, W. Holcomb, P.W.H. Habambe, J.W. Huckster, Mrs. Mary Hinson, C.J. Henry

C. Isgett

A. Jones, Miss Jones, Henry Jones, T. Jordan, Mrs. A.A. Jones, Mrs. E. Johnson, Mrs. P. Jones

John D. King, T.K. Kornegay, H. Koonts, John D. King

W.C Lee, W. Langley, J.P. Lee, M. Lile, J.C. Lovely, Mrs. Mary Lynch

E. Miller, A. Mitchell, John Morong, J. Miller, Mrs. McCrane, A.G. M'Craw, W. Murphy, M. Mosley, J. McDaniel, Mrs. M. Moore, B.A. Mobley, Mrs. Sarah Minter, John McIver, W.T. Minter, J. McMullen, Mrs. Moussune, C. Mitchell, D. Morrow, R.R. Minter, T. McKane, Miss M. McCrane, J.K. Morrison, R.G. Metetheny, J.T. McCowalen

J. Nelson, D.H. Norwood, J. Noble

J. Owen, W. Ore

MISCELLANEOUS ALABAMA NEWSPAPER ABSTRACTS --- VOL 1

V. Pye, Miss M.A. Paul, Mr. Plattenburg, B. Pearson, J. Potent, A. Pegues, J.P. Prime, J. Poe, W.R. Picket, L. Parks, J.V. Pickens, Mrs. S. Porterent, F.A. Porter, F.M. Porter

D. Russell, Mr. Reves, J. Russell, B. Russell, D.W. Rather, J. Rosser, Miss N.B. Reeves, T.L. Rynolds, R. Ruttendge, J.W. Reynolds, Mrs. P. Rynolds, R. Rutledge, M. Rives, P. Ross, D. Robertson, R. Rains, A.V. Rowndtree, A.N. Rowndtree, J.D. Rowndtree

R. Sisor, J. Simpson, J.M. Savage, S. Sadrick, Mrs. S. Safford, Jas. Safford, S. Safford, Miss H. Shields, S. Suddth, T.M. Smith, V. Stone, W. Safield, W.H. Smith, R.H. Smith, J. Sims, Miss R. M. Stoudemire, Mr. Simmons, S. Smith, M. Sharber, J.A. Smith, W.T. Smith

Miss E. Taulon, Mr. Towchets

W.J. Verell, T. Ving, O. Vandeford

T.L. Waddell, G.W. Wills, W. Whitmore, C.R. Webster, J. Williams, J.C. Wear, D. Weaver, Mrs. R. Williams, Lewis Williams, C.J. Williams, J. Welch, C. Webster, W. Whatley, U. West, H. Walker, J.T. Walker, S. White

A. Zimmerman
James Cannte, Post Master

A list of letters remaining in the Post Office at Cahawba the quarter ending the 30th March, 1836:

Aseph Abby, A. Alexander, Mrs. P. Abbott

B. Bohonon, R.H.W. Begger, Jacob Brown, Miss Caroline Burket, E. Blan, Horatio Bonley, David L. Boon, James Beattie, Enoch C. Bell, William E. Bird, William Barnett, Washington Baby, Mrs. Lucretia Bohanon

James Craig, John Calleham, Wiley Cearley, James Campbell, John P. Carethers, Eli Campbell, Nathaniel Campbell, Sheppard & Cleavland, Allen Coleman, P.D. Coleman, David Carter, W.C.M. Cockron, P. Clark, R.H. Croswell or Jesse West

To: Isaac Davidson, Wily J. Sorell and Willis Carr; Jacob Denton, Samuel Davis, Benjamin P. Dow, Miss Caroline Davis, John Davis, Colin Dellard, Wm. V. Dennison

John A. English, Spencer Evans, Winston Estis, Obediah Earles

MISCELLANEOUS ALABAMA NEWSPAPER ABSTRACTS --- VOL 1

Charles Furr, Talford Forseth, Mr. Fletcher, Administrator of J. Fletcher; John T. Finly, Benjamin Freeman, Henry Franklin

George W. Gollsty, Levi Garner

N.R. Husted, Is. Clemon Hale, Benjamin Hatche, William Hunter, J.S. Hunter, Jesse Hendrick, J. Hall or Nancy Kornigay, John Hunter, Moses Haskin, Miss Mary Harrison, Willas Horne

William C. Jones, T.M. Jackson, H.B. Jones, Messrs. Jones & Abby, James Irwin, William Johnson

George Keaneer

Benjamin Logan, William N. Love, Daniel Long

Kineth McCoy, John Davis, B.J. Wright or Wm. P. Molette, Meret McDonald, Samuel A. Mays, Abram Mathews, Mrs. A. McDonald, Wm. T. Minter, James Morrison, Enoch Morgan, Thomas McFatter, Mrs. Martha McDonald, Thomas Mackharm, James Moads, Peter Mosly, Wm. Minter, Robert Miller, Daniel McFarline, H. McKinny, Miss Lucretia Murphy, James Marthhome, Thomas McKoun

Samuel Norwood, Robert Noline

Christopher Orsburn, Jesse Owins

Mathew Prun, Noel Pittes, Samuel Posby, James C. Pruett, F.M. Phillips, Lewis Parkham, Jesse Pitts, D.A.W. Patterson, Wm. V. Dennison, Jessee Pally

Prior Rieves, Robert Rolines, Mrs. A.E. Rivers, Thomas Read, Miss Eliser Rodgers, To some other Baptist or Divine besides Mr. Reves, Miss Francis Riddle

James Saffold, Richard Spencer, Asa Siks, Bryant Sholes, Young Smith, Miss E. or S. Saffold, J.S. Sorell, James W. Simons, William Smily, Abram Sheppard, John Smily, T.B. Sorells

E.C. Tillmon, R.E. Thompson, Miss Margaret Traylor, William Taylor, Miss Lucy B. Thomas, Thomas Taylor, Miss Mary Thompson, Joseph Taylor

Henderson Wade, W.H. Watson, James P. Waugh, Mrs. Jane Wallas, John Williams, Lemuel White, Jesse West or R.H. Croswell, or James Watson, J.G.

MISCELLANEOUS ALABAMA NEWSPAPER ABSTRACTS --- VOL 1

Campbell or John D. Womack, J.H.D. Womack, Kinchen F. McKinny, Phideus Rutherford, Wm. E. Weaver, Wm. Whitehead, John M. Williams, Wm. N. Williams

ISSUE 4-23-1836

Married, in Greene County, on Wednesday last, by the Rev. T. Alexander, Mr. Andrew C. Pickens of this county, to Miss Nancy daughter of the late Robert Bell.

(Married) On Thursday evening last, by the Rev. Mr. Averet, Doct. ___ Grant, to Mrs. Caroline C. Perry, of this county.

(Married) On the same evening, by the same, Mr. John W. Kelly of Perry County, to Mrs. Cassander Plunket of this county.

Married, by Sackfield Brewer, on Tuesday evening the 12th inst., William J. Davis to Miss Mary E. Lewis, both of the vicinity of Portland, Dallas County.

The Rev. Peyton S. Graves will preach the funeral of Mr. Richard Land, at Shady Grove on the Mulberry, on the second Sabbath in May next.

ISSUE 5-7-1836

Married, on Thursday the 28th ult., by Henry West, Mr. Wright Williams to Miss Marian Ellis, all of this county.

ISSUE 5-21-1836

Married, near Uniontown, Perry County, on Thursday last, by the Rev. S.M. Nelson, Mr. James M. Calhoun to Mrs. Ann M. Dickson, all of Dallas County.

Died in the vicinity of this place on thur. last, Mr. James Kimball, aged about 35 years.

Died in Cahawha on the night of the 5th inst., Matthew Plunket, aged about 35.

Ranaway from the subscriber, living in Livingston, Sumter County, Alabama, some time in February last, a negro boy about 16 or 17 years of age, dark complexion, round face, will weigh between 100 and 120 lbs. by the name of Buster. Said boy was taken up in Wilcox County.... he was brought from Georgia last fall by Messers. Warren and Walker, of whom I purchased said negro.... Livingston, May 11th, 1836, Wm. Earbee

Miscellaneous Alabama Newspaper Abstracts --- Vol 1

ISSUE 6-4-1836

Death of Col. Gwin: We are informed by a gentleman who left Tillatoba, Miss. about 10 days ago, that intelligence reached that place two days before he left, that Col. Samuel Gwin, the receiver of public money at Chockchuma, had died from the effects of the wound received in the duel with the late Mr. Caldwell.

Died, very suddenly, on Saturday the 28th ult., Mrs. _____ Sturdivant, wife of Robert Sturdivant, of this county.

(Died) On Sunday last, Miss Ann, daughter of Mr. John Erwin, of this town.

Died, on Friday the 27th inst., at the residence of Mrs. Mary Bonnell, after a short though painful illness, Mary Eliza Smith, consort of Mr. Baxter Smith of Lowndesborough, late of Dallas County, aged 17 years, 7 months and 7 days.....

Ad for new store of J.A. Jones, Selma
Ad for P.J. Weaver for Guns, Pistols.... Selma, Ala

I wish to sell seven valuable business and family residence lots in the town of Wetumpka.... Apply to Dr. E. Burrows and John Simms, Wetumpka.... June 4, 1836, A.E. Laughridge

ISSUE 6-11-1836

Married, on the 7th inst., in Dallas County, at the residence of Mr. James G. Cowan, by the Rev. S.M. Nelson, Mr. Cowan Mitchell, of Perry County, to Miss Ellen Cowan of Dallas County.

There will be a barbecue given at the residence of Buddy Bohannon on Mush creek, on Friday next (the 17th inst.) in honor of the Florida volunteers from Dallas.... June 11, 1836, B. Bohannon, G.A.B. Walker, H.J. King, Joel E. Mathews

The copartnership heretofore existing between the subscribers, under the firm of Berry & Weyman, have this day been dissolved by mutual consent.... Selma, June 9, 1836, P.A. Berry, Edwd. Weyman

ISSUE 6-18-1836

Married, on Thursday evening last, by the Rev. Mr. Larkin, Dr. Oliver G. Eiland of Marion, Perry County, to Miss Mary, daughter of Maj. James

MISCELLANEOUS ALABAMA NEWSPAPER ABSTRACTS --- VOL 1

Hatcher of Dallas County.

(Married) At Washington City, on the 5th inst., by Rev. Mr. Hawley, Andrew P. Calhoun, of South Carolina, to Miss Margaret M., daughter of Gen. Duff Green.

ISSUE 7-2-1836

Married, on Tuesday evening last, by the Rev. James C. Sharp, Mr. James A. Norris, Merchant, of this town, to Miss Sarah Ann, daughter of Henry Moss, of this county.

Ad for the law office of Charles Dear and David W. Sterrett

Pay your debts! All persons indebted to the late firm of Tredwell & Wills, either by note or account, are hereby notified that unless said debts are immediately liquidated, they will be placed in the hands of a proper officer for collection. It is necessary that the estate of the latter partner, deceased, should be settled.... Selma, June 18, 1836, Wm. Tredwell, surviving partner

ISSUE 7-16-1836

The Rev. James C. Sharp will attend the funeral of Mr. James Norwood, deceased, of Perry County, on the 4th Sabbath in July instant, at Childers' Chapel.

Persons indebted to Dr. John H. Miller, are requested to call on the subscriber (who has his papers in charge) for settlement. Selma, July 16, 1836, J.W. Lapsley

Dallas County Orphans' Court, July Term, 1836: This day came Jarvis Langford, Guardian of the persons and estates of Susannah Tarrence, Sarah Tarrence and John Tarrence, heirs of John Tarrence, deceased, and applied for a final settlement of said Guardianship..

The copartnership heretofore existing between the undersigned, was this day dissolved by mutual agreement. John Simpson, Presley A. Berry

ISSUE 7-23-1836

Died, at Wood-Lawn, Dallas County, on Sunday the 7th inst., Robert James, son of A.E. and Sarah Jane Loughridge.

Stolen from the town of Selma, on the evening of the 4th of July, a Roan

MISCELLANEOUS ALABAMA NEWSPAPER ABSTRACTS --- VOL 1

Sorrel Mare.... Thos. Kenan, Jun.

ISSUE 1-28-1837

Married, on the 18th inst., by the Rev. Mr. Walker, Ivey Russum, of this place, to Mrs. Mary Jones, daughter of Enoch Bell, of Bogue Chitto.

The Rev. D.M. Norwood will preach the funeral sermon of the late John C. Sims, his wife and daughter, at Childers' Chapel, on Sunday the 12th of February next.

ISSUE 8-5-1837

Caution: All persons are forewarned against trading for a note of hand for eleven hundred dollars, dated 7th March last, and due 1st January next, made by myself and payable to George O. Britt or bearer.... Wilcox County, July 24, 1837, H.T. Kimbrough

Lost or mislaid, a note of hand given by Uriah Harvey to me for $550.... Elijah Abston

Ranaway or stolen from the subscriber living in Perry County, on the 9th June last, a negro woman named Sarah, 19 or 20 years old, slim.... Saml. D. Jackson

J.A. Jones has just opened a splendid lot of Saddlery.... Selma, May 27th, 1837

ISSUE 8-12-1837

NOTICE: Left my bed and board on the 7th inst., my wife Mary Ann Benson, without any known cause to me. I therefore forwarn all persons from crediting her on my account, as I will not pay any debts of her contracting from the date of this advertisement. The circumstance of her leaving me is strange to me indeed, for if we ever lived affectionately it was at the time of her leaving me, and as the neighborhood is teeming with falsehoods against me on her account. One report is that I whipped my wife, abused and ill treated her. In answer to these charges I can say before God, I never did whip my wife since our marriage, for I married her for the best of motives, pure affection, which I never calculate entirely to loose. I am very proud to think I live where I do; I live in the village of Hamilton in Autauga County, Alabama, and within 360 yards of me lives seven families, and I defy my enemies to get a single head of a family or any branch of the families living in said village to say I have whipped or mistreated my wife.... July 8, 1837, W.H. Benson

MISCELLANEOUS ALABAMA NEWSPAPER ABSTRACTS --- VOL 1

Ad for the drug store of G.W. Seaman & Co., Cahawba

ISSUE 8-19-1837

Died, on Tuesday evening the 15th inst., Colonel Joab Pinson, a highly respectable citizen of this county.

(Died) On the same evening, William Thomas, son of Mr. Bartlett V. Gamage, of this vicinity, aged 4 years, 2 months and 10 days.

Doct. A.P. Manley would respectfully inform his friends and the public, that he has returned from his visit to Texas, and is now at his residence at Valley Creek Academy, ready for business in the practice of medicine, surgery & midwifery.

ISSUE 8-26-1837

Another victim to the bowie knife: Mr. Thomas Hayles of this county, in the neighborhood of this place, whilst in controversy with a man by the name of Funderburgh received a fatal stab in the abdomen with a bowie knife, of which he died the following day. Funderburgh has fled from justice.... (*Montgomery Journal*)

Col. George W. Owen, of Mobile, died at his plantation near that city, on the 18th instant.

Married, on Monday evening last, at the residence of L.B. Vasser, of this county, Mr. David R. Bell, of Cahawba, to Miss Caroline Davis.

Thomas Linticum, waggonmaker from Kentucky. Commerical business at Valley Creek Academy.

ISSUE 9-2-1837

Married, in Richmond, Kentucky, on the 15th ult., Mr. Singleton Shields, formerly of this place, to Miss Sally Ann Miller, of that place.

ISSUE 9-9-1837

Married, on Thursday last, by the Rev. S.M. Nelson, Mr. Laid Kirkpatrick to Miss Nancy Kallen, all of this county.

Died, near this place, on Sunday morning last, Mr. William Sutliff. He formerly resided at Louisville, Kentucky.

MISCELLANEOUS ALABAMA NEWSPAPER ABSTRACTS --- VOL 1

Ranaway from the subscriber, about the last of April, a negro boy named Carolina, about 19 years of age, 5' 8 or 9 inches high.... Brandon, Mi. Aug. 15, 1837, John A. Pearson

ISSUE 9-23-1837

Married, on Tuesday evening last, by the Rev. T.H. Porter, Mr. Andrew J. Hunter, of this town, to Miss Mary, daughter of the late Dr. George Phillips of this vicinity.

Died, at Wood Lawn, in this county, on the 18th inst., in the 23rd year of her age, Mrs. Sarah Jane Loughridge, wife of A.E. Loughridge, of that place, and daughter of Robt. Meken, of Oakmulgee, Perry County.... Member Baptist Church. Husband. Two small children.

(Died) Lately, in Macon County, in this State, Leonard Abercrombie, formerly a citizen of this county.

(Died) In New Orleans, on the 10th inst., of the prevailing fever, Col. John Wood, aged about 30 years, formerly one of the partners of the Commission House of Taylor & Wood in Mobile.

Caution: The public are cautioned against receiving or trading for, in any way, the following described notes: say one note payable to Osborn Vines for one hundred and twenty two 61/100 dollars, and one note payable to William Vines for fifty two 84/100 dollars, both dated July 13th and due 1st January next. The consideration for which these notes were given having failed, they will not be paid. Selma, Parkman & Miller

ISSUE 10-14-1837

Married, on Thursday evening the 12th inst., by the Rev. Dr. William Culverhouse, Mr. E.D. Green of Perry County, to Miss Jane Callen, of Dallas.

Died, on Sunday last, infant daughter of the Rev. P. Graves, of this county.

Departed this life, on Tuesday the 10th inst., at the residence of Mr. Willis Brown, near Centreville, Bibb County, Mr. William F. Hodges, formerly a merchant of this town.

ISSUE 10-21-1837

Married, on Thursday evening last, by the Rev. D.H. Norwood, Mr. Ambrose M. Chapman, of Macon, Ga. to Miss Sarah Ann, daughter of Henry Jordan,

Miscellaneous Alabama Newspaper Abstracts --- Vol 1

of Pleasant Valley, Dallas County.

The Rev. D.H. Norwood will preach the funeral of Colonel Joab Pinson tomorrow at Childers' Chapel.

Committed to the jail of Wilcox County, a negro man who says his name is Joe, and that he belongs to Dixon H. Lewis, of Lowndes County, Alabama.

Committed to the jail of Wilcox County as a runaway, a negro man who says his name is Ellick and that belongs to Henry Lewis of Lowndes County, Alabama. About twenty-five or thirty years of age.

Lost on the 2nd inst., on the road between John S. Pegues and Cahawba, a Calfskin Pocketbook, containing $300 in $20 notes on the branch bank of the State of Alabama at Montgomery.... Among the notes recollected, was two drawn by James and Henry Young.... to Spencer J. Adams.... one by Thomas J. Roberts.... payable to Spencer J. Adams.... one on Littleton Chambliss.... one on Charles Forness.... one on Older W. Caloway, near Athens.... one on Gayle & Bower.... and one on James Young and ____Hardaway.... one on B.N. Pegues. John Adams, Sen.

ISSUE 10-28-1837

Married, on Thursday evening last, by the Rev. P.S. Graves, Mr. William J. Norris, Merchant, of this town, to Miss R. Louisiana, daughter of Col. Wm. Rutherford of Pleasant Valley.

(Married) On the same evening, by the Rev. J.C. Sharp, Mr. Elijah Moseley, Merchant of Vienna, to Miss Mahala, daughter of Mr. John Campbell of this county.

(Married) On the Same evening, by James Cannte, Mr. David P. Harris to Miss Selina Riesor(n?) of this county.

Died at his residence in Mobile on Tuesday morning the 24th inst., John Chandler, late of this county, in the 66th year of his age.... Here where he long resided.

ISSUE 11-4-1837

Died, in Mobile, on the 29th ult., William J. Morgan, Commission Merchant, of the house of Morgan & Boykin.

By virtue of the will of Turner Ivy, deceased, we will expose for sale, on the premises, on the 23rd day of December next, a valuable plantation, containing 244 56/100 acres, more or less, situated on the east side of the Cahawba river....

ISSUE 11-11-1837

Married, at Marion, on Sunday morning, 29th ult, by the Rev. Mr. Larkins, Thomas Billingsly, of this co., to Mary Railand of Mobile.

ISSUE 11-25-1837

Died, on Monday morning last, after an illness of eight days, Mr. William Branch, a respectable citizen of this county.

ISSUE 12-2-1837

Married, on the 17th ult., by the Rev. Mr. McVail, Mr. Felix Adams of Linden, Marengo County, to Miss Huldah Ann, daughter of John Shields, of Perry County.

Doctor N. Childers having determined to make Selma his permanent place of residence, takes this method of tendering his services to the citizens of the place and its vicinity.... Doct. C. has been extensively engaged in the practice of his profession, in the States of Georgia and Alabama, for 34 years....

A Ball will be given at the Assembly Room of Mr. Richard Hall, at Vienna, on Tuesday evening the 26th inst.

Notice: This is to certify that I am about to leave the State. All persons indebted to me, and those to whom I am indebted, will please call on W.N. Williams or to Oliver Ellis. Wright Williams

ISSUE 12-9-1837

Judge Sullivan one of the representatives from Perry County in the legislature, died at Tuscaloosa on the 1st inst.... The Honorable Dunklin Sullivan no longer lives.... A native, if I mistake not, of Greenville or some immediately adjacent district of South Carolina; he removed at an early age to the State of Tennessee, where he acquired a valuable academical education...In the year 1819.... he removed and settled in the town of Cahawba, Dallas County.... He there engaged in the practice of the law, and in the year 1822 removed to the County of Perry.... To a wife and six little orphans, the loss is irreparable.

Miscellaneous Alabama Newspaper Abstracts --- Vol 1

Married, on Tuesday last, by the Rev. H. Williamson, Mr. Richard H. Hayes to Miss Ann H. Williams, all of Lowndes County.

(Married) On Thursday last, by the Rev. Mr. Rocket, Mr. Thomas A. Burgan of Tuscaloosa County, to Miss Martha A., daughter of Mr. John Davis of Dallas County.

Land Sale: By virtue of authority in us by the last will and testament of Burwell J. Fort, deceased, we shall expose to sale, on the second Monday of Jan. next, at the late residence of said Fort, the following described tracts of land, lying in Dallas County.... P.B. Traylor, P. Walter Herbert, Wm. Fort, Ex'rs

ISSUE 12-16-1837

Married, on Tuesday last, Major John Tipton, of this vicinity, to Mrs. Elizabeth Brown, daughter of Benj. Tarver, Sen. of Lowndes County.

Died, in this town, on Thursday last, after a painful and protracted illness, Maj. Ashley Wood, in the 63rd year of his age.

ISSUE 12-30-1837

Married, on the evening of the 20th inst., by the Rev. P.S. Graves, Mr. Madison L. Wilson to Miss Sarah Ann Chandler, both of Mobile.

ISSUE 1-13-1838

Married, on Thursday last, Mr. James Kave of Milton, Autauga County, to Mrs. Rebecca Gardner of Dallas County.

ISSUE 1-20-1838

We regret to learn that Col. Samuel W. Oliver departed this life on Thursday last, at his residence in this county.

Married, on Thursday evening last, by the Rev. Mr. Averett, Mr. William G. Hale, merchant of this town, of the firm of Douglas, King, & Co., to Miss Terather, daughter of the Rev. A.G. McCraw of Perry County.

(Married) On Tuesday the 9th inst., Mr. Nathaniel Reese, of Lowndesborough, to Miss Amy, daughter of Maj. Lewis Tyus of Autauga County.

MISCELLANEOUS ALABAMA NEWSPAPER ABSTRACTS --- VOL 1

ISSUE 1-27-1838

Committed to the jail of Dallas County, as a runaway, on the 15th Jan, 1838, a negro woman by name of Nancy... says she belongs to Dawson Sullivan, who lives in the Choctaw Purchase, and that she was aiming to get to Nathan Barrett's near Hayneville, Lowndes County, Ala., who she says bought her. Said negro is between 25 and 30 years of age, black and tolerable likely....

Sheriff's Sale: levied on as the property of Powell Williams and Braddock McDonald to satisfy an execution in my hands for collection in favor of Adam Crosby. Cahawba, Jan. 27, 1838

Dallas County Sheriff's Sale: ....levied on as the property of James A. Smith

Ad for Hilliard J. Brantley. Prepared to keep horses. Selma, Jan. 13, 1838

ISSUE 2-3-1838

Married, on Thursday evening last, by the Rev. A.G. McCraw, Mr. John Armstrong of Sumter County, to Miss Adeline G. Gilmer of Dallas County.

(Married) On Wednesday evening last, by the Hon. E. Pickens, Mr. James C. McNeil to Miss Emily, daughter of Mr. Levi Jordan, all of this county.

Married, on the 25th ult., by the Rev. J. Crumpton, Mr. Samuel Stewart to Miss Susan, daughter of Mr. John Johnson (not Col. Bernard Johnson as announced in our last) all of this county.

Take Notice: I have disposed of my interest in business, in this place, to Mr. James D. Monk.... Selma, Feb. 3, 1838, S.W. Murley

ISSUE 2-10-1838

Samuel W. Oliver is no more! Some time during the latter part of Aug last, he was visited with an attack of the fever... born according to his own register of his age in Charlotte County, Va., on the 8th of June 1799, removed to Georgia in 1806, entered college in 1812, graduated at the Univ. of Georgia in 1816, read law in the office of Augustus S. Clayton in Athens, completed law studies at Litchfield, Conn., removed to Ala. in this county in 1821... (lengthy)

Committed to the jail of Wilcox County, on the second day of December, 1837, a negro man who says his name is Isaac, and that he belongs to William Saunders of Perry County. Said negro is about 5' 8 or 9 inches high,

Miscellaneous Alabama Newspaper Abstracts --- Vol 1

dark, and about 30 years old.

Committed to the jail of Wilcox County, on the 13th day of January, 1838, a negro man who says his name is Jonathan, and that he belongs to Captain Rambart of Marengo County, near Linden. Said negro is totally black, 5' 6" high and about 20 or 21 years of age....

ISSUE 2-17-1838

Died, on Tuesday last, Mrs. Mary Tate, wife of Major Caleb Tate, of Pleasant Valley.

Absconded from the plantation of Abel Lancaster, deceased, in Dallas County, Alabama, a negro fellow named Limus, who can read and write.... Saml. Dorroh, George C. Phillips

ISSUE 2-24-1838

Died, in Mobile, on the 10th inst., Mr. David H. Burke, formerly a respectable citizen of this town, but for the last 6 or 8 years has resided in Mobile.

ISSUE 3-3-1838

Married, in Perry County, by the Rev. Robert Martin, on Monday evening the 26th ult., Mr. T.S. Driskill of Centreville, Talbot County, Georgia, to Miss Emily S., daughter of Davis McGee and Sarah McGee.

ISSUE 3-10-1838

A shocking occurrence took place in Tuscaloosa on the evening of the 28th ult. Thomas Shores was shot down with a pistol, at the corner of the Indian Queen Hotel, by Martin Goodman. Shores expired immediately.

The undersigned have this day taken into copartnership Mr. Thomas Durden of Montgomery, Ala., the business will be conducted at the same stand, under the firm of Kirk, Harris & Durden. Mar 1, 1838, Wm. Kirk, M. G. Harris, Mobile

ISSUE 3-17-1838

Died, in Montgomery, on the 8th inst., Lucy, only daughter of Col. A.A. Dexter, Chief Engineer, Selma and Tennessee Railroad, aged 2 years and 8 months.

Died, at the residence of his son, at Centre Ridge on the 2nd ult., Mr. James

MISCELLANEOUS ALABAMA NEWSPAPER ABSTRACTS --- VOL 1

Womack, aged 70 years. Mr. W. had been afflicted with the consumption for 16 years.... He has left a large circle of friends in North Carolina and Tennessee....

ISSUE 3-31-1838

Married, on Thursday evening, the 2nd inst., by the Rev. Isaac Suttle, Mr. A. E. Loughridge, of Woodlawn, to Miss Margaret E. Reed, both of this county.

Died, on Sunday evening, the 18th inst., Dr. James M. Newman, aged 27 years, a practicing physician and much esteemed citizen of Woodlawn in this county.

ISSUE 4-7-1838

BLOODY TRAGEDY: One of the most fatal and most lamentable occurrences which this community has ever been called to witness, took place in this city on Wednesday afternoon, the 28th ult., in front of the Montgomery Hall. At the time and place above stated, a rencontre took place between William J. Mooney, and Kenyon Mooney, his son, upon one side, and Edward Bell, and his brother, Bushrod Bell, Jun., upon the other. During the affray, three pistols were fired, and knives or daggers were resorted to. Edward Bell was shot in the throat and neck with three balls which penetrated to the vertebrae. Kenyon Mooney was shot through the right arm, the ball grazing his breast; he also received a stab in the same arm, which passing through, wounded him slightly in the right side. Wm. J. Mooney was stabbed in two places in the abdomen, entirely dividing the stomach. The young Bell was, we understand, uninjured. The above particulars are from the *Montgomery Journa*l, which adds, that William J. Mooney and Edward Bell have since died of their wounds. Intemperance was the leading cause of this fatal affray.

ISSUE 4-14-1838

Committed to the jail of Dallas County, as a runaway, on Wednesday, the 4th inst., a negro wench, by the (name) of Beckey, and says she belongs to John Bruce, near Linden, Marengo County. The said negro wench has two children with her, one a boy about 6 years old, by the name of Aaron, the other a female child, about 3 or 4 months old by the name of Melissy....

Dallas County estray notice: Taken up by Waid Scott.... a roan horse poney....

Dallas County estray notice: Taken up by John Roller.... a blood bay horse

List of letters remaining in the Post Office at Valley Creek, April 1, 1838:

MISCELLANEOUS ALABAMA NEWSPAPER ABSTRACTS --- VOL 1

Micajah J. Blakey, David Cummings, Isaac Canterberry, James Chambliss, Daniel Green, L.B. Johnson, H.G. Johnson, James B. King, Geo. C. King, Geo. Leffers, Martha Middleton, Ephraim Mitchell, Dr. Geo. Phillips, Geo. C. Phillips, Martha Pinson, Setenah H. Sneed, Washington Willis, Geo. W. Willis J.V. Pettibone, P.M.

Dallas County: Selma Beat, J. Hinds & Co., McKinnon & Murley, James Cannie and E. Parkman vs Willie Brooks Levied on a lot of leather, saddler's tools and sundry other articles.

ISSUE 4-28-1838

Married, on Thursday evening last, by the Rev. J.C. Wear, Mr. L. M. Harris Walker to Miss Sarah R. Bowie, both of Dallas County.

(Married) On the 10th inst., by the same, Mr. Jonathan A. Brantley to Mrs. Rebecca B. McMillan, both of Wilcox County.

Died, at the residence of his brother, Mr. James G. Cowan, in Lowndes County, Mr. John D. Cowan, in the 21st year of his age. Consumption for nine months.

Notice: All persons indebted to the estate of Dr. Joseph M. Newman, are requested to come forward and make settlement.... Woodlawn, Geo. S. Newman, Adm'r

ISSUE 5-5-1838

Letters of Administration on the estate of Benjamin J. Wright, late of Dallas County, deceased, were on the 2nd inst., granted to the undersigned.... Henderson S. Wade, Adm'r

Absconded from my plantation on the 10th ult., a negro fellow named Calvin, about 26 years old, stout built, weighs about 170 lbs.... Having a wife some where in Green County, he may try to get there, or to North Carolina, from whence he was brought about 18 months ago.... address to me at Selma, Dallas County, Ala. Anthony M. Minter

The undersigned having purchased of his late partner, Mr. Wm. H. Boyd, his entire interest in the accounts, notes and dues of every kind, of the late firm of Parsons, Ferguson & Boyd, and Ferguson & Boyd, all sums due said firms must be paid to him or to his authorized agents.... Selma, April 28, 1838 Thomas P. Ferguson

MISCELLANEOUS ALABAMA NEWSPAPER ABSTRACTS --- VOL 1

ISSUE 5-12-1838

Married, on Tuesday evening last, by the Rev. J.C. Sharp, Mr. Alfred Gibson, to Miss Catharine, daughter of Mr. James Thompson, all of this county.

Departed this life on the 4th inst., after a very short attack of that fell disease, consumption, Mrs. Mary Arnold, consort of Mr. A. W. Arnold of Lowndes County, aged 22 years.

Committed to the jail of Dallas County, as a runaway on the 3rd inst., a negro woman, by the name of Minty, and said she belonged to Dr. Marshall of Cahawba, but recently confesses that she belongs to Dr. Withers of Green County, Ala., about 5 miles from Erie. The said negro woman is large and likely, and about 30 years old, and had several marks of the whip on her back....

Committed to the jail of Dallas County, on the 7th inst., a negro fellow by the name of Randell, and says he belongs to Col. Lee, who lives near Livingston, Sumter County, Alabama; said boy is stout made, black and likely....

Committed to the jail of Dallas County, as a runaway, on the 7th inst., a negro man by the name of Bill, and says that he belongs to Col. Lee, who lives near Livingston, Sumter County, Alabama; said boy Bill is about 23 years old, and a light complected negro....

Committed to the jail of Dallas County, Alabama, on the 10th inst., a negro fellow by the name of Jesse, who says he belongs to Geo. C. King, of Pleasant Valley, Dallas County, Alabama; and said negro is about 20 years old, small and slim made, but likely, light complected for a negro, a scar on his right wrist from a burn....

A man calling himself Caleb Hanford came to Selma between the middle and last of March, and was employed to work as a house carpenter in the shop with me. He worked until the 17th of April, and after having received some $15 or $20 more than his wages, Hanford asked me for the loan of my horse to ride about 4 miles into the country, saying that he would return in the course of three or four hours. The next news I heard of him he was in Columbus, Georgia, where I understand he sold my horse and rigging.
Hanford will weigh about 180 lbs., well made and good looking, has a dark skin, black eyes and black hair. I believe he is a good carpenter, but a most accomplished swindler. He said he was born and raised in the city of New York, where I suppose he is aiming for.... Selma, May 5, 1838, Thomas H. Lee

Miscellaneous Alabama Newspaper Abstracts --- Vol 1

ISSUE 5-26-1838

Ranaway from my plantation in Marengo County, about the 15th inst., a negro woman whose name is Mary. She is very black, about 24 or 25 years of age, large and likely. When formerly runaway, she claimed Mr. H.H. Chapman of Georgia (the gentleman of whom I purchased her) as her master. P.J. Weaver

ISSUE 6-2-1838

Married, on Wednesday evening last, by James Nelson, Mr. John M. Walker, of Dallas County, to Miss Isabella J. Walker, of Perry County.

(Married) On Thursday last, by the same, Mr. ____ Holloway, to Miss Elizabeth Palmer.

ISSUE 6-16-1838

Married on the 7th inst., by the Rev. Levi Parks, Abram L. Pope of Perry Co. to Ann Pegues of Dallas Co.

ISSUE 6-23-1838

Married, at the residence of the Rev. Fleming Freeman, of Dallas County, on the evening of the 14th inst., Col. James K.T. Walton, of Sumter County, to Miss Mrs. [sic] Mary Ann Sutton of Mobile.

ISSUE 7-28-1838

The Nashville Wig announces the death of the last soldier of the old French war in Canada, at the advanced age of 104 years. His name was John Lusk, of Warren County, Tennessee, and a native of Staten Island, N. York....

Married, on Thursday evening last, Mr. Horotio Baxley, to Mrs. Sarah Clinton, daughter of Capt. Williams Hendrick, all of this county.

Died, near Selma, on the ?3rd July, inst., after an illness of 17th days, of bilious fever, Mrs. Martha P. Beale, wife of James W. Beale, aged 27 years.

The Rev. D.H. Norwood will preach the funeral of Mrs. Mary Tate, on Sabbath the 5th August, at Childers' Chapel.

MISCELLANEOUS ALABAMA NEWSPAPER ABSTRACTS --- VOL 1

ISSUE 8-8-1838

Married, on the 2nd inst., by the Rev. S.M. Nelson, Rev. J.C. Wear, to Miss Hannah Lucia Scever, both of Wilcox County.

ISSUE 8-25-1838

Died, on Friday evening the 10th inst., Miss Caroline Jane, youngest daughter of R. McLeod, of this vicinity, aged about 15 years.

Died, on the 22nd inst., by congestive fever, Fleming Joseph Freeman, son of the Rev. Fleming Freeman, aged 17 years and 7 months.

ISSUE 9-1-1838

Died, at the residence of his father, in this county, on Sunday evening last, Mr. John R. Woods, formerly of this place, aged about 25 years.

The undersigned having qualified as Executors of the last will and testament of James Hatcher, deceased, late of Dallas County.... Martha Hatcher, Robert S. Hatcher, Fielding Vaughn

Committed to the jail of Dallas County, on the 15th of August, 1838, a negro wench who says her name is Jane, and that she formerly belonged to Mr. John Mathews of Meriweather County, Georgia, and was brought from Georgia by a man by the name of Smith, who sold her in Montgomery, Ala., to a man whose name she did not know, who took her to Selma, Ala., and offered her for sale.... the said negro wench is about 20 years old....

ISSUE 9-8-1838

Died, on Monday last, Rebecca Jane, daughter of Benajah and Rebecca King, of this county, aged 9 years 7 months and 3 days.

Married, on Thursday evening last, by the Rev. D.H. Norwood, Lewis Thomas, to Miss Jane N., daughter of James Craig, all of this county.

(Married) In Fayetteville, N.C., on the 30th ult., by Rev. Buxton, S.W. Murley, Postmaster of this town, to Miss Ann, daughter of Asa Bebee, of that place.

ISSUE 9-15-1838

Departed this life in Selma, on Tuesday evening, the 11th inst., after a painful illness of 10 days (from bilious fever) Mrs. Jane Blunt, widow and relict of the late Capt. Richard Blunt, of Southampton County, Virginia. Tears of three daughters. 60th year.

Died, in this city, on Wednesday morning inst., after a brief illness of remittent fever, in the 45th year of his age, Alexander M. Robinson....

ISSUE 7-3-1841

Departed this life, on Monday evening the 28th ult., after a painful illness of only three days, Captain Alexander Hamilton Conoley, aged about 30 years, a native of North Carolina, but for the last 6 years a resident of this town.... Masonic Brethren....

Ad for river plantation for sale.... The plantation is situated two miles above Cahawba.... Edward T. Watts

The undersigned having associated themselves in the mercantile business, will conduct the same under the name and style of Conoley & Boyd.... John F. Conoley, William H. Boyd

The copartnership heretofore existing between Strong & Murley is this day dissolved.... Jno. M. Strong, S.W. Murley

Dallas County Orphans' Court, June, 1841: This day Pumroy Cormichael, administrator of the estate of Hannah Cormichael, deceased, and applied for final settlement of said estate....

Dallas County Orphans' Court, May Term, 1841: This day came Robert R. Nance, administrator of the estate of Robert Dunlap, deceased, and applied for a final settlement of said estate....

Dallas County Regular Court, May Term, 1841: This day came Robert C. Morrison and Benjamin A. Glass, executors of the last will and testament of William Morrison, deceased, and applied for final settlement of said estate....

Sheriff's Sale: levied on as the property of James W. Kelly, to satisfy an execution in my hands for collection in favor of John M. Terry. Sheriff's Sale: levied on as the property of Peter Robertson to satisfy an execution in my hands in favor of the Planters and Merchants Bank at Mobile, and against said Robertson. Sheriff's Sale: levied on as the property of James H. Lucas in the hands of John M. Lucas, Guardian &c. to satisfy an execution in favor of Edward Grumbles in my hands for collection.

$100 will be paid for the apprehension and delivery to me of John Erwin,

MISCELLANEOUS ALABAMA NEWSPAPER ABSTRACTS --- VOL 1

Jun., who on yesterday shot at me with (as I believe) the intention of taking my life.... P. J. Miller, Selma

Sheriff's Sale: Will be sold before the courthouse door in Cahawba, on the first Monday, of August next, the plantation of John H.D. Womack.... Sheriff's Sale: Levied on as the property of John E. Barnes to satisfy executions in my hands for collection. Sheriff's Sale: Levied on as the property of Jacob Hoot, to satisfy sundry executions in my hands for collection. Sheriff's Sale: Will be sold before the court house door in Cahawba.... the plantation of Angus McRae, lying on Chelatchen Creek, in the County of Dallas County.... Sheriff's Sale: Levied on as the property of Benjamin Day to satisfy an execution in my hands in favor of James Grumbles, for the use of Wm. Brown. Sheriff's Sale: Levied on as the property of Washington Hardy to satisfy an execution in my hands in favor of Samuel Quarles. Sheriff's Sale: Levied on as the property of Hiram Tipton, to satisfy an execution in my hands for collection in favor of Green Underwood. Sheriff's Sale: Levied on as the property of Samuel H. Taylor, to satisfy two cases in my hands for collection against said Taylor. Sheriff's Sale: Levied on as the property of David Lauderdale to satisfy sundry execution in my hands for collection.

Notice: Loss or mislaid, a note made by Livingston Gardner, in favor of the subscriber for $72.30.... Chas. H. Houston

CAHAWBA PRESS AND ALABAMA STATE INTELLIGENCER

ISSUE 9-27-1823

Will be sold on the 3rd Saturday in October next, fraction 8 in range 11, township 6, on the east Alabama river, containing 333 acres.... James L. Cowan, Rosanna Cowan, Adm'r & Adm'x of J. Cowan, dec.

Perry County, Special Probate Court, June Term, 1823: On representation of Duncan Sullivan, administrator of Henry Bernhard, dec'd the said estate is insolvent and unable to pay the debts thereof....

Geo. M. Rives intends removing to Mobile on the 1st of October next, for the purpose of transacting commission business. Cotton may be shipped to me through Messrs. F. Vaughan & Co. of Cahawba....

Letters of Administration on the estate of Michael Pearson, deceased, were granted to the subscriber on the 18th inst. by the County Court of Marengo County.... Henry Pearson, Adm'r

Letters testamentary on the last will and testament of Stephen Potts, deceased, hath by the Judge of Bibb County Court, been committed to the undersigned executrix and executor of the last will and testament of the deceased, on the 16th day of July 1823. (Ex. names illegible)

Whereas my wife Elizabeth having absented herself from my bed and board, without any just cause, the public are hereby warned against harboring or trusting her on my account, as I am determined not to pay any debts of her contracting, after this date. Dallas Co., Sept. 13, 1823, Shadrach Martin

Perry County, Special Probate Court, July Term, 1823: On the representation of Jeseph Brown, administrator of the estate of Thomas Means, deceased, that the said estate is insolvent and unable to pay the debts thereof.

Doctor Cantt has removed to Selma and offers his medical services to the town and vicinity.

For sale, two likely young negro fellows, apply to Thomas H. Wiley.

$100 reward will be given by the subscriber living in Dallas County, State of Alabama, for the apprehension and delivery or confinement so that I get a large, likely yellow young negro fellow named Smith, about 24 years old, a little cross eyed, speaks quick, looks shy, has short thick feet.... Leo. Abercrombie, June 28th

Ranaway on the 25th ult., two negro men, Ned, an old offender and artful rascal, about 30 years of age, 5' 6 or 8 inches high....; Jim, a stout, likely young fellow, a little inclined to be bald headed, has lost the middle finger of his right hand.... J.S. Walker

Ranaway from the subscriber on the 23rd ult., near Tuscaloosa, a negro woman, named Maria; tolerably tall, very nice made, yellow complexion, about 27 years of age, often has her hair platted.... William Bryant

Notice is hereby given that I have made application to Andrew McBride and Jeremiah Loftin, for the benefit of the insolvent debtors act; and that I shall proceed on the 8th of October next, at Andrew McBride's office, in the town of Montgomery, to make before them a surrender of my goods and estate, (excepting such as are by law reserved) for the benefit of all my lawful creditors, and obtain a discharge from arrest and confinement. Sept. 27th, P.(?) K. Brummitt

This is to forewarn all persons from trading with my wife Silvy Wooten, as I do not mean to pay her contracts any more. Bibb Co., Sept., Wm. Wooten

MISCELLANEOUS ALABAMA NEWSPAPER ABSTRACTS --- VOL 1

Will be sold at public auction on Saturday the 4th of October next, at the old court house, in Perry County, a complete assortment of Drugs & Medicines, being the stock of Dr. Wm. Carr, late of said county, terms made known at the place of sale. C. Humphries

I hereby forewarn all persons from trading for a certain note given by the subscriber to Thomas Willis, for five hundred dollars, due the 25th of December next.... J.V. Perryman

Married, at Tuscumbia, on the 21st August, Mr. Richard B. Brickell, junior editor of the Alabamian to Miss Margaret Commons.

Died, on the 30th Aug., in Knoxville, E. Tennessee, Mrs. E. Armstrong, wife of Maj. F.W. Armstrong, of Mobile. She had been a bride but a few months.... In Selma on the 19th inst, Mary Ann, wife of.... she has left a husband and child, and an aged mother.... she was the idol of her husband, and the comfort and support of her doating mother, who has now consigned the last of three daughters to the silent tomb.

(Died) In Mobile, on the 17th inst., Doct. John Mcoker, a native of New Jersey, but for the last six years a resident of St. Stephens, from whence he removed to Mobile in February last.

(Died) Same day, Don Miguel Eslave, a native of Mexico.

Montgomery County: Notice is hereby given that I have made application to Jeremiah Loften and Andrew McBryde.... for the benefit of the insolvent debtors act.... Wm. Bell

ALABAMA STATE GAZETTE

ISSUE 4-3-1825

Ranaway from the subscriber, living in Dallas County, near Cahawba, on Tuesday night, the 26th ult. Two negroes, to wit: Jim, a small African fellow, about 25 years of age, of black complexion.... Nelly, the wife of Jim, about 20 years of age.... John B. Norris

Strayed or stolen, from the house of Bolling Hall, Autauga Co., about 4 weeks since, a large mare....Subscriber, living near Portland, Dallas County, Leo Abercrombie

I have lost three mules, and will give ten dollars a piece to any one who will return them to me.... A. Pope

MISCELLANEOUS ALABAMA NEWSPAPER ABSTRACTS --- VOL 1

Dallas County, Circuit Court, October Term, 1824: Russell Stebbins, surviving &c. vs Ebenezer J. Bower: Foreign Attachment.

Bibb County: Ordered, that the time given by order of the Orphans' Court, at its sittings in May last, for the creditors of the estate of Henry W. Stephens, reported insolvent....

State of Alabama, Dallas County, October Term, 1824: John M. Sims vs Allen Sims et al : Bill in Chancery.

Information Wanted: George D. Davenport left this place 12 or 15 months since, and is supposed, if living, to be in the State of Alabama. Should he see this advertisement, he is requested to communicate with his brother, J.D. Davenport, at the office of the *Pensacola Gazette*.... Pensacola, Dec. 24th, 1824

All persons indebted to the estate of Edward Lane, dec'd., are requested to come forward and make immediate payment.... David White, Thomas Lesly

Sale of Real Estate: four lots, in the town of Cold Water or Tuscumbia.... all belonging to the estate of George V. Dick, deceased.... Alexander Pope, Adm'r

ISSUE 4-28-1825

The undersigned, executor of Col. Edward Conway, deceased, late merchant at Selma, finding it indispensable to have concerns of his estate brought to a speedy close, give notice that the books, accounts and papers of the said deceased are placed in the hands of Mr. E. Parkman of Selma, for settlement and collection.... Charles T. Porter, Wm. C. Hogan, Ex'rs of E. Conway, deceased

The subscriber having obtained letters of administration on the estate of Joseph Gee, deceased.... Wilcox County, Sterling H. Gee

AMERICAN WHIG

Published by Lumpkin & Dodson

ISSUE 1-7-1826

Letters of Administration on the estate of Randle West, deceased, were granted to the subscribers on the 6th of September last by the Judge of the County Court of Washington County.... John McElroy, Administrator, Rachael

MISCELLANEOUS ALABAMA NEWSPAPER ABSTRACTS --- VOL 1

Hunnicutt, Administratrix Executor's Sale: On Wednesday the 25th of January next, will be sold to the highest bidder on the plantation on which Armistrad Russell, late of Autagua County, deceased, land, negroes, and furniture.... Burnell Russell, Lewis Tyus, executors

$400 Reward.... for the apprehension of one David Henry Moore, charged with being an accomplice with one Edward Broughton in the murder of a negro man named Mitchell, the property of James H. Richardson of Sumpter District and state of S. Carolina....

SEMI WEEKLY DALLAS GAZETTE

ISSUE 11-29-1845

Died, in this place on Wednesday night the 27th inst., Mr. H.M. Elder, aged about 3? years.

Executor's Sale: Will be sold by order of the Orphan's Court of Dallas County, on the premises of the late Danniel H. Norwood, deceased, on Saturday the 27th of December next, 10 or 12 likely negroes. I will also sell at private sale the plantation of said Daniel [sic] H. Norwood, deceased, consisting of 500 acres.... John Paulling, executor of D.H. Norwood, dec'd

The firm of Steitz & Howlett was dissolved by mutual consent on the 20th day of September 1845.... Wm. H. Steitz, Robert Howlett

Tax Collector's Sale: levied on as the property of James Goodwin's heirs....
Tax Collector's Sale: levied on as the property of John Steele of Autauga County.

Whereas the undersigned was on the 18th day of Nov., 1845, appointed administrator de bonis non of the estate of Morgan Mills, deceased, by the Orphans' Court of Dallas County, Alabama. John M. McGehee, Adm'r

Trustees' Sale: In pursuance of a certain deed of trust, made by Leonard A. Weissenger, to the undersigned trustees, which was executed on the 12th day of July last, and recorded in the office of the County Court of Perry County, Alabama in Book G page 564, 565, 566, and 567.... mentions lands formerly owned by Geo. Weissinger, dec.; .... N. Lockett, Geo. T. Johnson, A.B. Moore, J.R. Goree, Trustees

In Chancery at Cahawba, before the register in vacation, Monday Nov. 24th, 1845: Eliza Allen pro. amie vs Martin Allen.... the defendant Martin Allen is not a resident of the State of Alabama, and that the place of his residence is

MISCELLANEOUS ALABAMA NEWSPAPER ABSTRACTS --- VOL 1

unknown to the complainant or her next friend.... The bill states that in July, 1839, complainant intermarried with the defendant, in Dallas County. That they lived together as husband and wife until some time in August, A.D. 1842, when defendant absconded from the State of Alabama.... Bill prays for final hearing for a divorce..

Sheriff's Sale: levied upon as the property of Edward B. Holloway to satisfy executions in my hands against Thomas O. Holloway and Edward B. Holloway for collection.

Sheriff's Sale: Dallas County, the following negroes, Will, Charles, and Honry, levied upon as the property of Thomas O. Holloway the satisfy an execution in my hands in favor of Will E. Bird, use &c., against said Holloway.

Committed to the jail of Dallas County, a negro man calling his name Phil, who says he belongs to Dr. Robert J. Ware, of Montgomery County. Phil is of a copper color, about 5' 10" high. He says he formerly belonged to the estate of Thomas O. White, of Dallas County.

Tax Collector's sale: The owner of said land is unknown; it was interred by Anderson Motes, and is levied on as his property.

J.T. Allen, respectfully informs the public that he has removed his shop to Cahawba....

Tax Collector's Sale: Said land was granted to William Richardson, and is assessed as his property.

Tax Collector's Sale: The owner of this tract is unknown; it was entered by Jonathan Sims, Reddie Sims, and David Butler.

Tax Collector's Sale: Dallas County....The owner of said tract is unknown; it was entered by John Reed, and is appraised at $640.

Tax Collector's Sale: Dallas County, This tract is known as _____ Ambler of Virginia.

Dallas County Estray notice: Taken up by Isaac Moore.... one gray mare....

Administrator's Sale: Will be sold under an order of the Orphan's Court of Dallas County, on the premises of the late Elizabeth Vincent, on the 3rd Monday in December next.... John Vincent, Admr, with the will annexed of Elizabeth Vincent

Miscellaneous Alabama Newspaper Abstracts --- Vol 1

Dr. R.W. Safford tenders his professional services to his friends. Dr. John T. Bickley, formerly of Lowndes County, having permanently settled himself at Cahawba, tenders his professional services....

Letters of Administration were granted to the undersigned, on the estate of Rowe Harris, deceased, by the County Court of Dallas County.... M.D. Thomason, Adm'r

Executor's Notice: Letters testamentary were granted to the undersigned, on the 24th of October, 1845, by the County Court of Dallas County, on the estate of John Chambers, deceased.... John H. Chambers, Ex'r

Orphans' Court Dallas County, Oct. term 1845: In the matter of the estate of W.J. Underwood, this day came Green Underwood, administrator de bonis non of the estate of Wiley J. Underwood, deceased, and filed his allegation in court, setting forth that said estate is insolvent....

The subscriber is desirous of selling his plantation, situated about 4 miles east of Cahawba, adjoining lands of Capt. R.S. Hatcher, J.W. Kelly, and Henry Adams.... September 25, 1845, E.W. Hamilton

Letters testamentary having been granted to the undersigned by the judge of the County Court of Dallas County, on the 18th day of August, 1845, upon the estate of Jesse Hardy, deceased.... John Lee, Ex'r

On the 24th day of July, 1845, letters of Administration were granted to the undersigned on the estate of John W. Campbell, late of Wilcox County, deceased, by the judge of the County Court of said county.... James M. Campbell, John Scott, Adm'rs

Will. E. Bird and J.W. Outlaw have formed a copartnership in the practice of the law.

Ad for C.C. Sellers, Attorney at Law, Camden, Wilcox County, Alabama
Law notice of G.W. Gayle, W.W. Gayle & Horace Cone
Law notice of Thos. H. Watts & Ashley W. Spaight
Ad for the Law office of Hood & Lodor, Cahawba
Ad for Law office of Downman & Walker
Ad for law offices of A.W. Ellerbe & C.C. Peguse
Ad for law offices of J.W. Bridges & S.G. Cochran

Orphans' Court for Dallas County, Oct. Term 1845: In the matter of the estate of Robert B. Carnahan. This day came Elisha Carnahan, administrator of the estate of Robert B. Carnahan, deceased.... estate declared insolvent....

MISCELLANEOUS ALABAMA NEWSPAPER ABSTRACTS --- VOL 1

Chancery Sale, James D. Roberts, Amaranth E. Roberts, et al vs Elizabeth Harrison, et al

Orphans' Court for Dallas County, Oct. term, 1845: Estate of Archibald Butler, determining the allegations of insolvency....

THE CAHABA GAZETTE

ISSUE 7-13-1860

Married, in St. Luke's Church, Cahaba, on Wednesday evening last, July 11th, 1860, by Rev. Geo. F. Cushman, Rector of the Parish, James Shepherd Diggs, of Cahaba, to Miss Kate Evans, daughter of the late Benj. W. Evans, of Louisiana.

Died, on last Thursday evening, July 5th, 1860, at her residence in Dallas County, Mrs. Mary Saffold, widow of the late Hon. Reuben Saffold, in the 67th year of her age.

Died, in Cahaba, Ala., on Saturday night, July 8th, 1860, Mrs. Mary M. Lake, in the 48th year of her age. She was born in Tennessee, where she resided many years, but, since 1849, she has been a resident of Cahaba...

Ad for new clothing store of Sam'l M. Hill & Co.
Ad for Dr. E.H. Fournier, office at Hudson's drug store
Ad for A.I.F. Coleman
Ad for Cahaba Insurance Company, Directors: A. Saltmarsh, E.M. Perine, S.M. Hill, James D. Craig

Letters of Administration on the estate of Mrs. Elizabeth B. McCurdy, deceased, were granted to the undersigned on the 15th of June, 1860, by the Probate Court of Dallas County. Wade H. Griffin, Administrator

EUTAW WHIG AND PUBLIC ADVERTISER

ISSUE 5-28-1842

Greene County, In Chancery, at Eutaw, 21st District in the Middle Chancery Division: Edward F. Holcroft vs John Skinner & John Cathey

Taken up by Gen'l Patrick May.... two stray horses....
Taken up by Hugh A. Watson.... a gray mare mule....

Joseph S. Simmons is my authorized agent during my absence. Allen A.

MISCELLANEOUS ALABAMA NEWSPAPER ABSTRACTS --- VOL 1

Johnston, auctioneer for Greene County.

Married, on the 24th inst., by the Rev. Mr. Nash, Dr. B.J. Algood, to Miss Caroline, daughter of Col. Blake Jones, all of Sumter County.

Greene County, in Chancery, at Eutaw: William J. Steel vs the Heirs of William Houlditch, et al.

Ad for Tin Ware Manufactory of C. S. Martin

Greene County Orphans' Court, May 16th, 1842: This day came Thomas H. Hernden, executor of the last will and testament of Enoch Stringfellow, dec'd., and filed his account and vouchers for final settlement.

Greene County Orphans' Court, May 9, 1842: This day came William B. Inge, administrator, and Rebecca E. Inge, administratrix, of the estate of Richard Inge, deceased, and reported the estate of their said interstate insolvent..

Greene County Orphans' Court, May 9, 1842: This day came William C. Logan, administrator of the estate which were of James C. Logan, deceased, and filed his account current for final settlement of said estate...

Greene County Orphans' Court, May 9, 1842: This day came Nicholas Arrington, administrator of the estate which were of John D. Arrington, deceased, and filed his account for final settlement.

Greene County Orphans' Court, May 9, 1842: Bluford Hopson vs Daniel Eddins, adm'r of Allen Lee, dec'd.

Ranaway from my plantation, on Sunday night, the 15th of May, two negro fellows, of the following description: One named Isam, of rather light complexion, between 5' 4" and 6' high; will weigh about 165 lbs., about 25 years old: The other named Lewis, a very black, likely fellow, about 20 years old, about 6' high, will weigh about 165 lbs. They both carried their budgets and are supposed to be making their way back to South Carolina, whence they have recently been brought. Daniel's Prairie, Ala., A.B. Brown

Greene County, Orphans' Court, May 9, 1842: Henry Dance, executor of the last will and testament of John Watkins, deceased....final settlement of estate.

Greene County Orphans' Court, May 9, 1842: The estate of David E. Hyde, deceased, having been reported insolvent by William Huntington, the administrator.

MISCELLANEOUS ALABAMA NEWSPAPER ABSTRACTS --- VOL 1

Greene County Orphans' Court, May 9, 1842: This day came Nevin Phares, administrator of the estate which were of Mary Phares, deceased, and filed for final settlement of estate....

Greene County Orphans' Court, January 3, 1842: This day came Sidney S. Perry, administrator of the goods and chattels, rights and credits which were of Alvah Perry, deceased, and reported the estate of his said intestate insolvent....

Ad for Wm. B. McKee, Eutaw, May 7, 1842
Ad for J. Seligman & Brothers, Eutaw
Ad for Addison Fike, Clinton, Alabama
Ad for William Kennedy
Ad for Alexander Jarvis, baker & confectioner

Notice: The co-partnership heretofore existing between Charles W. Cadle and George W. Whaley.... is this day dissolved. Cha's W. Cadle, George W. Whatley, Eutaw, May 10, 1842

All persons indebted to the estate of the late Thomas Riddle, either by note or account and also, to the late firm of Riddle and Chiles, will please call on my agent, William P. Webb, in Eutaw.... Thompson Chiles, adm'r

Greene County Orphans' Court, April 16, 1842: Mary Hill, administratrix of Greene Hill, deceased, filed for final settlement of estate.

Greene County Orphans' Court, May 3, 1842: Christopher C. Gewin, administrator of the estate of which were of Elizabeth Gewin, dec'd., filed his account for final settlement....

Greene County Orphans' Court, May 3, 1842: This day came Catharine Harrison, executrix, & William S. Harrison, executor, of the last will and testament of Mary Foster, deceased, filed for final settlement of estate....

In Chancery, at Eutaw, 21st District in the Middle Chancery Division first Monday in March, 1842: Crumbly & Draper, and L.H. Hamilton vs Henry F. Arrington, Robert Arrington, John C. Gillespie, & Jesse Womack.

Greene County: Norman P. Dunham vs Gaorge A. Liber, Willis Logan, Garnishee: Garnishment

Greene County Orphans' Court, April 11, 1842: petition of James C. Locke, administrator of the goods and chattels, rights and credits of Tambolin Jones, deceased, to sell the real estate of said decedent, consisting of two lots of

MISCELLANEOUS ALABAMA NEWSPAPER ABSTRACTS --- VOL 1

land, in the town of Erie, Greene County, Alabama.... that Joshua G. Jones and Mary Ann Jones, the brother and sister of said decedent, are the heirs at law, and live beyond the limits of this state....

Taken up by Lawrence Williams.... 4 head of horses....
Taken up by Robert Craig.... a bay mare mule....

Sale of real estate, Greene County: all the right, title, and intense of William Tasker, deceased.... A.M. McDow, A.P. Barry, O.M. Birchett, Comm'rs

Ad for G.W. White, Eutaw, Alabama

THE ALABAMA WHIG

ISSUE 9-29-1853

Ad for Wm. H. Fowler, Eutaw, Sept. 20, 1853

Sheriff's Sale, Greene County: against the goods and chattles, lands and tenements of Nathaniel G. Friend, et al. Sheriff's Sale: By virtue of an execution in my hands from the Circuit Court, Greene County, in favor of M.B. Stapler vs Jno. H. Hord, I have levied on and will sell on Monday the 10th of Oct., 1853, the distribution, share and entire interest of defendant in both real and personal property, in the estate of his father William Hord, deceased.

Sheriff's Sale: By virtue of sundry executions in my hands from the office of the clerk of the Circuit Court of Greene County, Alabama, in fovor of John Nelson, J.N. Chadwick, and T.L. Ratcliffe against Nathaniel G. Friend, et al. I have this day levied on the following named slaves, to wit: Lucy, age about 55; Tempy, age about 50; Viny, age about 7; Charles, age about 5; Charlotte, age about 7; William, age about 5; Edmund, age about 55; Betsey, age about 40; Jinny, age about 12; Tener, age about 7; Maria, age about 16; Ursey, age about 30; Jimmy, age about 60; Josephine, age about 5; Ciawley, age about 40; Tom, age about 9; Frank, age about 30; Caroline, age about 14; Edmund, Jr., age about 18; French, age about 20; Moses, age about 40; Amy, age about 43.

Greene County, Probate Court, September 3, 1853: This day came Dempsey Eatman, Guardian of Wiley A. Williams, Mary A. Williams, Emerson Williams, and Jemison Williams, and filed his account for final settlement of his said Guardianship.

The undersigned having purchased the stock of Johnston and Bostick, have this day formed a new copartnership under the name and style of W. Barnes,

MISCELLANEOUS ALABAMA NEWSPAPER ABSTRACTS --- VOL 1

& Co. W. Barnes, J.T. Bostick, W.H. Lewis

Greene County: On the 18th October, 1852, I was appointed administrator of John Mobley dec'd.... W.C. Oliver, Admr.

Ad for James Meacham & Wm. R. Gully, Eutaw, Jan. 13th, 1853
Ad for J.B. Smith, cabinet making
Ad for Chas. A. Van Doorn, cabinet making

Greene County, Special Term, Sept. 1853: A.R. Davis, adm'r. John Edmiston, dec'd.: petition to sell land.

Administrators sale of land: Greene County; By virtue of an order of sale made by the Probate Court of Greene County, I shall proceed as administrator of Wright W. Smith, deceased, on the 10th day of Oct. next, ... sell the lands belonging to the estate of said decedent. John J.A. Smith adm'r, of Wright W. Smith, dec'd

Public Sale of Real Estate: John C. Phares vs Robert Leachman, adm'r., Charles L. Roberts, dec'd. et al.

Greene County Probate Court: A.R. Davis, administrator of Sam'l S. Leigh, dec' d.: petition to sell land.

Public Sale: Greene County.... sale at public auction to the highest bidder, a negro woman, Nancy Greer, about 23 years old, and her four children. Mary, about 5 years old, Brittan, about 3 years old, Jacob about 18 months old, and Miranda, an infant. S.F. Hale, Guardian minor heirs of G.L. Hill, dec'd

Greene County Probate Court Sept 13, 1853: A.R. Davis, adm'r. Abram Hester, deceased vs the heirs at law of Abram Hester, dec'd: petition to sell land.

Greene County Probate Court, Sept. 13, 1853: This day came Clemens Logan and David T. Williams, administrator of the estate of Charles Williams, dec'd., and filed for a final settlement of said administration....

Greene County Probate Court, Sept. 13, 1853: This day came William W. Long, Guardian of Lunsford Long, and filed his account for an annual settlement of his said Guardianship.

Greene County Sheriff's Sale: against the lands and tenements of Pleasant Gills in favor of Ralph S. Hunt.

MISCELLANEOUS ALABAMA NEWSPAPER ABSTRACTS --- VOL 1

Sheriff's Sale, Greene County: By virtue of an execution in my hands from the Circuit Court of Greene County in favor of J.H. Street, adm'r, for the use of Joel E. Pierson against John Cameron, Martha Street, and Mathew S. Cameron....

ISSUE 5-17-1855

Tribute of respect from George Washington lodge #24 upon the death of John Eatman.

Greene County Administrator's sale: all the remaining stock of goods and perishable property belonging to the estate of Charner G. Brown, deceased.... Wm. S. Price, Adm'r of C.G. Brown, dec'd

Administrator's Sale: On Monday the 4th day of June 1855, by order of the Probate Court of Greene County, I will sell.... as the administrator of W.R. Hassell, dec'd, a negro girl named Lucy aged about 18 years, for cash, at the risk of the former purchaser, J.D. Holly, who bid her off on the 9th day of April 1855, and failed to comply with the terms of sale. F.M. Kirksey, Adm'r of W.R. Hassell, dec'd

The firm of Hankins and Cook is this day dissolved by mutual consent. Eutaw, May 8, 1855, Wiley Hankins, Wm. A. Cook

Greene County: Letters of Administration on the estate of Wm. Dougherty, dec'd, were granted to the undersigned.... Andrew Johnston, Adm'r

Greene County: Letters of Administration on the estate of G. Brown, dec'd, were granted to the undersigned.... Wm. S. Price, adm'r

Greene County Probate Court: Anderson Thetford, Guardian of Josephine, Harriet and Wm. E. Holloway, and filed his accounts for final settlement of his Guardianship.

Greene County Probate Court: Thomas T. Tyrce, executor of the last will and testament of Amos Lay, dec'd, filed for final settlement of said executorship.

Taken up by I.S. High, a light sorrel mare mule. Taken up by Peter Stokes, two bay mules.

Greene County Probate Court: A.R. Davis, administrator of the estate of James Key, deceased, filed for final settlement of his administration.

Greene County Probate Court: Cornelia A. Bragg, administratrix of John H.

Miscellaneous Alabama Newspaper Abstracts --- Vol 1

Bragg, dec'd, filed her accounts for final settlement of her said administration.

Greene County Probate Court: Mary A. Chadwick, administratix of the estate of Shelby W. Chadwick, dec'd, filed her account and vouchers for an annual settlement of said administration.

Greene County Probate Court: P.N. True, Guardian of J.Q.A. True and W.L. True, filed his accounts for a final settlement of his Guardianship.

AMERICAN WHIG

ISSUE 6-7-1855

Married, on the 31st ult., at the residence of Mr. J.C. Phares, by Rev. F.M. Grace, Mr. R.A. Markham and Miss Eliza Phares, all of this county. (*Sumter Democrat*)

Departed this life at Harwinton, Connecticut, on the 28th of May, 1855, ?????, wife of Luther Hondley.

Died, in Wharton County, Texas, at the residence of J. Hardy, on the 16th of April, of pneumonia, John Buckley, formerly of this county. He leaves a widow and three children now residing in this county.

The subscriber having purchased the interest of Messrs. W.H. Lewis and James T. Bostick, in the accounts and notes of W. Barnes & Co.... Eutaw, June 5, 1855, Wm. Barnes

Greene County Probate Court: Hope Borden, administratrix of the estate of David W. Borden, dec'd, filed her account for an annual settlement of her administration.

Greene County Probate Court: Margaret James, Guardian of Margaret E. James, filed her account for final settlement of her Guardianship.

Greene County: To the creditors of Benj. S. Logan, dec'd. You are hereby notified that Attoway R. Davis administrator of the estate of Benj. S. Logan filed his allegation and settlements.... showing the insolvency of said estate....

Greene County Probate Court: A.R. Davis, adm'r of the estate of James Turner, dec'd: petition to sell land.

Greene County Probate Court: Patience Bizzell Guardian of Julia A. Bizzell filed for settlement of Guardianship.

Miscellaneous Alabama Newspaper Abstracts --- Vol 1

Greene County Probate Court: A.M. Pippen, administrator of the estate of Bethena Pippen, dec'd, filed for settlement of his administration.

Green County Probate Court: Augustus M. Pippen, administrator de bonis non of the estate of Peleg P. Pippen, dec'd filed his account for an annual settlement of his said administration.

Greene County Probate Court: David D. Harriss, Guardian of John R. Harriss, Mary J. Harris and Laodicia Harriss, and filed his accounts for annual settlements of his said Guardianship.

ISSUE 6-14-1855

Died, at the residence of Maj. James G. Stuart, near Huntsville, Walker County, Texas, on the 18th inst., of pulmonary disease, Daniel W. Tilman, in the 25th year of his age. Mr. Tilman was a native of Greene County, Alabama, and removed from thence to Texas in the fall of 1854.... Mr. Tilman died as he had lived, a useful and consistent member of the Christian Church. (*Huntsville,Texas Item*)

Greene County Probate Court: Petition to sell land: Ann T. and Richard Randolph, executrix and ex'r of R.C. Randolph, dec'd.

Administrator's notice: letters of administration on the estate of Simeon Lester, dec'd, were granted to the undersigned.... Holland Little, adm'r

Married, on the 7th inst., by the Rev. J.R. Bowman, at the residence of Bradley Ridgway, in the Fork of Greene County, Mr. William F. Lewis and Miss Mary Ridgway.

(Married) On the 6th inst., by the Rev. A.P. S?liman, Mr. Alison Bolton and Miss Jimsey Horn, of this county.

Greene County Probate Court: Sarah Allen, Guardian of Margaret E. Allen and George Anna Allen, and filed her account for an annual settlement of her Guardianship.

ISSUE 7-19-1855

Died, at the residence of her father, Col. Wm. H. Bullock, in Greene County, Ala., on Thursday morning July 12th, Miss Lucy Ann Bullock, in the 29th year of her age. The earliest years of the deceased were spent in Granville County, N.C.; whence her parents removed to Ala., in the ninth year of her age.... became a member of the Presbyterian Church.

Miscellaneous Alabama Newspaper Abstracts --- Vol 1

Died, in Marion, on the 11th inst., of typhus fever, Miss Mary J. Harkness, daughter of Wm. B. Harkness of this county.

(Died) On the 18th ult., at the residence of his uncle, near Greensboro, Mr. Paul Hatch, in the 23rd year of his age.

(Died) On the 12th inst., Miss Jane Wright, daughter of Mr. P.T. Wright, aged about 18 years.

Greene County Probate Court: Attoway R. Davis, administrator of the estate of Frances Philips, deceased.... petition to sell land. Where upon it is ordered by the court that the second Monday in September next, be set for the hearing of said petition, and that citations issue to Robert H. Philips, Jane Hughes and John Hughes, her husband, Elijah A. Philips, Arterberry Phillips, Charlotte Philips, Henry Jackson Philips, Diana Coleman, Mary King, Zachariah Philips, Uriah Philips and Maria Lewis, resident heirs of said decedent; and that notice to Ryal M. Philips, a non-resident be given by publication for three successive weeks in the *Alabama Whig*...

Greene County Probate Court: This day came Attoway R. Davis, administrator of the estate of Frances Philips, deceased, and filed his petition to sell the following named slaves belonging to said estate, for a distribution among the heirs of said decedent, viz: Viney, a woman and her children; John, a boy; Caroline, a girl; Sarah, a girl; Tom, a boy; Erronia, a girl; Jim, a boy; Margaret, a girl; Hugh, a boy; and Jane, a girl.

Greene County Probate Court: Attoway R. Davis, administrator of the estate of Robert H. Philips, deceased, petition to sell land...

Greene County Probate Court: Attoway R. Davis, administrator of the estate of Robert H. Philips, deceased, petition to sell the following named slaves: Island, Sally and Matilda.

Greene County Probate Court: This day came Rufus M. Brassfield administrator de bonis non with the will annexed of the estate of John R. Brassfield, dec'd and filed for a final settlement of his said administration.

Greene County Probate Court: This day came Volney Boardman executor of John Locke, who was executor of the estate of James C. Locke, dec'd and filed his account for a final settlement of the executorship of John Locke, executor as aforesaid.

Greene County Probate Court: This day came Green B. Mobley, administrator of the estate of Wiley Mobley, dec'd and filed his account for a

MISCELLANEOUS ALABAMA NEWSPAPER ABSTRACTS --- VOL 1

final settlement of his administration.

Administrator's Notice: Letters of Administration on the estate of William Martin Dr., dec'd were granted to the undersigned .... James Martin, John Martin, adm'rs

Administrator's Notice: Letters of Administration on the estate of James Wilson, dec'd were granted to the undersigned.... W. A. Jones, adm'r

Greene County Circuit Court. April 23, 1855: James D. Webb vs Alexander Springs.

Greene County Circuit Court, April 23, 1855: Wm. B. Johnston & Co. vs Royal M. Phillips.

Greene County Probate Court, July 9, 1855: W.W. Story, administrator of the estate of Benjamin Love, dec'd, filed for a final settlement of his said administration.

Ad for S.S. Murphy & Co., Eutaw
Ad for R.E. Watkins, dentist, Eutaw, Alabama

Greene County Probate Court: This day came Howel L. Kennon Guardian of Garland H., Lucy A.E., John T. and Mary J. Hendly, and filed his accounts for a final settlement of his said Guardianship.

Greene County Probate Court: This day came John H. Parish, Guardian of Frederick and Ann Amelia Peck and filed his account for annual settlement of his said Guardianship.

Administrator's Notice: Letters testamentary to the will of John Estes dec'd were granted to the undersigned. Evans Estes, Margaret Estes, ex'r and Ext'x

Administrator's Notice: Letters of Administration on the estate of Alexander Springs, dec'd, were granted to the undersigned.... A. R. Davis, adm'r

ISSUE 6-11-1857

Suicide in Cuthbert: We learn from the Cuthbert Reporter that on Friday morning last, Mr. Martin D. Hendrick, an old resident of Cuthbert, committed suicide by cutting his throat with a razor. His body was found, a short time after the deed was done, in a thicket near his residence, with the razor still in his hand. It is supposed that he did not live longer than one minute after the stroke was made, as the carotid artery was completely severed. Mr.

MISCELLANEOUS ALABAMA NEWSPAPER ABSTRACTS --- VOL 1

Hendrick made a similar attempt some weeks since, by opening an artery in the arm. (*Sun*)

Bloody Affray: A store keeper named Stribling, in Belmont, Texas, was attacked a few days ago by two men named Fisher and Kirkpatrick. Knives and pistols were freely used. Kirkpatrick was wounded and Stribling and Fisher both killed.

Died, on the 2nd inst., at her residence in this county, after a short illness, Mrs. Elizabeth M. Thomas, consort of the late Theophilos Thomas. The deceased was born in Oglethorp County, Georgia, on the 24th January, 1802, was married in 1819, and removed to this county in 1835. By the death of her husband in 1849, she was left in charge of a large family.... For 25 years she sustained a connection with the Cumberland Presbyterian Church. A short time preceding her last illness, she was gratified with the visit of her only daughter from a distant part of the state.... Athens, Ga., and Huntsville, Ala., papers will please copy.

Died, at her residence on the 23rd of April, in Vienna, Jackson Parish, La., Mrs. L.E. Quinn, (formerly Miss L.E. Otts) wife of Dr. M.P. Quinn, in the 25th year of her age. Mrs. Quinn was a member of the Presbyterian Church, having made a profession of religion, she attached herself to that Church in Greene County, Ala., in the fall of 1851. Some time after this she came to the west on a visit to her friends, near this place. She was married to Dr. M.P. Quinn, July 12th, 1854, and they settled in Vienna, where they resided until her death.... leaving her husband and dear little babe....

Greene County: Thomas J. Anderson, trustee of William Anderson and his wife Martha Anderson and their children....

Greene County Probate Court: Attoway R. Davis, Guardian of Jemima A. and Martha R. Meriweather, filed account for final settlement of Guardianship.

Greene County Probate Court: Attoway R. Davis, Guardian of Louisa A. Thornton and Arthor F. Thornton, filed for final settlement of Guardianship.

Greene County Probate Court: D.H. Williams, Guardian of Wm. B. Hutton, A.W. Hutton, A.D. Hutton, and E.C. Hutton, filed for final settlement of said Guardianship.

Greene County Probate Court: Chas. L. Stickney Guardian of Sarah McCarty, now Sarah Johnson, and Geo. McCarty, filed for final settlement of said Guardianship.

Miscellaneous Alabama Newspaper Abstracts --- Vol 1

Executrix's Notice Greene County: Letters testamentary on the estate of Edwin N. Thompson, dec'd, were granted to the undersigned.... June 1, 1857, Nancy M. Thompson, executrix

Administrator's Sale of Negroes: Three negro slaves, the property of the estate of Mary E. Beazley, deceased, namely: Mary, a woman, and her two (boy) children Richard and Bryant.... A.R. Davis, Admr

Greene County Circuit Court, April Term, 1857: J.H. & E.J. Butler vs John Willis: Attachment.

Greene County Circuit Court, April Term, 1857: John A. Baskin & Co. vs John and Ellen Willis.

Greene County Circuit Court, April Term, 1857: Jesse W. Fulgham vs John Carpenter. Attachment levied on the indebtedness in the hands of Simeon Carpenter, administrator of Pricilla Carpenter, dec'd....

Greene County Circuit Court, April Term, 1857: The Bank of Wilmington N.C. vs John A. Avirett.

Greene County Probate Court, May 28, 1857: Harriet Stickney and Chas. L. Stickney executrix and executor of Joseph B. Stickney.

Administrator's Notice, Greene County: Letters of Administration on the estate of Sarah A. O'Neal, dec'd, were granted to the undersigned.... A.R. Davis, adm'r

Administrator's Notice, Greene County: Letters of Administration on the estate of Raynes P. Travis, dec'd were granted to the undersigned.... Wm. F. Kennon, adm'r

ISSUE 6-18-1857

Married, on the 16th inst., near Forkland, in this county, by Rev. R.M. Saunders, Mr. Richard F. Irby, of Noxubee Co., Miss., to Miss Mary P. Kennon, of this county.

Died, of consumption at his residence in Greene County on the 8th day of June 1857, Isac C. Snedecor, aged 57 years. *Observer* and *Beacon* please copy.

Ad for C.A. Sheldon, Greensboro, Alabama

MISCELLANEOUS ALABAMA NEWSPAPER ABSTRACTS --- VOL 1

ALABAMA WHIG

ISSUE 2-3-1859

Married, in Montgomery on the 27th ult., by the Rev. Mr. Tichinor, Mr. Allen W. Glover, of this county, to Miss Kate Molton, of that city.

The copartnership hitherto existing between the undersigned is this day dissolved by mutual consent. J.C. Anderson, J.S. Meriweather, Jan. 1, 1859

Greene County Probate Court: Wm. R. McGowen, administrator of Wm. McGowen, dec'd, who was Guardian of Alexander, Susan, Francis, Kity, Cora and James Danrimple, filed his account for a final settlement of his said Guardianship.

Notice: Mrs. Saunder's school accounts, are in the hands of Jos. W. Taylor.

Notice: The notes of Zilia(?) A. Walker, adm'x of Jamesison Walker, dec'd, are left with me for collection.

New Firm: The undersigned have associated themselves as co-partners, in the carpentering business. P. Schoppert, R.P. Schoppert, P.C. Schoppert.

Issue Date Unknown, Vol. XXI, No. 46

Married, on the 20th inst., by Rev. J.M. Patton, Mr. Samuel T. Carpenter and Miss Clementine C. Hamlett.

Married, on the 20th inst., by S.F. Crawford, Mr. William M. Spencer and Miss Grizzy Richardson.

Married, on the 20th inst., by Rev. J.C. Wright, Mr. Meeady M. Williford and Miss Mary C. High, all of Greene County, Alabama.

Ad for Marengo Nursery: R.J. Manning

Negro Hiring: I will hire out before the court house door on the 1st day of January next, 20 negroes, belonging to the minor heirs of Wiley G. Bullock dec'd. J.R. Evans, Guardian, Dec'r. 18th, 1860.

MISCELLANEOUS ALABAMA NEWSPAPER ABSTRACTS --- VOL 1

EUTAW WHIG AND OBSERVER
ISSUE 2-9-1865

Married, in Bibb County, on the 18th ult., by the Rev. James McLean, Mr. Madison Jones, of this place, and Miss Alice McLean, of Mississippi (*Greensboro Beacon*)

Died, at the residence of Mr. F.F. Hill, in this vicinity, on the 26th ult., Wm. Tacitus Hill, in the 37th year of his age. (*Greensboro Beacon*)

Died, suddenly, from the effects of measles, on Saturday the 28th day of January, 1865, Ada Gertrude, youngest daughter of Dr. R.H. and Mrs. Mary Jackson, aged 11 years and six months. (*Greensboro Beacon*)

Died, in this vicinity, on the 20th ult., Willie, son of Mr. Robert Lewis, aged 7 years. (*Greensboro Beacon*)

Died, near Newborn, on the 26th ult., of diphtheritic croup, Minte N., aged 3 years 7 months. Also, on the 28th ult., of same disease, Lillie, aged 1 year 10 months, children of Dr. A.W. and Minnie Higgins. (*Greensboro Beacon*)

Committed to the jail of Greene County, Alabama, on the 4th day of February 1865, as a runaway slave, a negro man who says his name is Boston, and that he belongs to George Kidd, of Lagrange, Ga., and has been hired to Daniel Parker, who is in the Confederate Army. Said man is 5'5" high, weighs about 150 pounds, about 25 years old and of copper color.

Wanted, by a gentleman who has had several years experience in the business, and is not subject to military duty, a situation as overseer. Address J.H. Pritchett, Hollow Square, Alabama, February 7, 1865

Committed to the jail of Greene County, Ala., on the 20th day of August, 1864, as a runaway slave, a negro boy who says his name is Henry and that he belongs to John Jackson, near Jackson, Mississippi. Said boy is 4' 9" high, 120 lbs., about 14 years old and black.

Committed to the jail of Greene County, 8th of December, 1864, a negro man who says his name is William and he belongs to James Powell of Talladega, AL. Said man is 5'4" high, 150 lbs., 45 or 50 years old, and of copper color.

Greene County Adm's Notice: the undersigned appointed administrator of the estate of Frederick Meriwether, deceased. Willis Meriwether, Administrator

Greene County Administrator's Notice: T.J. Sorsby appointed administrator of B.A. Sorsby, deceased.

Greene County Administrator's Notice: Jno. T. Richardson appointed administrator of Wm. H. Richardson, deceased.

Greene County Administratrix's Notice: Martha E. Kirkland appointed administratrix of Isaac W. Kirkland, deceased, on the 19th day of Dec., 1864.

Greene County Administrator's Notice: J.M. Hall appointed administrator of George L. Pearce, deceased, on the 19th day of Dec., 1864.

Greene County Probate Court, Jan. 20, 1865: Susan Eubank, administratrix of Jno. M. Eubank, dec'd filed for settlement of said administration.

Greene County Probate Court, Jan. 20, 1865: J.T. Martin, Guardian of F.M. Martin and Laura J. Martin, filed for final settlement of his said Guardianship.

Greene County Probate Court, Jan. 20, 1865: J.T. Martin, Guardian of Martha J. Martin, C. G. Martin and Mary J. Martin, and filed for an annual settlement of his said Guardianship.

Greene County Probate Court, Jan. 16, 1864: T.C. Clark, administrator of J.P. Clark, deceased, filed his account and vouchers for an annual settlement of his said administration.

Administrator's Notice, Greene County: J.M. Hall appointed administrator de bonis non of Andrew Norwood, deceased, on the 27th day of Dec., 1864.

Administrator's Notice, Greene County: J.M. Hall appointed administrator de bonis non, with will annexed, of Isaac Brown, deceased, on the 31st day of Dec., 1864.

Administrator's Notice, Greene County: J.M. Hall appointed administrator of Nancy C. Brown, deceased, on the 31st day of Dec., 1864.

Administratrx's Notice, Greene County: Therresa Lay appointed administratrix of Sylvester F. Lay, deceased, on the 16th day of January, 1865.

Administrator's Notice, Greene County: John Bouchillon appointed administrator of the estate of William F. Bouchillon, deceased, on the 2? day of November, 1864.

Greene County Probate Judge's Office: R.F. Shelton, administrator of Jno. R. Shelton, dec'd, who was administrator of R.W. Garrett, dec'd, filed his

MISCELLANEOUS ALABAMA NEWSPAPER ABSTRACTS --- VOL 1

account and vouchers for a final settlement of said administration.

Greene County Probate Judge's Court: Virginia McAlpine, administratrix of Solomon McAlpine, dec'd, filed her account and vouchers for a final settlement of her said administration.

Greene County Probate Judge's Office: Jan. 17, 1865: J.J.A. Smith, Guardian of J.C.W. Smith and C.C. Smith, filed his account and vouchers for a final settlement of his said Guardianship.

Greene County Probate Judge's Office, Jan. 14, 1865: Wiley Coleman, executor of Rhoda Coleman, deceased, filed for final settlement.

Ad for Turner's Tan Yard, S.L. Creswell
Ad for Iron, wholesale and retail, J.J. Porter, Selma, Alabama

ISSUE 3-9-1865

Lost by the subscriber, a small calfskin pocket book, containing a plain note of hand given by Thomas H. Watkins to the undersigned on the 10th day of Feb. 1859, for $386 and due one day after. Also 2 50/100 dollars in money. Thos. I. Anderson, Hollow Square, Alabama, Feb'y 9, 1865

Executrix's Notice Greene County: Mary J. Freeman appointed executrix of Peter L. Mabry, deceased, on the 1st day of Feb'y, 1865.

Executor's Notice Greene County: W.P. May was appointed executor of Luke Thornton, deceased, on the 8th day of Feb'y, 1865.

Executrix's Notice Greene County: Eliza G. Watson was appointed executrix of the estate of David Watson, deceased, on the 30th day of January, 1865.

Administrator's Notice Greene County: W.W. Paschall was appointed administrator of John Norwood, deceased, on the 8th day of February, 1865.

Greene County Probate Court, Feb. 14, 1865: T.J. Drummond, executor of Geo. W. Drummond, deceased, filed his account and vouchers for a final settlement of his said executorship.

Notice: To Robert P. Walker, of Rapides Parish, La., John L. Walker of Winn Parish, La., and to the children of Thos. W. Walker, deceased, Viz: Herbert F. and Henry Walker and their mother, of Athens, Ga. On the 27th day of February, 1865, Mary A. Walker, widow of Sanders Walker, dec'd, filed in the Probate Court of Greene County, Ala., for propounding an instrument in writing purporting to be the will of the said Sanders Walker, dec'd. The second Monday in May next is set for hearing. Take due notice.

TAX SALE: On Monday the 24th day of April, 1865, I will sell publicly, to the highest bidder, before the court house door, in the town of Eutaw, the following described parcels of land for the state and county tax due thereon for 1864, Viz:..... Assessed to Wm. T. Watt; town lot in Greensboro assessed to William Dorris; town lot in Greensboro assessed to Stephen Mullins; town lot in Greensboro assessed to Rebecca E. Briggs; 45 acres in N 1/2 Sec 19, township 20 range 5 east assessed to Keziah A. Croom; 14 acres S.E. Corner Sec 21, township 19, range 5 East.... assessed to Lucy A. and Richard Croom; NW 1/4 less 20 acres S.W. Corner, Sec 4 township 22, range 2 East.... assessed to David H. Coleman; N.E. 1/4 N.E. 1/4 Sec 6, township 23, range 2 East assessed to J.B. Tynes; S.W. 1/4 S.W. 1.4 Sec 24, township 23, range 1 West.... assessed to Doss & Tierce; S.E. 1/4 N.W. 1/4, Sec 2, township 23, range 1 East assessed to estate of Mourning Crumpler; S.W. 1/4 and W 1/2 S.E. 1/4 Sec 25, township 21, range 1 East..assessed to est. Peter Martin; Town lot in Greensboro assessed to Isaac Ullman; W 1/2 S.W. 1/4, Sec 28, township 19, range 3 East.... assessed to Littleberry Mason; N.E. 1/4 Sec 1, township 20, 5 East.... assessed to Albert Smith; N.E. 1/4 S.E. 1/4, Sec 36, township 22, range 4 East assessed to Wm. T. Harper; W 1/2 S.W. 1/4, Sec 5, township 19, range 1 East assessed to Matilda LaBrouse. Newton F. Smith, Tax collector, G.C., March 1st, 1865

Greene County Probate Judge's Office: William Miller, administrator of James M. Free, deceased, filed his account for final settlement of his said administration.

Greene County Probate Judge's Office: John W. May, administrator, with will annexed, of Jonathan May, deceased, filed his account and vouchers for final settlement of his said administration.

Greene County Probate Judge's Office: Dempsey Harrison, administrator of Thomas A. Thompson and Joseph W. Thompson, dec'd, filed his account and vouchers for a partial settlement of his said administration.

Greene County Probate Judge's Court, Feb. 20th, 1865: Thos. C. Clark, administrator of Judith P. Clark, dec'd, filed his account and vouchers for a final settlement of his said administration.

Greene County Probate Court, Feb. 13, 1865: Zylphia McCrackin, administratrix of Jno. C. McCrackin, dec'd, filed her account and vouchers for an annual settlement of her said administration.

MISCELLANEOUS ALABAMA NEWSPAPER ABSTRACTS --- VOL 1

Greene County Administratrix's Notice: Martha Ann Horn, appointed administratrix of Leroy W. Horn, deceased, on the 27th day of February, 1865.

Administrator's Notice, Greene County: Jno. H. Hargrove, appointed administrator of Sarah A. Hill, deceased, on the 27th day of Feb., 1865.

Greene County Probate Judge's Office, Feb. 24, 1865: Noah Harris, executor of Clement Logan, dec'd, filed his account and vouchers for a final settlement of his executorship.

Col. Simeon Maxwell, the subject of this notice, was born in Elbert County, Ga., June 24th, 1792, married Miss Elizabeth Fortson in 1819, emigrated to Ala., in 1820, united with the Clinton Baptist Church, 1835, and died at his residence in Greene County, Ala., Feb. 15th, 1865, in the 72nd year of his age.

We are pained to announce the death of C.A. Scarbrough one of the most worthy and excellent young men of our town. He died at his fathers residence in this place on the 2nd inst., of pneumonia.

Died, near Union, on the 24th ult., Caroline Birchett, daughter of William H. and Sarah A. Birchett, aged 10 years, 1 month and 26 days.

ISSUE 3-16-1865

$300 Reward: Stolen from me on the night of the 1st of March, a light sorrel horse mule... N.T. Sorsby, Forkland, March 2nd, 1865

Shoe Making: The undersigned is prepared to make all kinds of men's, women's and children's shoes, at the residence of Mrs. E. W. Gould, near Boligee. Le Fleur, March 4th, 1865

The subscriber has a Steam Boiler, weighing about 800 pounds, suitable for making ploughs, which he would barter for provisions. W. Croom

Died, of pneumonia, on the 2nd of March, 1865, at his father's residence, in Eutaw, Ala., Charles A. Scarbrough, aged 32 years, 10 months and 22 days....

Wm. R. Hardaway a candidate for Sheriff of Greene County. E. Nutting a candidate for Sheriff of Greene County.

Committed to the jail of Greene County, on the 8th day of March, 1865, as a runaway slave, a negro man who says his name is Moses, and that he belongs to John E. McLemore, of Carrol County, Mississippi. Said man is 5' 5" high, weighs about 150 lbs., about 21 or 22 years old and black.

SELMA WEEKLY MESSENGER

ISSUE 11-10-1866

We learn that an old gentleman named Davenport, residing near Brandidge, in this county, was last week, found drowned in a mill creek, in the vicinity of Monticello. He was very old and decrepit. It seems that he had started from where he was living to visit a daughter near Monticello. The creek in which he was found is very small, and not at all swollen with water, because of the very long dry spell in that section. We have heard of no one being accused of having drowned him, though it is believed that a violent hand brought him to his death.

Dallas County Probate Court, October 9, 1866: Charlotte M. Bissell granted letters of administration upon the estate of Henry C. Bissell, deceased.

Dallas County Probate Court: H.B. Rives granted letters of administration upon the estate of Thomas Rives, deceased, 9th day of October, 1866.

Dallas County Probate Court, October 19th, 1866: Moses A. Nunnelly, administrator of the estate of Wm. A. Spears, deceased, filed his application for sale of lands belonging to said estate for the purpose of paying debts, upon the grounds that the personal property is insufficient .

Dallas County Probate Court, October 15, 1866: Wm. E. Boyd, Guardian of Nancy, Mary, Martha, Anderson, George and Elizabeth Templin, filed his statements, accounts, vouchers for a final settlement of said Guardianship.

Dallas County Probate Court, October 15, 1866: Benj. L. Saunders, deceased, estate of: This day came the administrator of said estate and filed his statements, accounts, vouchers, and evidences for a final settlement of his said administration.

Administrator's Sale of Land: Probate Court of Dallas County: I will sell to the highest bidder all the real estate of Samuel S. Johnson, deceased, in Dallas County, consisting of 153 acres lying about 2 miles north of Burnsville. 63 acres of said land will be sold subject to the dower interest of the widow of said estate.... E.A. Mixon, Adm'r de bonis non

On Friday, the 16th of November, at Pleasant Hill, Dallas County, I will rent to the highest bidder, the three plantations belonging to the estate of S.B. Vasser, deceased, known respectfully as the Home Place, the Saffold Place, and the Smyley Place.... Jno. T. Morgan, Adm'r of estate of L.B. [sic] Vasser, deceased

Administrator's Sale: By virtue of an order granted on the 10th of September, 1866, to the undersigned, as administrator of the estate of Dr. John H. Jones, deceased, by the Hon. Bush Jones, Judge of Probate of the County of Perry and State of Alabama, I will offer for sale, to the highest bidder at public auction...(lands in Dallas and Perry Counties) F.A. Bates, Administrator

Dallas County Probate Court, October 13, 1866: Edward W. Marks, dec'd, in the matter of the probate of his will: This day came Mrs. Martha A. Marks, and filed her petition, in writing, therewith producing, and filing in this court, an instrument of writing purporting to be the last will and testament of said Edward W. Marks, deceased, and praying for such order, decrees and proceedings as may be proper and requisite for the due probate and record of said will in this court.

Mortgage Sale: By virtue of a mortgage to the undersigned, executed by P.G. McCuary, on the 19th of February, 1858, we will sell at public outcry, to the highest bidder for cash, on the premises in the town of Summerfield, at 12 o'clock M., on Saturday the 17th day of November, 1866, lot #11, in said town, lying immediately north of the Methodist Episcopal Church, and containing one acre more or less. White & Blake, Selma, Ala.

Dallas County Probate Court, Oct. 31, 1866: Robert Hinton, administrator of the estate of Christopher Fitzgerald, dec'd, and filed his accounts and vouchers for a final settlement of his said administration.

Dallas County Probate Court, Oct. 31, 1866: Robert Hinton, administrator of the estate of Elizabeth Fitzgerald, dec'd, filed his accounts and vouchers for a final settlement of his said administration.

Dallas County Probate Court, October 24, 1866: William Cox, administrator of the estate of J.B. Cox, deceased, filed his accounts, vouchers, evidences, and statements for a final settlement of his said administration.

On Saturday, 17th November next, I will rent to the highest bidder, at Boykin & Kenan's store, in the Boykin settlement, in Dallas County, the place known as the "Bonner Plantation," 8 miles from Portland, containing about 2,200 acres.... Mrs. E.M. Boykin, administratrix of estate of Burwell Boykin, deceased

MISCELLANEOUS ALABAMA NEWSPAPER ABSTRACTS --- VOL 1

All person having claims against the estate of Andrew Bogle, deceased, are requested to present the within the time prescribed by law.... W. Ditmar, administrator

Administrator's Sale of Land: By virtue of an order of the Probate Court of Perry County, I, as administrator de bonis non, of O.T. Jones, deceased, will sell, on Wednesday, November 28, 1866 between the usual hours of sale, on the premises, the plantation owned and occupied by the said Jones at the time of his death. Said plantation lies on the road from Hamburg to Craig's Ferry, about 4 miles east of Hamburg, and the same distance from Harrell's Cross Road's, on the Selma and Meridian Railroad, and contains 1,030 acres, more or less.... N. Lockett, adm'r of Osmond T. Jones, deceased

ISSUE 11-17-1866

Married, at the residence of the bride's father, on the 1?th inst., by the Right Rev. Bishop Wilmer of Alabama, Capt. Wm. M. Polk son of the late Bishop Polk, and Miss Ida Lyon, daughter of Hon. F.S. Lyon, of Demopolis, Alabama.

ISSUE 11-24-1866

Died, at Cambridge, Ia., Saturday, Nov. 17th, Theodora, only child of H.C. and S.G.M. Purple, aged 9 years and 1 month.

Married, at Jacksonville, Ala., on the ??, by the Rev. J.J.D. Renfro, Mr. T. S. Bowen, of this city, and Miss S.C. Snow, of the former place.

(Married) On the 22nd inst., by Rev. W.J. Lowry, at the residence of Captain Otey, in Uniontown, Mr. J. Scott Carter and Mrs. Carrie Gol?man.

ISSUE 12-1-1866

Dallas County Probate Court, Nov. 12, 1866: The estate of T.J. English, dec'd declared insolvent by said court.

Dallas County Probate Court, Nov. 12, 1866: The estate of John H. Stone, dec'd declaired insolvent by said court.

Dallas County Probate Court, Nov. 17, 1866: James Gilmer, the administrator of Samuel Donaghey, dec'd, filed his statements, accounts, and vouchers for a final settlement of his administration.

Dallas County: Whereas Lucy S. Hatcher and Julia Hatcher have this day filed with me their petition in writing, setting forth that they are citizens of this

Miscellaneous Alabama Newspaper Abstracts --- Vol 1

county, and of full age, are jointly interested in certain lands located in this county belonging to the estate of John Hatcher, deceased, and praying that the said land may be divided and allotted to the said Lucy S. Hatcher and Julia Hatcher....

Dallas County Probate Court, Nov. 17, 1866: James Gilmer, as administrator of the estate Samuel Donaghey, who was the administrator of Miller Edwards, dec'd, filed his accounts, vouchers, evidences for a final settlement of said administration.

Dallas County Probate Court: John T. Heflin, and S.N. McCraw appointed administrators de bonis non, with will annexed, on the estate of Fredrick S. Becton, deceased.

Dallas County Probate Court: Lewis Griffice, administrator of the estate of Thomas Ethridge, deceased, petition for sale of real estate.... upon the grounds that said real estate cannot be equitably divided.

Ad for Charles F. Brown, watchmaker, Selma, Alabama

Dallas County Probate Court: Samuel Donaghey, Guardian of minor heirs of Zachariah A. Bennett, deceased: In matter of settlement. This day came James Gilmer as the administrator of the estate of said deceased, and filed his accounts, vouchers and evidences for a final settlement of said Guardianship of Samuel Donaghey, as Guardian of the minor heirs of Zachariah A. Bennett.

Dallas County Probate Court, Nov. 23, 1866: Thomas J. Portis and M.R. Rixey, Guardians of Sallie Ann and Drury Fair Jones: In matter of settlement.

Dallas County Probate Court: Letter of administration being granted to W.S. Knox upon the estate of Richard M. King, deceased.

Dallas County Probate Court: Letters of Administration being granted to Wm. C. Ward upon the estate of Jesse C. Lord, deceased, 6th day of November, 1866.

The undersigned Guardians of the minor children on J. Bruce Gill, dec'd, will rent for the year 1867, on Monday the 10th day of December 1866, the plantation known as the "Bruce Gill Place," 7 miles from Cahaba.... W. H. Hammock, S.J. Hammock, Guardians.

Ad for N.D. Johnson and R.A. Pettibone, successors to L.W. Pettibone, Selma, Alabama

Miscellaneous Alabama Newspaper Abstracts --- Vol 1

ISSUE 12-22-1866

Married, at the Church of the Holy Cross, Uniontown, on the 6th inst., by the Rev. R. H. Cobbs, Major F.C. Randolph, of Montgomery, Alabama, to Miss S. T. Nicolson, daughter of R.W. Nicolson of Perry County.

THE DEMOCRATIC WATCHTOWER

Published at Talladega, Talladega County, Alabama, by M'Afee, Griffin & Co.

ISSUE 7-29-1840

A list of letters remaining in the Post Office at Talladega, on the 1st day of July, 1840:

Joshua Averett, William Allen, Senor Pedro Alberty

H.G. Barclay, F.N. Brown, Dan'l Brigman, A.R. Barclay, Louisiana Bradford, Bradford & Lawler, Jos. Bradford, Spencer Ball, Henry Brown, F.N. Brown, Mrs. Hannad Brock, Miss L.L. Bowie, Miss L. Brotnam, Jas. J. Britt, Sam'l C. Baskin, John Brown, Charles Bennett, David M.B. Boring, James Barnett, Henry L. Brown, Gen'l T. Bradford, J.R. Bracken

Tho's Cook, W.S. Carpenter, Wm. C. Crenshaw, C.W. Chaney, R.B. Carey, Pinekney D. Casper, Mrs. Nancy A. Cunningham, G.W. Copeland, Wm. Cobb, Tho's Cox, Tho's Cunningham, John Casey, Matthew Carter, Wm. Cameron, Ja's L. Chandler, C. Carptem, Ja's Chandler, Jacob Cunningham

Simeon Douglass, Jesse Daniel, Miss S. Dixon, Wm. R. Dodson, William Davis, M.M. Duncan, P. Davis, Baker Dulaney

John G. Eve, George Elrod, Wm. G. Embry, Z.A. Edwards, Henry F. Evans, Ellington, Dewo? Ellington

Edmond Foreman, Elijah Foreman, John M. Funderburg, Ja's J. Forman

Alford Gaylor, Mrs. Margaret Gray, Reuben A. Golding, Mrs. Margarett Graham, James Graham, Talifarro Grimbs, Miss Charlotte Gaines, Ja's A.H. Givens, Rob't Giag, Tho's Garner, Robert Gray, Norvell Ganaway, William E. Grady, Mrs. Cyntha Gray, Washington Goodman, John Gaines

John J. Henderson, R.J. Harrison, John Hill, John Hardie, William Holmes,

Miscellaneous Alabama Newspaper Abstracts --- Vol 1

Abner Howard, C. Haynes, Ewel S. Harrison, J.B. Henry, Ambrose Hendon, J.H. Hill, John Haughton Jr., John Harman, William Hogan, Tho's L. Holly, William H. Hudson, William Hall, Rob't K. Hampson,

J.D. Inger

Sam'l Johnson, Tho's W. Jones, Mansfield Jenkins, Mrs. M.W. Johnson, Miss Margarett Johnson, Sam'l J. Jones

William King, Shelton Kenerly, William Kenida

J.T. Leftwich, W.Y. Lundie, J.R. Lawler, Abraham Leveret, Francis Lee, Mrs. E.A. Lewis, Matthew Lee

Wm. J. MacLin, Wm. A. Mason, George C. Metcalf, M.L. McGuire, William Miller, Ja's McDonald, Nath'l Malory, Dan'l McLeod, Rob't McRight, W.H. Moore, G.T. McAfee, H. McAden, Tho's J. Monk, Wm. T. McGrew, Wm and Isaac McCarter, William Moore, William A. Martin, William McPherson, Rich'd Miller, Ja's M. McCann, Wm. McLemore, Wm. McDonald, Elizabeth Moore, Miss Elvira F. Morgan, Frances Mitchell, Tho's McCulloch, Seaborn McCane

Alex'r Nicholson

David Owen

B.M. Pace, B.F. Powell, B.F. Powell & Co., Lewis E. Parsons, Alex'r Porter, William C. Price, Seaborn Parmer, Cornelius Price, Washington Philips, Reuben Philips, G.P. Ploughman, Edward W. Parker

Asa Rowe, Mary Richey, Henry A. Rutlidge, Eskidge Robinson, S.F. Rice, Wm. A. Reavis, Ja's C. Reed, David Rolies, Cha's Rutledge, Robert Rodgers, Obadiah Rayford, J.P. Rowden, Cha's D. Reed, Thomas Rollins, D. Rather, Geo. L. Ragland

T.H.P. Seales, Benj'n Spence, John Scott, Ja's M. Smith, Kyro Smith, Dan'l Smith, J.D. Shelley, Wm. A. Scott, Cha's P. Shelley, Albert G. Sims, Jesse Steed, Wade H. Sims, E. Sawyer, Miss Lucy A. Scott, Shelton & Borum, Tho's M. Smith, Solomon Spence, Kyle Smith, H. Sims

John Tant, Mrs. M.M. Tomkies, Mrs. Martha Talmage, Tho's Terry, Wm. G. Thompson, J.F. Tomkies, Hiram T. Taylor, F.M. Thomason, Sabry Thompson

John Vensey

MISCELLANEOUS ALABAMA NEWSPAPER ABSTRACTS --- VOL 1

William A. Willson, Walter West, Frances Whitworth, William H. Watson, H.P.S. Watson, Henry Weaver, Rob't C. Willson, Bennett Ware, Edw'd Williams, Wm. H. Williams, Dan'l Welch, Jesse M. Willson, Oliver Welch, William Willson, George T. Watkins, Willis Wood, H.J. Welcker, Rob't N.C. Ware, H.G. Woodard, James Wheeler
F.G. McConnell, P.M.

ISSUE 5-12-1841

Jas. Adair, Tandy W. Arnold, ???? Armbre?ster, Mrs. Elizabeth Ashley

James Bailey, Stephen Bishop, Alfred Blackwell, David Blackwell, Mrs. Sarah C. Baily, A.R. Barclay, H.L. Brown, Mrs. Frances Bryan, Henry W. Baskin, Tarpley Barber, J.T. Bradford, Jas. H. Bradford, James Brock, Neil Buie, Jas. A. Brady, Frederick N. Brown, J.F. Bumgardner, Bradford & Lawler, Mrs. Jane Burns, Mrs. Sally Brooks, John Brooks, Raymond Blankinship

H.W. Coleman, W.H. Campbell, Henry Carter, Thos. W. Coker, Thos. Chilton, Jno. W. Carter, Wm. Camel, T.W. Cox, John Chappell, Wm. S. Carpenter, William Coldwell, Syrus W. Cotten, John Coffee, James W. Clements, John Clark, Nicles Cales

Hugh S. Darby, Simeon Douglass, Baker Dulaney, Danl Dulaney, Robert Dodd, Thos Derrick, Jas. Dorsey, Cornelious Dancy, David Dulaney, Marcus M. Duncan

Richard Evans, D.B. Elliott, Allen Elston, Jesse Ellis, Geo. Elrod, Nancy Embry

Willis Franklin, Larkin Ferguson, Robert Fountain, E. Foreman, Benjn. Foreman, James W. Furlow

D.A. Griffin, Jas. S. Guthrie, John N. Golden, Thos. or Wm. Garner, Robert Gray

John Harman, John F. Henderson, Saml. Henderson, James Headen, Jacob Hall, John Hill, Jas. H. Hill, John Hardie, Jas. Hancock, C. Haynes, J. & J. Harman, Geo. Hill, Thos. L. Holly, Wm. Henderson, Hill & Rice, A.R. Houston, James Hill, Isaah Holas, Andw. or Cagia Hughs, Ambrose Headen, H. Hill, James Hollmark, Nathan Y. Hunter

Seaborn Jones, Rowland R. Jones, Patrick Johnson, Gerdine Johnson, Willis H. Jones

MISCELLANEOUS ALABAMA NEWSPAPER ABSTRACTS --- VOL 1

Dr. J.H. King, Shelton Kenerly, Wm. King, Wm. Kilgore

Thos. Lynch, Jacob Ledbetter, Wm. Liles, Isaac Lawler, Mrs. Wm. Lewis, Francis Lee, Irwine Lambert, Thos. F. Lundie, Robert Lundsay, Levi W. Lawler, J.T. Leftwich, Abner Lawler, Rewben Lenear, Wm. W. Lane, Benjn T. Long, Daniel A. Long, Jeremiah Long, Matthias Lee, John Long, James Long, John or James Long

Simon Morris, E.G. Morris, W.H. McElheney, McAlister Mayfield, Jas Mallory, Francis Mitchell, James Meadows, Wallace Mygate, A.H. Moss, Jas. M. Moore, Geo. McLeod, T.S. Morgan, Jas. Montgomery, Thos. McCulloch, Thos. McEldry, Henry Malory, Wm. Miller, T. Moody, Benjn Miller, Solomon Martin, W.H. Moore, Mr. Mitchell, William Montgomery, Danl. McLeod, Wm. McKee, G.T. McAfee

Ephraim Osborn

H. Pearse & Co., J.H. Pearse, B.F. Powell & Co., B.F. Powell, John Patterson, Lewis Pyles, William Pew, Thos. W. Price, Reuben Philips, Reuben Patterson, P.E. Pearson, R.F. Pollard, Andrew Pauley, Ross Philileps, G.W. Penn

Alexr. Riddle, H.A. Rutledge, Miss Sarah A. Robeson, S.F. Rice, John Rhoden, Danl Robeson or Danl Allison, Addison Roseman, Polard Roads, John Rentfrow, Hugh Rhea, J.A. Rowe, H.C. Robinson, Obadiah Radford, Seth L. Randall, Martin K. Ryan, Robert Rodgers, A. & J. Riezer, H.W.W. Rice, John Robberson

Solomon Spence, Wm. Shaffer, J.D. Shelley, Benjn. Smoot, Elisha Simmons, William Sumners, Henry Sims, G.W. Stone, Wm. E. Stubblefield, Rufus Stinnett, Isaac Stone, Wylie Sanders, Lorenzo Stover, John G. Smith or Jas. Hill, John Sloan, Henry Strictland, Ansol Sawyer

Southan Thomason, A.S. Terry, Henry Taylor, Josiah Terry, John H. Townsend, William Turner, J.P. Taylor, F.M. Thomason, Majr. Tremore

John Williams, Benjn Willson, John White, H.P. Watson, S.M. Welch, Matthew Wood, John Wheeler, Samuel Watson, John B. Willson, Oliver Welch, Mr. Rev. Watson, W.A. Willson, Ezekial Wilder, Jesse M. Willson, Edward Wesson, Jno Write, R.C. Wilson, Francis Watkins, John Watkins, L.W. Willson, John D. Willson

Mrs. Rebbecca Young, John Yarborough, J.C. Young, Saml H. Young

MISCELLANEOUS ALABAMA NEWSPAPER ABSTRACTS --- VOL 1

ISSUE 8-16-1843

The subscriber has in his possession an offer of one thousand acres of land for the apprehension and delivery of Mark W. Doss, into the custody of the keeper of any jailer in the Republic of Texas. This Mark W. Doss married Jane Langston; she is known by the write of this article to be an excellent woman and of a good family. During the winter of 1838, and when Judge Summers was at Tuscaloosa engaged as a Representative of the County of Bibb, Doss went to Judge Summers, and Summers' wife being a sister to his wife, he prevailed on her to loan him the Judge's waggon and team. He then started off under a pretext of a prospect of making some money by wagoning and has never returned since. He went directly on to western Texas where he turned his attention to preaching, and was very religious outwardly and a strict member of the Baptist Church. He finally on being received into the house of a ???? widow by dint of slight of hand, pocketed her gold watch and suddenly disappeared from that part of the country. He then went on to eastern Texas to Jacob Blanton's, who was another brother-in-law to Obediah Langston of our neighboring County Bibb. He here represented his wife to be dead, had said he had left his children with her friends in Bibb County, Alabama. He here became as usual very pious, and finally married a woman a shade deeper than would pass for white folks. After he had resided there for some time, a misunderstanding took place between him and Jacob Blanton, and he concealed himself in the bushes on the road side where he knew Blanton would pass, and from his hiding place he shot Blanton dead. He was arrested and broke jail twice in Texas, and it is supposed that he is now in Tennessee or Mississippi lurking about, or probably acting the part of a Baptist preacher under a new name. He has a good voice and sings well, and when he resided in Bibb, he frequently taught singing schools. He was then a member of the Baptist Church but never attempted to preach. He is 6'1" high, has a thin sharp looking face, a sharp looking nose, and is about 45 years of age. One of his big toes has been broken and turns up so as to be plainly seen with a shoe on. If he should be discovered by any person seeing this, let him address a letter to Obadiah Langston, of Bibb County, Alabama, and he will furnish them with the written offer of reward of one thousand acres of land. This is the same Mark W. Doss who has for some time past been noticed in the papers of this country as the murderer of Blanton, and his having broke jail the second time and his final escape. Obadiah Langston, Bibb County, Alabama

$25 Reward: Runaway from my plantation, on the 9th inst., a negro girl Jane about 18 years old, slender built, and stands about 5'6" high. She is of a dark complexion.... Jane has been decoyed off by a free negro calling himself John Stewart, who is thin visaged and of yellow color.... Madegan & Devan, or by me Thomas Merriweather, August 16th

MISCELLANEOUS ALABAMA NEWSPAPER ABSTRACTS --- VOL 1

Committed to the jail of Talladega County, Alabama, on the 20th day of July inst., a runaway negro man who calls his name Daniel, of dark complexion, 5' 8" high, about 45 years old, he say he belongs to William Israel of Macon County, Alabama.

ISSUE 9-3-1845

Died, in this place on Sunday morning last at 3 o'clock August 31st, of a long and painful illness, Mrs. Mary Catharine Chilton, consort of William P. Chilton, and eldest daughter of George and Frances Morgan. Mrs. Chilton contracted the illness, which has at last terminated her earthly career, about two years ago.... Mrs. Chilton was born in Nashville, Ten. on the 16th of October 1814, (and was married in Athens on the 26th of February 1833) consequently she was in her 31st year when she died. She has left behind her an affectionate husband and five little children.... Member Baptist Church....

Departed this life on Tuesday the 19th inst., in this city, after an illness of 14 days, Florida Louisa, daughter of Charles and Cintheha E. Yancey, aged 1 year, 4 months and 9 days. At New York, on the 6th inst., Mr. Wm. H. Cook, printer, aged 36.

ISSUE 3-8-1848

Married, near Ashville, St. Clair County, on the 25th ult., by the Hon. John I. Thomason, Mr. G.O. Taylor to Miss Martha Joiner, all of that county.

ISSUE 4-5-1848

$10 Reward, ranaway from the subscriber on the 7th inst., a negro man named Gre
en, about 22 years old, yellowish complexion, 5' 9" or 10" high, straight and slender made. He was purchased by me, on the day he left, at the sale of the administrators of David Walker, deceased.... his delivery to me at my residence in Talladega County. Joseph Keith

Ad for Franklin W. Bowdon & Tignal W. Jones, attorneys at law, Talladega, Alabama
Ad for the Alabama House, in Jacksonville, Eliza Jane Tate

ISSUE 7-12-1848

Ad for Watch repair, T. Warwick, Talladega. Apprenticeship in England & devoted 30 years exclusively to the business
Ad for the law offices of Thos. G. Garrett and Wm. C. Hill, Talladega, Ala

MISCELLANEOUS ALABAMA NEWSPAPER ABSTRACTS --- VOL 1

Ad for the Mardisvile Academy, Wm. A. Stewart

ISSUE 8-30-1848

Died, on last Monday, at the residence of B. Eason, near this place, Mrs. Harriet Swan, aged about 39 years.

ISSUE 9-27-1848

Died, on Monday the 25th inst., John D., infant son of Alexander White, aged about 15 months.

ISSUE 10-2-1850

Died, near this place of pulmonary consumption, on Wednesday July 24th, between 8 and 9 o'clock P.M., Mrs. Mary Riddle, consort of Col. Riddle. Mrs. Riddle was, at the time of her death, in the 49th year of her age. She was a South Carolinian by birth, but from Talladega County, Alabama, to this state in 1848.

Talladega County Executors Notice: Letters testamentary having been granted to the undersigned upon the estate of Samuel Cunningham, deceased.... J.Q. Cunningham, Executor, September 10, 1850

ISSUE 4-29-1857

Married, on Thursday, 23rd inst., at the residence of James McCann, by Rev. F.M. Grace, Mr. H.H. Hamill to Miss Virginia Alabama Stephenson.

ISSUE 6-29-1859

Married, at the residence of Mrs. Frances Simmons, by W.H. Thornton, W.A. Roberson, of Memphis, Tenn., to Miss Phereby Stocks, of Oxford, Mississippi.

Married, on Tuesday evening, the 28th inst., at the residence of the bride's father, by Rev. A.B. McCorkle, W.N. Boynton, of Cahaba, to Miss Fannie, daughter of Major James Isbell, of this place.

Homicide: Mr. Thomas Gooden, was stabbed, and almost instantly killed by Hiram Morris at Eastaboga, in this county, on the 24th inst. The weapon used was a common pocket knife, which penetrated the left side of the chest, at a point between the second and third ribs, ranging down towards the heart, severing the large artery in that region, and perhaps penetrating the base of that organ. Morris was arrested immediately by Deputy Sheriff Renfro, who

MISCELLANEOUS ALABAMA NEWSPAPER ABSTRACTS --- VOL 1

happened to be on the ground.... Bail 2,500 & lodged in co. prison....

Talladega County Probate Court, June 24, 1859: the estate of Anthony Morgan, deceased, declared insolvent. Joseph N. Savery, adm'r of said estate.

ISSUE 3-21-1860

Died, at Arbacoochie, in Randolph Co., on the 12th ult., Mr. Andrew H. Charrow, aged about 40 years.

ISSUE 3-28-1860

Balloon Ascension: Mons. Wells made a most beautiful and successful balloon ascension, from the lot in the rear of Gen. Thomason's livery stables, on Saturday evening last....

Boarding can be obtained at the subscribers.... residence one mile from the court house, J.L. Davis; references: J.G.L. Huey, Joiner & Taylor

ISSUE 4-25-1860

Died, near this place, on the morning of the 22nd inst., Mrs. Agnes, wife of John A. Winbourn and daughter of Col. Andrew Cunningham.

ISSUE 6-6-1860

Married, on the evening of the 24th ult., at the residence of the bride's father, by the Rev. A.B. McCorkle, Mr. J. Augustus Storey, to Miss Margarett, daughter of Col. Andrew Cunningham, all of this county.

Ad for W. & J.A. Curry's new store, Talladega, Alabama
Ad for James Isbell, Banking & Exchange Office, Talladega, Alabama

ISSUE 6-20-1860

Died, in the vicinity of this place on the 15th inst., Elizabeth Turner, wife of William Turner, in 61st year of her age. Mrs. Turner was born and reared in Tenn. where she resided until 1833 when the family moved to this place... a member of the Presbyterian Church almost from its organization in this town.

MISCELLANEOUS ALABAMA NEWSPAPER ABSTRACTS --- VOL 1

ISSUE 6-27-1860

Married at the residence of the bride's father, on the 20th inst., by Rev. A.B. McCorkle, Jno. W. Bishop, to Miss Olivia Montgomery, all of this county.

Died, in this place on Wednesday, the 20th inst., Edward Hooper, infant son of Dr. John L. and Mrs. Mary Harris. Aged six weeks.

Ad for the Baptist Male High School, James Headen, Pres't
Ad for ambrotypes, Mrs. Mosher, formerly Miss Augusta Wilde. C.S. Mosher

ISSUE 7-4-1860

Died, at her residence, in Claibourn Parish, La., on the 18th ult., Mrs. Esther A. Givens, in the 72nd year of her age. Mrs. Givens, was the wife of our former citizen, Jas. A. Givens.

Died, Sunday the 1st inst., Elizabeth Scott, wife of Wm. B. Scott and daughter of the late Jas. Barclay of this town. Many friends and relatives in Talladega.

Died. Also on the night of the 2nd inst., Rev. R. Finley, principle of the Presbyterian Collegiate Female Institute, of this place.

ISSUE 7-18-1860

Married, on the 16th inst., at the residence of Mr. E.A. Cowan, by the Hon. W.H. Thornton, Mr. James Linton to Miss Harriet V. Frazer, all of this place.

$50 Reward, runaway from subscriber in Noxubee County, Mississippi, Feby last, a negro boy named Isaac.... Said boy is a bright mulatto, medium sized, about 20 years, raised by Mr. Jerry Collins of this county, and is supposed to be lurking in this place or St. Clair County. A. C. Bush, Prairie Point, Miss.

Ad for White Chapel Female Seminary, T.A. Cook, Principal
Ad for Miss C.H. Pitts, teacher

Notice: The notes and accounts due Henderson & Moore, are in my hands for settlement, and if not paid by the first of August will be sued on without discrimination. Also all debts due me individually, and all debts due Henderson & Fitzgerald.. R.M. Henderson, July 3, 1860

ISSUE 1-16-1861

Married, on the 1st inst., Mr. G. A. Woodward, of this place, to Miss Charlotte

Miscellaneous Alabama Newspaper Abstracts --- Vol 1

E. Dunham, of Edgefield District, S.C.

Married, on Sunday morning, the 6th inst., at the residence of Mr. Samuel Hunter, by Rev. Wm. Hall, Mr. John J. Weatherly to Mrs. Margarett Howell, all of this county.

Died, in this place, on Monday, the 14th inst., Mrs. Elizabeth Nolen, wife of J.M. Nolen, aged about 27 years. Mrs. Nolen was a consistent member of the Baptist Church.... She leaves a husband, two children....

ISSUE 1-30-1861

Married, in this city, on the 22nd inst., by Rev. Stuart Robinson, Charles Pelham, of Alabama, to Miss Lulie Johnston, daughter of Hon. G.W. Johnston. (*Louisvile Courier*)

Ad for J. M. Nolen, boots and shoes, Talladega

Talladega County Probate Court, January 28, 1861: Mrs. Nancy C. Rice, adm'strx of the estate of John W. Rice, deceased (of the state of Mississippi)

ISSUE 2-27-1861

Died, at Selma, on the 23rd inst., Henry Fullenwider, in the 57th year of his age. The remains of the deceased were brought up and interred at this place yesterday. Deceased was born in Lincoln County, N.C. in 1804.

ISSUE 3-13-1861

Runaway from the subscriber, in Talladega County, about the last of December, 1860, a negro boy named Squire, about 26 years old, a dark mulatto, will weigh about 145 lbs., chunky built, and is exceedingly smart and shrewd. When he left he had a sore finger, the first joint being off, the result of a felon.

Also a negro woman whose name is Jane, who has been gone 8 or 9 years. It is thought she is in Mobile; her proper name is Frances; she is passing as a free woman; having relations in said city who pass as free, named Bryant. She is 27 or 28 years old, mulatto, chunky, medium height, full breast; very smart, a sister of the boy above described. The free negroes are said to be protected by one Norton, an engineer of some boat. Address the undersigned, at Fayettville, Talladega County, Alabama. Neadham Bryant, March 13, 1860

MISCELLANEOUS ALABAMA NEWSPAPER ABSTRACTS --- VOL 1

The undersigned have opened a Blacksmith Shop, on Main Street, in the town of Talladega, at the stand known as the Old Cain Shop.... Boswell & Dye, Talladega, Dec. 26th, 1860

ISSUE 3-20-1861

Died, near this place on the 18th inst., Wm. Barclay in the 85th year of his age. Member of Convention that formed the Constitution of this state.

Letter testamentary upon the last will and testament of Thomas Hall deceased, late of Talladega County, Alabama, having been granted to the undersigned.... Joseph Hall, executor, March 4th, 1861

ISSUE 4-17-1861

Mrs. Mary Ann Harris, wife of Dr. John L. Harris, and daughter of ?. A. & Harriett Pease, died suddenly, on the morning of April 12th, 1861. The deceased was born December 3, 1830, in Marianna, Florida, and completed her education at the Weslyan Female College, in Macon, Georgia. Connected herself with the Methodist Episcopal Church.

ALABAMA REPORTER

Published at Talladega, Alabama,
by T. J. Cross and J. D. O'Connell; Editor, Daniel Sayre

ISSUE 5-22-1845

Married, in this place, on the evening of the 15th inst., by Hon. H.W.W. Rice, Mr. Ira P. Culbreath, of Randolph County, to Miss Esther Givens, of Talladega.

The creditors of the estate of Garland Oldham, will take notice, that said estate has been declared insolvent.... John W. Sobury, administrator.... Orphans' Court, Shelby County, Alabama, May 22, 1845. Orphans' Court, Shelby County: Robert Oldham, administrator of the estate of Carter Oldham, deceased.... estate declared insolvent.

Sheriff's sale: By virtue of an execution to me directed from the County Court of Morgan County, against John W. Bishop, and John H. Townsend, and in favor of the Branch Bank of the State of Alabama, at Decatur, I shall proceed to sell ...in the town of Talladega, the NW 1/4 of section 22, township 21, range 8, in the Coosa land district. Also the lot in the town of Talladega, on which the Female Academy is built; levied on as the property of said Bishop and Townsend to satisfy said execution.

Ad for P.D. Simmons, saddler, Talladega, Alabama

Shelby County Orphan's Court, May 14th, 1845: Vincent J. Gragg, one of the executors of the last will and testament of Henry Gragg, deceased, offered said will for probate.

Wanted, in exchange for Iron at the Moriah Forge, any quantity of corn and bacon, for which a fair price will be given. W.D. Riddle, Talladega.

Sheriff's Sale: by virtue of an execution against Augustus E. Wood in favor of Sylvanus Walker, Talladega County.

Sheriff's Sale: by virtue of an execution for public sale.... land, levied on as the property of Henry Criswell, to satisfy two executions; one in favor of A. Rosaman, the other in favor of Abner Howard, assignee.

Sheriff's Sale, Talladega County: by virtue of a venditioni exponas, expose to public sale.... the lot numbered 154, in the plot of the town of Talladega levied on as the property of William Keating, to satisfy an execution in favor of Barclay Stinnett & Co.

Sheriff's Sale, Talladega County: Execution against Nicholas Scales, James B. Watson et al, and in favor of the State Bank of Alabama.

ISSUE 8-12-1847

Ad for James W. Riley, boot and shoe maker
Ad for E. & T.E. Williamson, boot and shoe making. Talladega
Ad for Eli E. Cowsar. Talladega. Will do job of writing with neatness and Dispatch, such as Posting Books, Writing deeds to Lands, deeds of Gifts, Trust & Mortgage

Talladega County Circuit Court: T. & W. Cameron, use of Jacob Freeze vs Daniel Fuller: Attachment against the property of Daniel Fuller.... mentions William McGuire, executor of the last will and testament of Tryon Fuller.

Ad for A.J. Weathers, Wagon and Carriage maker, Talladega, Ala
Ad for P.D. Simmons, Saddle, bridle, and harness maker, Talladega, Ala

List of letters remaining in the Post Office at Talladega, June 30th, 1847:

MISCELLANEOUS ALABAMA NEWSPAPER ABSTRACTS --- VOL 1

Martha Byers, Asa Barcalin, Wm. C. Brown, Benjamin Bledsoe

Lewis Carley, H. Chapin, Nathaniel Cox, Miss Elizabeth Cotton

Wm. Dixon, B.H. Dulany, John Dickey

Charles F. Elliott

Jesse or Elijah Foreman

James Harris, P.S. Harris, Miss Mary W. Hoyle

Archibald Jennings

John Lightsey, Miss A. C. Long

Robt. Miller, Mrs. Rosa Mayhew, Mrs. Mary Moore, Wm. Machurn, Daniel Mayness, J.P. Moore

Richard Neeley

Mrs. Frances Phillips

Geo. Richey, Watson Robbs, Jas. M. Roberts, Jacob Routh

Mrs. Mary Sims, Jackson D. Stewart

Dr. Henry L. Theus, Jesse Tanner

Samuel Wats, Samuel Watkins, A.C. Wood, Wm. H. Wyatt
Wm. R. Waldron, P.M., July 1st, 1847

Talladega, Fortieth Chancery District, Monday, August 2, 1847: Hudson Allen, complainant vs Elijah C. Walker, and David Conner, defendants.... the the defendant Conner, is a nonresident of the State of Alabama, and a resident of the State of Texas....

Northern Chancery Division, Talladega, Fortieth Chancery District: William McPherson vs David A. Griffin, H.M. Cunningham, A.H. Rippetoe and others...that Archer M. Maham, one of the defendants in this suit, is a non-resident of the State of Alabama, and resides in the state of Mississippi....

Northern Chancery Division, Talladega, Fortieth Chancery District: July Term, 1847, William Easley, Guardian of James T. Barnes vs Lawrence Bass,

Miscellaneous Alabama Newspaper Abstracts --- Vol 1

William Davis, and Henry Davis.... that the defendants are nonresidents of this state and residents of the State of Texas....

Ad for J. Donley's store, A.M. Breedon. Tennessee Hams, shoulders, & Sides

Talladega County Orphan's Court, August 10, 1847: Thomas L. Best, as administrator of the estate of Thomas Goodwin, deceased, late of said county, has filed his accounts and vouchers for a final settlement.

ISSUE 10-11-1848

Died, at his residence, in this county, on Sunday morning, the 7th inst., Mr. George W. Kennedy, tax collector for this county.

ISSUE 7-20-1852

Married, on the 12th inst., by the Rev. H.E. Taliaferro, the Rev. L. Law, of Tuscaloosa County, to Miss Martha A. Bell, of Talladega County.

(Married) On the 13th inst., by the same, Mr. Franklin Acker, to Miss Susan, daughter of the Rev. Wm. McCain, all of this county.

(Married) On the 15th inst., in this place, by J.D. Copeland, Mr. Jesse V. Smith to Miss Eliza F. Bently.

Announcement of Presbyterian Collegiate Female Institute: On Wednesday night the anniversary address will be delivered by Jabez L.M. Curry. Thursday night, concert, J. Hoyt.

ISSUE 7-?-1852

Walter Dulaney Riddle is dead. He departed this life at Maria Forge, Talladega County, on the 16th June, in the 39th year of his age. He was the son of Samuel and Marion Riddle, and was born in Bedford, Pa.____. In 1842 he moved to Alabama, and settle in this county. Since that time he has been employed in large contracts on the Montgomery and West Point Railroad...When Samuel S. Riddle was on his death bed in August last, he committed his beloved wife, soon to be a widow, and his children, soon to be fatherless, to his brother Walter.... of eleven children, only one brother and one sister survive. One fell by the hand of Santa Anna, in Fanning's massacre; one died when he had just entered with brilliant prospects on the legal profession; and three in the meridian of life have been laid beside their godly mother, at Maria Forge.... Widow and orphan....

Miscellaneous Alabama Newspaper Abstracts --- Vol 1

Died, on Sunday 26th ult., Laura Talmadge, daughter of Dr. Henry McKenzie, of this place, aged 10 years....

ISSUE 3-22-1860

Married, on the 7th ult., by the Rev. Mr. ___, Mr. Samuel T. Poole, to Miss Frances M. Skinner, all of Randolph County.

Died, at the family residence on Saturday night, the 10th inst., Mrs. Jane P. Fant, wife of Mr. Joseph C. Fant, of this place. Mrs. Fant had been a resident of Talladega for about 23 years.... Mrs. Fant was a member of the Baptist Church.... a native of Fairfield District, South Carolina and was about 40 years of age.

Died, at her mother's residence in this county, on Tuesday the 13th inst., Miss Adelaide, daughter of A.H. and James G. Hancock, in the 28th year of her age.

At Arbacoochee in Randolph County, on the 12th ult., Mr. Andrew H. Oharrow, aged about 40 years. The deceased was a member of the Methodist Church....

My friends and customers and the public generally, are hereby informed that having purchased the house known as the "Old Drug Store," I have moved my stock, and will hereforth carry on the mercantile business there, in all its various branches. J. Freudenberger

ISSUE 3-29-1860

Committed to the jail of Talladega County, Ala., a negro man, who says his name is Felix, and belongs to Jas. H. Vaughn, of Dallas County, Ala. Felix is dark complected, 5' 8" high, and weighs 170 lbs.... J.F. Puckett, Jailor

Accidentally killed at Selma: Dr. Dickinson, of Radfordsville in Dallas County, was killed at Selma on Thursday evening of last week. It seems that a difficulty between Mr. Joseph R. Curtis and a Mr. Goldsby was on hand and the former fired a pistol at the latter the shot passing through the hand of Mr. Goldsby and striking Dr. Dickinson in the temple inflicting a wound from which he died in about 36 hours. The doctor was not a party to the difficulty but stepped up.

Died, at his residence in this county on Tuesday the 20th inst., Mr. Thomas W. Turner, aged about 40 years.

MISCELLANEOUS ALABAMA NEWSPAPER ABSTRACTS --- VOL 1

Also, (died) at her residence in Madison County, Ala., on the 17th inst., of pneuralgia of the brain, Frances J. Van, in the 19th year of her age, consort of L.H. Van. Mrs. Van formerly resided in this place.

Ad for J.E. & C.M. Shelley, Talladega, Feb. 21, 1860. Brickwork, plastering

ISSUE 4-12-1860

Committed to the jail of Talladega County, Ala., a negro boy who says his name is Philip and belongs to Patrick McKinney who lives near Sockopatoy, in Coosa County, Ala., said boy is black, 18 or 19 years old, 5' 6 or 7 inches high, weighs about 140 lbs, has two scars on his right leg, one from a cut, the other from a burn.

Ad for lumber, J.S. Lane
Ad for clothing, hats.... J. & J.B. Huey

ISSUE 4-26-1860

Married, in Lowndes County, on the 19th inst., by Rev. J.A. Heard, Mr. S.A. Darby, of Montgomery to Miss Barbary C. Besseant, of the former place.

Died, in this place, on Sunday morning the 22nd inst., Mrs. Agnes Winbourn, wife of J.A. Winbourn, and daughter of Mr. Andrew Cunningham, of this county.

Ad for penmanship and card marking, D.F. Walker

ISSUE 5-3-1860

Married, on the 24th ult., in Sparta, Georgia, by Bishop Pearce, Rev. J.S. Lane, pastor of the Methodist E. Church, in this place, to Miss Sephronia J. Audis, of the former place.

Also, (married) on the 26th ult., at the residence of the brides father, by Rev. S.E. Swope, Merrit Street, of this county, to Miss Martha Dunn, of Tallapoosa County, Ala.

(Married) At Selma, on the 30th inst., by the Rev. Dr. Dorman, Mr. J.W. Blandin to Miss Belle John, eldest daughter of Joseph R. John, all of that city.

Died, in Talladega, April 22, in the 21st year of her age, Mrs. Elizabeth Ann Agnes Winbourn, wife of John A. Winbourn, and daughter of Andrew and Jane Cunningham.

MISCELLANEOUS ALABAMA NEWSPAPER ABSTRACTS --- VOL 1

ISSUE 5-24-1860

Died, at the residence of her husband in this county, Mary A. Butler, wife of George Buttler, aged 28 years, of Rheumatism of the heart. She was a member of the Presbyterian Church.

(Died) On Monday the 21st inst., at Cave Spring, Georgia, Lillian, daughter of Dr. Joseph H. and Mrs. Emily Johnson, of this place, aged about 2 years.

Ad for M.M. Slaughter, wholesale and retail grocer, Talladega

Talladega County Probate Court: Sarah A. Turner, Adm'x, Frances A. Turner, Adm'r of the estate of Thomas W. Turner, deceased.

$50 Reward, ranaway from the plantation of the undersigned 8 miles west of Marion in Perry County, 2 negro men Isaac and William, William was arrested at the Coosa Bridge on the Ala. & Tenn. R.R. and says they were bound for North Carolina, travelling at night and laying by in the day time. Isaac is a well built fellow about 25 years old and weight about 175 lbs. This boy ran away before and was put in jail at Augusta, Ga. W.B.de Yampert

ISSUE 5-31-1860

Died, at his residence in this county, on Sunday the 27th inst., Mr. William Fain.

ISSUE 6-7-1860

Married, at the residence of the brides father on Thursday the 24th inst., by the Rev. A.B. McCorkle, Mr. J. A. Storey, of this place, to Miss Margaret Cunningham, daughter of Mr. Andrew Cunningham of this place.

Ranaway from my plantation 6 miles below Gadsden, on Coosa river, a gray horse mule.... address me at Cave Creek P.O., Calhoun Co., Ala., J. W. Whisenant.

Ad for W. G. Venable, decorative and house painter, Talladega, Ala

ISSUE 6-21-1860

We regret to learn of the death of William E. Burnett, of Glennville, Ala., which occurred of consumption, at the residence of his father in Russell County, on the 13th inst. Mr. Barnett was a member of the bar of Barbour County.... Mr. Barnett whose death is noticed in the foregoing paragraph, was the gentleman who married Miss Julia Spyker, formerly of this place.

THE CELEBRATION: The joint committees of the "Talladega Artillery," and citizens would respectfully solicit the aid and cooperation of the citizens of the town and vicinity, in furnishing a basket dinner on the occasion of the 84th anniversary of American Independence.... The following gentlemen are respectfully solicited to act as committee on part of citizens: M.H. Cruikshank, mayor; Maj. J.G.L. Huey, J.N. Savery, J.H. Joiner, A. Bingham, L.G. Dye, Jas. E. Shelley, Josiah Terry, Thomas W. Curry, Micah. Taul, C.P. Samuel, X. Willman, John Donohoo, W.G. Rhodes, Geo. L. Ragland, R.M. Henderson, James C. Burt, W.A. Welch, L.W. Lawler, Col. Wm. Mallory, Gen. W.B. McClellen, P.D. Simmons, G.P. Plowman, J.L. Elston, Tipton Bradford, Sam'l Jemison, E.C. Turner, N.D. Johnson, W.A. Morris, Houston Isbell, Robert Douglass, J.M. Skaggs, A.W. Bowie, Geo. S. Walden, W.J. Cunningham, M.L. Wilson, T.H. Reynolds, H.P. Oden, Maj. J.G. Swain, J.H. Johnson, Chairman

Died, at the family residence near this place, on Friday the 14th inst., Mrs. Elizabeth Turner, wife of Mr. William Turner. Mrs. Turner was one of our oldest citizens, having removed with her husband from the State of Tennessee, and settled in this neighborhood, some twenty seven years ago. She was a member of the Presbyterian Church, established at Talladega, almost from the date of its organization...

ISSUE 6-28-1860

Married, at the residence of the brides father, on Wednesday the 20th inst., by the Rev. A. B. McCorkle, John W. Bishop, of this place, to Miss M. Olivia, daughter of Mr. James Montgomery, of this county.

Talladega County Probate Court, June 27, 1860: Bolivar Eason, administrator de bonis non of the estate of Mrs. Margaret Millican, deceased, filed for final settlement of estate.

Died, in this place, on Wednesday the 20th inst., Edward Hooper, infant son of Dr. John L. and Mary Harris.

ISSUE 7-26-1860

Married, at the residence of the brides father on Wednesday the 18th inst., by the Rev. A.B. McCorkle, Mr. Wm. B. Palmer, to Miss Mary Cunningham, daughter of Mr. Wm. J. Cunningham, all of this place.

Died, of consumption, on the 21st inst., in the 33rd year of her age, Evelina

MISCELLANEOUS ALABAMA NEWSPAPER ABSTRACTS --- VOL 1

Roena Turner, wife of Joseph Turner, and daughter of James Montgomery. She was from early years a member of the Presbyterian Church of Marble Spring.

ISSUE 8-2-1860

Married, by the Rev. Robert Nall, D.D. at his residence, in this place, on Wednesday the 25th inst., Mr. A. Spencer, to Miss Jane H. Nall, daughter of the officiating clergyman.

(Married) On Tuesday the 24th inst., at the residence of the brides father, by the Rev. T.A. Cook, Mr. Warren F. Lyman to Miss Virginia Stone, daughter of Mr. Isaac Stone, all, of this county.

(Married) At the residence of the brides father, on Tuesday evening, the 24th ult., by the Rev. O. Welch, Dr. S.M. McAlpin to Mrs. H.G. Wallis, daughter of Col. Wm. Mallory, all of this county.

Died, on Sunday morning, the 29th of July, Jackson Thomas, son of J.L.M. and Ann A. Curry, aged 9 months.

William Curry, son of Thomas and Eliza Caver, of Calhoun Co., Ala., was drowned on the 26th inst., in Choccolocco Creek, near Boiling Springs.... Little William was in his 10th year.

ISSUE 8-9-1860

Married, on Sunday night last, at the Methodist Episcopal Church, by the Rev. James S. Lane, Dr. C. H. Simmons to Miss Anna Martha, daughter of Mrs. Frances Simmons.

Also, (married) at the residence of Mrs. Beavers, on the 2nd inst., by Rev. J.J.D. Renfroe, Mr. Henry Fitzgerald to Miss Martha Castleberry, all of this county.

Also, (married) on the 24th ult., by Joseph S. Hubbard, Mr. James M. Hare to Mrs. Rebecca J. Trammel, all of this county.

ISSUE 8-16-1860

Committed to the jail of Talladega County, Ala., a negro man, as a runaway slave, dark complexion, about 33 years of age, 5' 10" high, weighs 165 lbs, 2 scars on his breast, who says he belongs to Dr. M. Moore, of Wetumpka, Alabama.

Miscellaneous Alabama Newspaper Abstracts --- Vol 1

Committed to the Jail of Talladega County, Ala., on the 12th inst., a negro runaway slave, dark complexion, about 30 years of age, 5' 11" high, weighs 175 lbs, a scar on his right side, made by a blister, some scars on his back, who says he belongs to Wm. P. Brown, of Montevallo, Alabama.

ISSUE 8-23-1860

Died, on the 14th inst., in Marshall County, Ala., of consumption, Mrs. Jane G. McGa?a, eldest daughter of W.R. and C.G. Stone.

ISSUE 8-30-1860

Committed to the jail of Talladega County, Ala., on the 27th inst., by James Lawson, J.P., a negro man, Solomon, 18 years of age, 5'5" high, weighs 150 lbs, dark complexion, heavy, bushy head, and says he belongs to Jesse Delony, of Columbus, Georgia.

Committed to the Jail of Talladega County, Ala., on the 25th inst., by James Lawson, J.P., a negro man, John, about 35 years old, 5'10" high, weighs 155 lbs., dark complexion, 3 scars on the left hip, caused by a dog bite. He says he belongs to Joseph S. Powell, of Russell County, Alabama.

ISSUE 9-13-1860

Married, at the residence of the brides father, on the 6th inst., by the Rev. J. D. Renfroe, Mr. James W. Riley, of this place, to Miss M. D. Bailey, daughter of Mr. Wyatt Bailey, of this vicinity.

Married, on the 2nd inst., at the house of James Foster, by B. F. Holly, Aaron Sizemore and Mary Elizabeth Foster.

(Married) By the same, at the same time and place, James Foster and Jemima Sizemore, all of Blackankle.

Lucius M. Finley, son of John and Lucretia Finley, was born, in Talladega County, Ala., June the 12th, 1849, moved with his parents, near Marshall, Harrison County, Texas, in the fall of '59, was called by death, away from those he loved.... brothers and sisters.

ISSUE 9-20-1860

Married, at the residence of Mr. James A. Turner, on the 4th inst., by Thomas J. Brewer, Mr. Joab B. Lawler, to Miss Rebecca Hudson, all of this county.

MISCELLANEOUS ALABAMA NEWSPAPER ABSTRACTS --- VOL 1

Died, on the 6th inst., at 5 o'clock P.M., Joel Smart Cunningham, infant son of Wm. N. and Mary E. Cunningham, aged 1 year, 1 month, and 1 week.

Committed to the jail of Talladega County, Ala., on the 11th of Sept. 1860, a negro man who says his name is William Wesley Webb, and that he belongs to Daniel Visher, of Chambers County, Alabama. Said negro is of a yellow complexion, 6' high, weighs 165 lbs.

ISSUE 9-27-1860

Married, on the 18th inst., at the residence of the brides father, by the Rev. O. Welch, Mr. John T. Caldwell to Miss Susan A. Cliatt, all of this county.

Married, at the residence of the brides father, in St. Clair County, on the ___ inst., Mr. R. M. Henderson of this place, to Miss Castleberry, daughter of Mr. Howard Castleberry, of St. Clair Co.

Died, at his father's residence on the 21st inst., of fever, Mr. John H. Lawler, in the 34th year of his age. The deceased had just arrived here from Bienville Parish, La., on a visit to his relations.

Died, in this place, on the 22nd inst., Willie Anna, youngest daughter of J. W. & M. R. Martin, aged 3 years, 8 months and 14 days.

ISSUE 10-4-1860

Deaths and murders at Tuskegee, Tuskegee, Ala., Sept. 1860: Our town today is shrouded in gloom and mourning; three of our citizens, young and healthy men have passed to the spirit land since yesterday morning; two of them dying from disease, the third brutally murdered by a negro Lucius Bryan, brother of our representative Charlie Bryan from this county, died today, Dr. Isbell on Yesterday, will be buried this evening. Two noble young men, just starting in the career of life, with the brightest of prospects before them, suddenly cut off from existence. The other, Mr. James Davis, overseer on the plantation of N. W. Cocke, near Tuskegee, was murdered yesterday by one of Cocke's negroes. The negro had stolen a hog, a few days before, and Davis had proved it upon him so clearly that he felt justified in correcting him for it. Davis went into the field for this purpose. The negro, anticipating such a termination of the difficulty had, with his wife, gone some hundred or more yards from the other negroes, all of whom were picking cotton. Davis went to the boy and took hold of him, when the boy with a heavy knife, severed the jugular artery in Davis' neck at the first thrust of his knife, and did not stop until he had inflicted some dozen wounds on Davis. The humeral artery of the arm, and femoral of the thigh, with the carotid or jugular, were all separated. Davis was a corpse in five minutes. A number of our citizens with dogs are hunting for him, and his speedy arrest is most sanguinely expected and hoped for, from present indications if he is arrested a judge and jury will never be troubled with his trial. Mr. Davis was a noble and humane man, highly respected by all who knew him. He leaves a young wife and two children to weep for him. (*Columbus Enquirer*)

ISSUE 10-25-1860

Married, at the residence of the bride's father on the 18th inst., by the Rev. James S. Lane, Mr. Ranson Williams to Miss Susan A. Martin, daughter of Mr. John W. Martin, all of this place.

(Married) On the 2nd inst., in Carrolton, Ga., by the Rev. C. A. McDaniel, Dr. B. S. Smoot of this county, to Miss Anna Bonner, of the former place.

(Married) In Montgomery County, Ala., on the 11th inst., by R. Olin, Mr. J. B. Gay, of this place, to Miss Fannie J. Wright, of the former place.

A CARD: The undersigned adopts this method of expressing his heartfelt thanks to the citizens of Talladega, for their kind and noble efforts to preserve his dwelling from destruction by fire during his absence. Respectfully, N. D. Johnson, Talladega, Oct. 21, 1860.

ISSUE 11-1-1860

Married, on the 22nd ult., by John T. Ragan, Mr. Ignatius Russell, to Miss Amanda M. Cargile, all of this county.

(Married) On the 11th ult., by John T. Ragan, Gabriel C. Ingram to Miss Sarah Ogle, all of this county.

(Married) On the 18th ult., by the same, Mr. Madison B. Green to Miss Sarah F. Dixon, all of this county.

ISSUE 11-8-1860

Died, on the 27th Oct., near Lebanon, DeKalb County, Ala., of neuralgia of the heart, Rev. Peter J. Walker, in the 58th year of his age.

Died, in this place on Thursday, the 25th inst., Mrs. Lavinia McCann, wife of Mr. Jas. McCann, aged about 50 years....

Miscellaneous Alabama Newspaper Abstracts --- Vol 1

ISSUE 6-5-1862

The following is a list of killed and wounded of the Bibb Greys, 11th Ala. Regiment on May 31st: Killed: Sergeant M.J. Carson, J.M. Davis; Mortally Wounded: Barney Kournega; Wounded Badly but not mortally: J.D. Maberry, Henry Davis, G.F. Woodruff, J. Moses, W. Smitherman, D.A. Griffin, John Henry. Slightly Wounded: M. Hogan, Wm. Greene, H. James, J.N. Suttle, J. Spinks, W.H. Brown, Louis Taylor, J.N. Suttle

From the Cahaba Rifles; the killed and wounded: The Fifth Alabama Severely Cut Up: Richmond, June 1st To the citizens of Cahaba: The Cahaba Rifles were under a galling fire all day yesterday. Killed: W.O. Bradley, W.A. Moore, W.A. Wilcox, W.C. Thrash, Joe Curtis, John Gardner Wounded Severely: Thos. Mays, John Bradford; Slightly Wounded: H.H. Hatcher, H. Booth, Jas. Matheson, John Babcock, Dr. Thos. Hunter, Robt. Kenan, Sneider, R.D. Gayle, E.B. Mosely, Capt.

Married, on the 28th ult., at the residence of the bride's father, by the Rev. J. Mays, Mr. A.T. Rhodes to Miss Sallie C. Pitts, all of this place.

Died, at the Alabama Institute for the deaf and dumb, in this place, Monday the 3rd inst., Miss Minerva Yateman of this county. The deceased was an estimable young lady and had been for several years a pupil of the Institute. This is the first death which has occurred among the mutes since the establishment of the Institution.

ISSUE 1-7-1864

Cropwell Lodge # 218, St Clair Co., Ala. Dec. 27th 1863. Whereas it becomes the painful duty of the members of this lodge to record the death of our brother Absolam S. Hull, who volunteered in Capt. N.D. Johnson's Co., 51st Regt. of Ala. cavalry about the 1st of August last; and having fought many battles, fell at Kingston on the 24th of November while bravely defending the flag of his country. Eminently worthy and exemplary Mason.

Ranaway from the subscriber about the 1st of Dec last, a negro boy named Ely, sometimes called Pondy. The said boy Ely, is about 12 or 13 years old, dark color, has a very broad mouth, is quick spoken and smart. Abner Wynn

ISSUE 1-28-1864

Broke jail on the 10th inst., a white man and a negro, J. B. Jordan, a deserter from the 10th Confederate Regiment and confined in jail charged with horse stealing. Jordan is fair complected, blue eyes, weighs about 170 or 180 lbs., dark hair, about 6' high, 25 or 30 years old. Webster, a mulatto boy, raised in this town, known as Webster Blythe confined for stealing and breaking open houses; he is very bright mulatto, nearly white, about 22 years old, 5' 10 or 12 inches high, weighs about 160 lbs.

ISSUE 2-4-1864

The subject of this notice, sister Nancy A. Moxley, consort of brother J. A. Moxley, was born Dec. 20, 1835; was married to her now bereft husband July 9, 1851, and died Jan. 10, 1864. Sister Moxley was a member of the C. P. Church....

ISSUE 2-11-1864

Died, Feb. 2nd, Emma J., infant daughter of Jno. B. and Ellen E. Huey, aged 3 weeks.

ISSUE 2-25-1864

Committed to the jail in Shelby County a negro boy who says his name is Stephen, and that he belongs to the estate of John Watson, of Mississippi, and that he was under the control of John Morgan, executor of said estate. Said boy is about 21 years old, 5' 4 or 5 inches high, yellow complexion with a large scar over his right eye caused by a kick from a mule. Said boy was stolen from Columbus, Mississippi, by Franklin Law....

ISSUE 3-3-1864

Died, at his residence 8 miles east of this place, on Monday the 29th ult., Mr. Thomas L. Owen, for many years a citizen of this town and county.

ISSUE 5-26-1864

Ranaway from our Iron Works, about the 5th day of last March, a negro boy named Fed, aged 24 years. Color black, stutters badly. He belongs to Mr. Charles Sherrod of Columbus, Mississippi.

ISSUE 6-2-1864

We are sad to learn of the death of Lieut. J. F. Turner, by a letter received a few days since, from Capt. Thomas Haley, of the 12th Texas Cavalry, to Mr. Joel Higgins of Texas. The letter was forwarded by Mr. Higgins to Mr. William Turner, near this place, the father of Lieut. Turner. Lieut. Turner was raised near this place, he with his brother-in-law Joel Higgins removed to

Texas, some five or six years since.... He died near Vienna, La., on the 5th of Sept. 1863, of congestive fever.

Ranaway from the subscriber at or near Alpine, on the 28th day of May, a negro boy named Levi, sometimes called Pondy, aged 13 years, dark copper color, with a very large mouth. He is a very smart boy. When last heard from he was near Talladega claiming to belong to a wagon train. His intention is to go to Rome, Ga. Abner Wynn, Alpin, Ala., Jun 1, 1864

Committed to the jail of Shelby County, on the 25th of May, a negro man, who says his name is John and that he belongs to James Trewitt of the State of Tennessee and that he was hired to Capt. Jones of Selma. Said boy is of dark complexion, about 3' 4 or 5 inches high; says he is 28 years old, has a bad stoppage in his speech, weighs about 150 lbs.

Committed to the jail of Talladega County, Ala., on the 27th day of May, 1864, by H.H. Hamill, a runaway negro man named William, who says that he belongs to Mr. Frank McIlhenny, of Auburn, Macon County, Ala., aged 22 years, 6' high, complexion black, and weighs about 170 lbs.

ISSUE 6-30-1864

(Died) Mrs. Mary C. Franklin, wife of Dr. Willis Franklin breathed her last at her residence in this county on the 8th of June in the 67th year of her age.

Died, in this place on Wednesday morning last, Capt. Jas. E. Peebles, Post Quartermaster of the Tax in kind for this district. He leaves a wife and five children to mourn his loss. His remains will be carried to Jacksonville for interment.

Died, near this place, on the 24th inst., Dr. Robt. H. Scales.

Ranaway from the Choccolocco Iron Works on the 26th of June, a negro man named Albert, aged about 45 years, 5' 3" high, black complexion, hump shouldered, slow spoken, weighs about 125 lbs. Also Isaac, aged about 28 years, 5' 6" high, black, weighs about 180 lbs. Has one finger bent backwards (think it is forefinger on right hand). These negroes belong to D. C. Topp, Duck Hill, Miss., and will probably make their way for home. June 30, 1864, J. B. Knight & Co.

ISSUE 8-18-1864

Died, on Thursday the 15th inst., of chronic diarrhea, at the residence of Uriah Dulaney, Lt. J. E. Spence, of Co. A., 29th Ala. Regt....

Miscellaneous Alabama Newspaper Abstracts --- Vol 1

Married, on Sunday night, the 14th inst., at the residence of Dr. Culverson, of this place, by the Rev. R. B. Crawford, Lt. John L. Bartow, of St. Louis, Mo., to Miss Etta E. Jones, formerly of Cave Spring, Ga.

Committed to the jail of Talladega Co., August 3rd, by H. H. Hamill, a runaway slave named William, who says he belongs to James McCowan of Itawambia County, Mississippi. Said boy is about 6' high, weighs about 160 lbs.,

Committed to the jail of Talladega Co., Ala., a negro woman named Christian, who says she belongs to Willis Roberts of Wetumpka. She is 23 years old, copper color....

Committed to the jail of Talladega Co., Ala., on the 5th inst., by H. H. Hamill, a runaway negro named Bruce who says that he belongs to Lieut. James Tunstall of Green County, Ala. Said boy is a mulatto, about 20 years old, 5' 8" high, weighs about 130 lbs.

ISSUE 9-15-1864

Married, on the 6th inst., by R. Allen, at the residence of Lieut. W. E. Sawyer, Mr. Sim Florence to Miss Fannie E. Curry, all of this place.

Married, on the 4th inst., at the residence of the bride's father, by W. M. Hearn, Mr. David Garigus to Miss Licena Tyler. All of this county.

Died, in this place, on the 14th inst., Louisiana, infant daughter of Taul and Mary I. Bradford. Aged 1 year and a few months.

ISSUE 10-27-1864

Committed to the Jail of Talladega Co., Ala. a runaway slave named John, who says that he belongs to R. C. Goodgame, who resides 7 miles from Rockford, Coosa County, Ala. John is about 5' 9" high, copper color, about 26 years old.... Said boy says he was hired to one John Logan, 4 miles above Hatchett Creek.

ISSUE 4-19-1866

Died, at his residence, about 4 miles from this place, on Tuesday, the 17th inst., of Small Pox, Mr. L. B. W. Howell.

Also, (died) at the residence of E. R. Wood, on the 12th inst., Albert, infant son of E. R. and S. E. Wood, of this place.

Miscellaneous Alabama Newspaper Abstracts --- Vol 1

ISSUE 5-24-1866

Married, on the 22nd of May, by the Rev. O. Welch, Mr. N. Woodruff to Miss S. Keith. All of this county.

(Married) On the 25th ult., at the residence of the brides father, in Gadsden, Ala., Mr. Junlus Hart to Miss Mattie Edwards, daughter of Dr. Thos. Edwards. All of Gadsden.

ISSUE 5-31-1866

Married, at the residence of the bride's father, Talladega County, Ala., May 29th, 1866, by Rev. O. Welch, Mr. A. F. Hardie, to Miss Lizzie D. Mallory, daughter of Col. James Mallory.

ISSUE 7-19-1866

Married, July 12th, 1866, by the Rev. J. J. D. Renfro, at the residence of Maj. Jas. Headen, Mr. W. G. Leonard to Miss Annie E. Pound. All of this county.

Died, near Guntersville, Ala., on the 9th of July, Dr. W. B. Harrison, of this place. Though the Dr. had resided here but a short time, he had won the confidence and esteem of the entire community, and his death is felt to be a public calamity. Dr. H. was a member of the Episcopal Church.... He has left a widow and three children.... Huntsville papers please copy

ISSUE 8-2-1866

Married, in Selma, at the residence of the bride's father, on the evening of the 30th, by the Rev. W. J. Lowry, Mr. John G. Bell to Miss Emma Edwards. All of that city.

Died, at Columbiana, Ala., on the 20th of July, Miss Allie Sterritt, of Shelby County, aged about 20 years. Daughter of Judge Sterritt.

ISSUE 8-16-1866

Sudden death of Maj. Gen. M. L. Smith: This gentleman, who was at the close of the war, chief engineer of General Lee's army, and recently appointed engineer of the railroad from Selma to Dalton, died at the Tennessee House, in this city on Sunday morning....

MISCELLANEOUS ALABAMA NEWSPAPER ABSTRACTS --- VOL 1

ISSUE 9-13-1866

Died, at residence of her father, the morning of the 4th inst., Mary Alice, only daughter of J.J. and Margaret Weatherly, aged 3 years, 11 months, 21 days.

ISSUE 7-8-1868

Married, on Thursday evening the 2nd inst., at the residence of the bride's mother in this county, by the Rev. A. B. McCorkle, Cyrus R. Smith, of Cameron, Texas, to Miss Mary Cornelia Orr.

(Married) On the 5th July 1868, at the residence of Mr. Sanford Smith the brides's father, by Rev. J. J. D. Renfroe, Mr. N. W. Phillips of Dallas County, to Miss Fannie D. Smith, of this county.

Married, July 7th, 1868, at the residence of Mrs. Tanner, the bride's mother, by Rev. J.J.D. Renfroe, Mr. Joseph L. Bently to Miss Falba L. Tanner of this place.

ISSUE 7-29-1868

Died, at the residence of Mr. Jarred Thompson, on Thursday last, Johnny Simpson, aged __ years. He came to this place from Montgomery last week seeking a home. Mr. Thompson took him home... soon after he was taken sick with congestion of the stomach and lived only a few days. He said he came from New York to Montgomery where he has relatives. Information about him can be obtained by addressing Mr. Thompson at this place.

Died, at the residence of Mrs. Albert Jones, near Marion, on the evening of the 22nd inst., W. W. Brickell, of Huntsville, Ala. At the King House, Marion, Ala., on the 23rd inst., Mr. Timothy Byrne, of Ireland, aged about 50 years. (*Marion Commonwealth*)

ISSUE 8-12-1868

We regret to learn that Miss Sue Groce, daughter of Judge J. E. Groce, died, on the road from Chandler's Springs to her father's residence, on Monday last. She had been in feeble health for some time; her father carried her to Chandler's Springs some two months since, thinking it would benefit her....

ISSUE 8-19-1868

Died, on Tuesday, August 11th, 1868, infant daughter of J. M. and Lucy M. Nolen.

MISCELLANEOUS ALABAMA NEWSPAPER ABSTRACTS --- VOL 1

ISSUE 9-9-1868

Died, on Tuesday the 1st inst., Mrs. Eva Curry, daughter of the late Hugh G. Barclay, and wife of the Rev. J. T. Curry of this vicinity. The deceased was born and raised in Talladega and leaves a large circle of friends to mourn her death.

ISSUE 9-16-1868

Married, at the brides residence in Calhoun County, on the 8th inst., by Rev. W. R. Kirk, Thos. T. McAdams, of this place, to Miss E. C. Allen, of Calhoun.

ISSUE 9-23-1868

Died, in this place on Friday morning, the 18th inst., Paul F., infant son of J. F. and Mrs. Ida Shanklin. Aged 1 year and 2 months. *Russellville* (Ky) *Herald* and *Jackson* (Miss.) *Clarion* please copy.

ISSUE 9-30-1868

Died, in this place, on Friday night, the 25th inst., Mattie A., only daughter of R. A. Jr., and Mrs. ???sie W. Moseley, aged 4 years, 9 months and 19 days.

ISSUE 10-7-1868

On the second day of August 1868, after a short illness, fell sweetly asleep in Jesus our beloved neighbor and sister Elizabeth F. Albright, consort of S. A. Albright, born in the State of Tennessee, Bedford County, March 18, 1832. She leaves a kind and devoted husband, and five sweet and interesting children.... Sisters residing in Texas, Tennessee, and Alabama.... The subject of this notice embraced religion and joined the Methodist E. Church South when about 14 years of age. D.M. Stovall

ISSUE 10-21-1868

Mr. Frank McAnana, a conductor on the Mobile and Ohio Railroad, was this morning about 9 o'clock, run over by a switch engine while walking on the track near the depot and instantly killed, his body being cut completely in two.

Married, on Tuesday morning the 20th inst., at the residence of the bride's father, by the Rev. F. T. Brandon, Dr. J. T. Harrison, of Marshall County, to Miss S. S. Groce, daughter of Hon. Jared E. Groce.

MISCELLANEOUS ALABAMA NEWSPAPER ABSTRACTS --- VOL 1

ISSUE 10-28-1868

Died, on the 19th inst., at the family residence in this county, Annie E. Stockdale, youngest daughter of Mrs. Sarah L. Stockdale in the 11th year of her age.

ISSUE 11-11-1868

Married, near Talladega at the residence of the brides father, Tuesday morning, the 28th inst., by the Rev. T. A. Cook, Mr. Dallas B. Smith, of Opelika, to Miss Josephine Bingham.

ISSUE 12-2-1868

Batesville, Ark., Nov. 27th: Capt. Edward W. Thompson, acting District Attorney, was shot and mortally wounded for politics. He was a son of A. B. Thompson, of Brunswick.

Married, at the residence of the brides father in this place, by the Rev. J. D. D. Renfroe, Mr. R. P. Henderson, of Tennessee, to Miss Nannie A. McNalley.

Also, (married) at the residence of the brides father on Wednesday the 25th ult., by the Rev. Mr. Odom, Mr. Henry Mauldin to Miss Evelina Fain, daughter of Mr. Jessie Fain of this county.

Mr. James Dye, Senior died at his residence in this county, on Thursday last the 26th ult., aged 84 years. He was an old line Whig and proud of his consistency refused to be called by any other party name to the day of his death.

ISSUE 12-9-1868

A man by the name of Gideon Muncos of Wickers precinct, Clay County, was shot and killed about the middle of last week.

ISSUE 12-16-1868

Died, on the 9th inst., of consumption, Miss Ann Eliza Jackson, daughter of Daniel and Julia Jackson, in the 22nd year of her age.

ISSUE 12-23-1868

Married, at the residence of Mr. J. L. Stone, the bride's father, on the 16th inst., by the Rev. J. J. D. Renfroe, Mr. M. P. McClusky to Miss Mary B. Stone.

MISCELLANEOUS ALABAMA NEWSPAPER ABSTRACTS --- VOL 1

ISSUE 1-6-1869

Married, at the residence of Mrs. Hill, on the 23rd inst., at 7 o'clock P.M., by the Rev. Samuel Henderson, Mr. C. C. Douglass, of Huntsville, Ala., and Miss Amelia C. Hill, of Talladega County.

Also, (married) on the 24th, at residence of Mr. J. Martin, the bride's father, by Rev. J.J.D. Renfroe, Mr. James B. Whitten and Miss Sarah E. Martin.

Also, (married) on the 27th, at the residence of Mr. A. Bingham, Mr. John R. Guinn and Miss Elizah C. Morgan.

Also, (married) on the 24th, at residence of H.G. Robertson, in this county, by Wm. Montgomery, Mr. William Blair and Miss Elizabeth C. Robertson.

Also, (married) at the same time and place, by the same, Mr. R.G. Brewer and Miss Susan R. Robertson, all of this county.

ISSUE 1-20-1869

Married, at the residence of the bride's father, in Yadkin County, North Carolina, on the 22nd day of December, 1868, by Rev. Richard H. Griffith, George M. Duskin, of Greensboro, Ala., and Miss Mattie E., daughter of Tyre Glen.

ISSUE 1-27-1869

We learn from a citizen of that county, that Mr. McClarde, Sheriff of Pickens County, was killed on Sunday the 17th inst. While attempting to arrest a horse thief, the thief shot him dead. This was done at the house of Jesse Padget.... leaves a wife and two children (*Rome Courier*)

ISSUE 2-3-1869

Married, at the residence of the brides on the 28th ult., by the Rev. W. R. Kirk, Mr. William L. Terry to Miss Mary Seay, daughter of Mr. John L. Seay of this county.

Also, (married) at the residence of Judge Heflin in this place on the morning of the 30th ult, by the Rev. J. J. D. Renfroe, Mr. F. A. McClellan to Miss Florence Bowden, eldest daughter of the late Hon. Franklin W. Bowden.

Died, at his residence in this place, on Friday last, William T. Jenkins, aged about 30 years.

MISCELLANEOUS ALABAMA NEWSPAPER ABSTRACTS --- VOL 1

ISSUE 2-10-1869

Mrs. Mary Taul, widow of the Col. M. Taul, died at her residence, near Mardisville, on Thursday.

ISSUE 2-24-1869

We are pained to learn of the death of Judge B.B. Clitherall, a gentleman well known in Alabama.... It occurred this evening in this city at 1 o'clock.

We regret to learn that Mrs. Sophia Darby, wife of Col. Hugh Darby of this county, departed this life on Friday night last the 14th instant.

ISSUE 3-3-1869

Information Wanted: Mr. Donald McClellan, of 7th Con Minto, Castwald P.O. Ontario, Canada, wishes to find the whereabouts of Donald McClellan who left Islay, Argyleshire, Scotland, about 60 years ago, for one of the Southern States supposed to be one of the Carolinas. When last heard from he intended to remove to Alabama, somewhere in the neighborhood of Montgomery, or Talladega. If not alive, his family or heirs, by writing to the former Donald, will hear of something to their advantage.

Married, by the Rev. H. Clay Stone, at the residence of the bride's father, Feb. 23rd 1869, Mr. Robert Spence and Miss Emma Morris.

Also (married) by the same, and at the same time and place, Mr. Henry Cliett and Miss Eeily [sic] Winn.

ISSUE 3-10-1869

Married, near New Cave Springs, Ga., on the 2nd inst., by Rev. J. Courtney Brown, at the residence of the bride's father, Mr. Alexander White, Jr., late of Selma, and Miss R. Anna Prentice.

ISSUE 3-17-1869

Died, in this place, on Saturday, the 13th inst., Mrs. Susan Bowie, wife of Hon. Alexander Bowie deceased, aged 80 years.

Brutal Murder.... A Minister Shot While Performing The Marriage Ceremony: We were inexpressibly shocked, last night, to hear of the shooting, by a man whose name our informant could not give us, of the Rev. Samuel Anthony, one of the oldest, and most respected ministers of the Methodist Church in this state. The tragedy was enacted, yesterday, at Andersonville.... (*Macon Journal & Messenger*)

Married, Wednesday March 10th, 1869, at the residence of the brides father Col. J. W. Kidd, of Talladega County, by the Rev. Daniel Duncan, Miss Eloise Kidd, to Dr. Henry C. Bartherson, of New York.

ISSUE 3-24-1869

Died, on Sunday morning, the 21st inst., at the residence of Mr. James Montgomery, in this county, the Rev. R. A. Houston, pastor in charge of the Presbyterian Churches at Marble Springs and Oxford.

ISSUE 3-31-1869

Married, Thursday, March 11th, 1869, at the residence of the bride's father, J. W. Barton, of Clay County, by Eld. Wm. H. Burton, Miss Celia C. Barton to Mr. D. L. Campbell.

ISSUE 5-19-1869

Died, on the 25th ult., near New Market, Ala., Mr. James M. Chaney, formerly of this county.

ISSUE 5-26-1869

Died, at her residence, in this county, near Syllacauga, on the 15th inst., Mrs. Mary Cameron, aged about 90 years. She was a native of Inverness, Scotland, and for the last 27 years a resident of this country.

Died, at the Deaf, Dumb, and Blind Institution, in this place, on Wednesday the 12th inst., R. R. Asbury, Jr., infant son of R. R. and C. B. Asbury, aged 1 year and 14 days.

ISSUE 6-9-1869

Died, on Saturday morning last, in this county, Brown, son of Mr. John L. Seay, aged about 8 years.

The residence of Mr. John Johnson, near Oden's Mills, in this county, was consumed by fire on Sunday night last.

Mr. William Knox, one of the oldest citizens of Montgomery, died suddenly yesterday morning after suffering from disease a long time. Mr. Knox was the

Miscellaneous Alabama Newspaper Abstracts --- Vol 1

first and only president of the Central Bank of Alabama....

Our citizens were startled to hear yesterday of the murder of Hon. R. W. Flourney, on Tuesday last, at his plantation near Saundersville, in Washington County....

ISSUE 6-23-1869

Married, at the residence of the bride's father Col. Thomas McElderry, in this county on Thursday evening the 16th inst., by the W. R. Kirk, Mr. Thomas H. Jones, of Nashville, Tenn. and Miss Emma McElderry.

ISSUE 6-30-1869

Married, at the (residence) of the bride's father, Hon. F. T. McAtee, on the 16th inst., by Rev. J. J. D. Renfroe, Mr. A. D. Bennett, of N.Y. and Miss Lizzie L. McAfee, of Talladega.

Died, on the 15th of June, Josephine, infant daughter of J. F. and L. C. Baker.

ISSUE 7-7-1869

Married, at the Baptist Church, in Cave Springs, on the 27th ult., by Rev. J. C. Brown, Dr. G.T. Deason, of Alabama, to Miss Mattie Prentiss, of Floyd County, Ga.

ISSUE 7-14-1869

Homicide: Mr. Billy Satterwhite was killed yesterday by his father, who shot him with a shot gun loaded with buck shot, the load taking effect in the abdomen, killing him instantly. The difficulty originated, as we are informed, from a dispute in regard to some dogs. This was the only remaining son of Mr. Satterwhite, the other five being killed or died in the war. (*Elyton Herald*)

ISSUE 8-4-1869

At the public speaking at Ashland in Clay County, on Saturday last, a young man by the name of Nelson was badly stabbed in several places, by a young man named Brooks. It is said Col. M. J. Bulger who was present in attempting to suppress the difficulty received a cut in the hand.

MISCELLANEOUS ALABAMA NEWSPAPER ABSTRACTS --- VOL 1

ISSUE 8-11-1869

Died, at Silver Run, Ala., on Monday August 2nd, Miss Lucy J. Connally. She was born March 1839....

Married, at the residence of the bride's father, in Calhoun County, on the 27th of July, Mr. John F. Smith to Miss Guss Caver, daughter of Thos. Caver, all of Calhoun County.

Newton S. Fain born in Troup County, Geo., 13th of October 1842, and died near Floyd Springs, Geo., July 17th 1869, of that fatal disease consumption....

ISSUE 8-18-1869

A jury of inquest on the body of James Berrier deceased being summoned sworn and empaneled on the 16th day of August 1869 by me as Special Coroner for the County of Talladega and State of Alabama, at the house of Mrs. M.W. Dye....

Died, at residence of Rev. John L. Seay, in this county, on the 5th inst., Maggie M., daughter of John L. and Anna A. Terry, aged 1 year, 8 months, 24 days.

ISSUE 8-25-1869

The case of the negro, Alex Griffin, arrested on the charge of killing Capt. J. B. Harrison and John Stewart, which has been undergoing an examination before Judge Conoley of the County Court for several days past, terminated yesterday in the committal of Griffin to await his trial....

ISSUE 9-15-1869

On Friday evening last, Willie C. Otts, while on his way from Garland to his father's house near that place, was fired upon by some unknown individuals, who had waylaid the road for that purpose. Three guns were fired, the first two, it is supposed, having missed their intended victim, the last of which, however, took effect in his head, and proved fatal in about four hours. When the guns fired, two of his sisters had just started from home on an evening walk; hearing the guns, and knowing that it was about time for their brother to be on his way from Garland, they suspected that all was not right, and directed their steps toward the spot from whence the reports proceeded. But a short distance, and they came upon the lifeless body of the noble horse that had last carried their dear brother from his home. A little farther, and prostrate upon the ground was the expiring form of him whom they had so dearly and tenderly loved. He was carried home and expired. His remains were interred in this city on Sunday last.

ISSUE 9-29-1869

Married, at the residence of the brides mother in Calhoun County, on the 23rd inst., by the Rev. Wm. Taylor, Mr. Samuel Albright, of this vicinity, to Miss S. E. Neighbors.

ISSUE 10-6-1869

Married, on Tuesday, the 28th of September, at the residence of the bride's father, by Rev. G. J. Mason, Mr. J. H. Weathers to Miss Mattie E. Swope, all of Clay County.

ISSUE 10-13-1869

Deranged: Mr. Anderson Moss, an old and highly respected citizen of our County was brought before the Probate Judge last week, and after an inquisition of lunacy, was sent to the lunatic asylum at Tuscaloosa.

Died, at the residence of Capt. Shouse, in this place, on Thursday morning, 7th inst., Mrs. Susan Miller, wife of Mr. George Miller, aged 67 years.

ISSUE 10-20-1869

Married, on the 7th inst., at the residence of Mr. Thomas L. Best, of Talladega County, Mr. E. A. Crandall, of Calhoun, formerly of Memphis, Tenn., to Miss T. Anna Walker, of Talladega County.

ISSUE 10-27-1869

Married, in Montgomery, on the 20th inst., at the residence of the brides mother, by Rev. H. C. Townsend, Mr. Jas. H. Holly, of Selma, to Miss Georgia Lewis, of Montgomery.

ISSUE 11-17-1869

We learn that Mr. Jessie Cox, who lived near Childersburg, in this county, was killed by a negro man, on yesterday.

ISSUE 12-8-1869

We are informed, that the negro George Holly who killed Mr. Watson, near

MISCELLANEOUS ALABAMA NEWSPAPER ABSTRACTS --- VOL 1

Opelika, about a month ago, to get the proceeds of two bales of cotton was taken out of jail before day yesterday morning and killed.

We regret to announce the death of Mrs. Amanda B. Rice, consort of Judge Samuel F. Rice, after a long and painful illness.

ISSUE 12-22-1869

Mr. Thomas J. Coleman, an old citizen of this county, died at his residence near Kymulgee on Monday morning last.

Married, at the residence of the bride's father, in this place, on Wednesday morning last, by the Rev. A.D. McVey, Dr. J.C. Blake to Miss Mary Lawson, daughter of Andrew Lawson, all of this place.

GLOSSARY

Ad interim- "In the meantime." When an official is temporarily absent or incapacitated, an officer *ad interim* may be appointed to discharge his duties until the official returns.

Administrator- A person appointed by the court to administer (manage) the assets and liabilities of the deceased. Such person may be a male (administrator) or a female (administratrix). If the person performing these services is named by the decedent's will, he is designated as the executor, or she the executrix, of the estate.

Administrator ad litem- A special administrator appointed by the court to supply a necessary party to an action in which the deceased or his estate is interested.

Administrator de bonis non- Persons appointed by the court of probate to administer on the effects of a decedent which have not been included in a former administration.

Administrator with will annexed- Appointed as administrator of the deceased's estate after executors named in the will have refused or are unable to act.

Administratrix- A woman who administers, or to whom letters of administration have been granted.

Attachment- The act of taking persons or property into the custody of the law. Its perpose may be to bring before the court someone who is guilty of contempt of court, or, in the seizure of property, to provide security for payment of the judgment that the plaintiff expects to recover.

Ca.sa- Capias ad satisfaciendum. A legal writ or process commanding the officer to arrest the person named in it.

MISCELLANEOUS ALABAMA NEWSPAPER ABSTRACTS --- VOL 1

Congestive chills/fever-	Malaria.
Consort-	Companion. Spouse.
Consumption-	Pulmonary tuberculosis.
Deed of trust-	A type of mortgage. The title to properly is given to one or more persons to secure the payment of a debt.
Dower-	That share of or interest in deceased husband's real estate that is assigned by law to his widow for life.
Estate sale-	The sale of a deceased person's property to settle the estate. Usually conducted by the executor or administrator.
Estray notice-	A discriptive advertisement placed in a newspaper that an animal has disappeared.
Executor-	The individual appointed by the one making the will to dispose of his or her property after death in accordance with the terms of the will.
Executrix-	A female executor. A woman who has been appointed by will to execute such will or testament.
Fi fa-	Writ of fieri facias. A court order to seize and sell goods belonging to the loser in a court case to pay debts owed.
Fodder-	Feed.
Guardian-	One who is legally assigned care of the person or property of an individual not competent to act for himself, as an infant or minor.

MISCELLANEOUS ALABAMA NEWSPAPER ABSTRACTS --- VOL 1

Guardianship-	The office, obligations or authority of a guardian. The relationship existing between a guardian and his ward.
Hereditament-	Anything that can be inherited, whether real or personal property. Corporeal hereditament is tangible property; anything intangible, for example easement or rent, is incorporeal hereditament.
Inst.-	In the current month.
Intestate-	When a person dies without a valid will.
Letters of administration-	Formal document issued by probate court appointing one an administrator of an estate.
Letters testamentary-	The formal instrument of authority and appointment given to an executor by the proper court, empowering him to enter upon the discharge of his office as executor. It corresponds to letters of administration granted to an administrator.
Next Friend-	One who acts on behalf of another person if they cannot act for themselves, such as a minor or an incompetent.
Note of hand-	A popular name (now obsolete) for a promissory note.
Orphan-	A person, especially a minor or infant, who has lost one or both of his parents.
Overseer-	A person in charge of work on a plantation.
Petition-	A formal, written application to a court requesting judicial action on a certain matter.
Polemic society-	A debating society.
Relict-	Widow or widower.

MISCELLANEOUS ALABAMA NEWSPAPER ABSTRACTS --- VOL 1

Sheriff's sale- A sale, commonly by auction, conducted by a sheriff or other court officer to carry out a decree of execution or foreclosure issued by a court. Examples include sales pursuant to attachments, liens and mortgages.

Tenement- Any property that can be held but most often refers to house and land.

Township and range- Much of the area of the United States has been subdivided by a system of land survey in which a square 6 miles on one side is the basic unit, called a township, when measured north and south of a given baseline, and called a range when measured east and west of a given principal meridian. Each township is divided into 36 sections, usually 1 mile on a side. Each section may be further subdivided into half sections, quarter sections, or sixteenth sections.

Ult.- In the month immediately preceeding. Previous month.

Will and testament- A will is a document in which the testator distributes his or her real estate. A testament is the document in which the testator distributes his or her personal property.

NAME INDEX

?earing	103	Allison	78, 180
Abbey	20	Alston	72, 77
Abbott	129	Ambler	153
Abby	52, 129, 130	Anaraon	89
Abercrombie	45, 61, 73, 78, 100, 111, 126, 136, 149, 150	Anderson	4, 5, 32, 33, 46, 47, 65, 72, 78, 84, 93, 121, 127, 153, 160, 165, 167, 170, 173, 212
Abercromby	11		
Abercromie	20	Andrews	73, 85, 96
Abney	57	Antery	121
Abrams	108	Anthony	101, 122, 143, 184, 208
Abston	121, 127, 134		
Acker	26, 190	Armbre?ster	179
Acock	20	Armstrong	43, 67, 93, 97, 120, 125, 127, 140, 150
Adair	179		
Adams	2, 4, 7-9, 11, 17, 18, 21, 22, 28, 30, 35, 37, 38, 41, 46, 49, 51, 64, 66, 72, 77, 78, 91, 100, 110, 117, 118, 123, 126, 127, 137, 138, 154	Arnold	61, 82, 84, 85, 117, 127, 144, 179
		Arrington	156, 157
		Arterbury	95, 121
Addams	26, 32	Arthur	51, 92, 107
Adkins	79, 102	Artiberry	79
Adkinson	85	Asbury	100, 209
Akeson	73	Ashe	93
Akin	121	Ashley	72, 73, 139, 154, 179
Alberty	177		
Albright	205, 212	Ashworth	127
Aldridge	9	Audis	192
Alexander	2, 11, 13, 20, 21, 24, 31, 32, 38, 44, 46, 48, 53, 58, 60-62, 64-67, 72, 74, 77, 84, 86-88, 92, 94, 99-102, 104, 106, 117, 120-123, 127, 129, 131, 147, 151, 157, 164, 167, 183, 208	Austil	57
		Austill	85
		Austin	47, 127
		Averet	131
		Averett	139, 177
		Avery	26, 65, 73, 78, 85
Algood	156		
Alilard	11	Averyt	11
Alison	2, 18, 38, 162	Avirett	166
Allday	6	Avyrett	10
Allen	32, 61, 67-69, 73, 81, 93, 100, 127, 152, 153, 162, 177, 189, 202, 205	Babcock	2, 8, 11, 17, 20, 32, 38, 51, 117, 199

MISCELLANEOUS ALABAMA NEWSPAPER ABSTRACTS --- VOL 1

Baby	129	Bartherson	209
Backus	26	Bartlett	34, 100, 135
Badger	2, 72	Barton	83, 209
Bagby	89	Bartow	202
Bailey	46, 79, 106, 179, 196	Baskerville	61
		Baskin	166, 177, 179
Baily	179	Bass	11, 71, 127, 189
Baker	14, 20, 35, 84, 113, 121, 157, 177, 179, 210	Bassett	11, 121
		Batchelor	10
		Bates	51, 77, 174
Balch	95	Battle	11, 28, 88
Baldwin	2, 63	Batts	16, 116
Baley	72	Baxley	17, 18, 145
Balker	117	Baxter	2, 9, 10, 17, 25, 38, 51, 117
Ball	4, 23, 56, 138, 142, 177	Baykin	126
Ballard	66, 79, 99	Baylor	2, 26, 38, 51, 110
Bancock	2		
Banfield	79	Baylue	57
Banone	32	Baze	46
Barber	179	Beal	121
Barbour	73, 193	Beale	2, 145
Barcalin	189	Beasley	11
Barclay	51, 177, 179, 185, 187, 188, 205	Beattie	100, 129
		Beavers	195
		Beazley	166
Bare	61	Bebee	146
Barefield	99	Beck	2, 11, 20, 56, 57, 73
Barfield	66		
Barlow	26, 38, 46	Beckley	73, 86
Barnes	25, 26, 38, 40, 42, 53, 55, 72, 100, 148, 158, 159, 161, 189	Beckman	2
		Becton	27, 176
		Beddingfield	127
		Bedingfield	121
Barnet	2, 72	Beene	2, 10, 18, 22, 23, 29, 32, 34, 40, 51, 68, 71, 100, 127
Barnett	78, 79, 129, 177, 193		
Barney	72, 199		
Barns	26, 42, 92	Beers	2, 11, 40, 57
Barnwell	69	Beeson	93
Barrett	140	Begger	129
Barron	86	Bell	8, 11, 29, 51, 57, 68, 70, 100, 127, 129, 131, 134, 135, 142, 150, 190, 203
Barry	158		
Barther	127		

MISCELLANEOUS ALABAMA NEWSPAPER ABSTRACTS --- VOL 1

Bellengslea	86	Blackwood	11, 32
Belvin	66, 92	Blair	207
Bender	66, 78, 79	Blake	26, 174, 213
Bennet	62, 64, 66, 72	Blakely	13, 19
Bennett	50, 176, 177, 179, 210	Blakeslee	61
		Blakey	143
Benson	24, 93, 123, 134	Blalack	29
Bently	38, 190, 204	Blalock	31, 61, 100, 127
Berine	77	Blan	129
Bernhard	148	Blandin	192
Berrier	211	Blankinship	179
Berry	26, 117, 127, 132, 133	Blann	11, 32, 57, 109
		Blanton	181
Besseant	192	Blarson	121
Best	134, 190, 212	Blassengame	2
Bethea	46	Bledsoe	189
Bethel	20, 39, 40, 46, 49, 57, 73	Blevins	13, 95
		Blewford	92
Betts	51, 57	Blount	17, 81, 113
Bhland	117	Blue	117
Bickley	61, 154	Bluford	39, 156
Biddie	102	Blunt	146, 147
Bigelow	25	Blythe	79, 89, 200
Biggle	72	Boardman	163
Bigham	66	Boggan	61
Billingsley	100	Bogle	61, 67, 69, 72, 93, 175
Billingsly	138		
Bingham	194, 206, 207	Bohanan	38, 51
Birchett	158, 172	Bohannan	15, 26
Bird	10, 23, 29, 57, 62, 80, 85, 101, 121, 129, 153, 154	Bohannon	2, 20, 109, 117, 125, 127, 132
		Bohanon	129
		Bohonon	129
Birdsall	2	Bolan	73
Birney	56	Boles	51, 73
Bishop	57, 92, 179, 185, 187, 188, 194	Boling	57, 85
		Bolling	11, 150
		Bolls	11
Bissell	173	Bolton	3, 5, 26, 61, 162
Bizzell	161	Bolware	121
Black	78	Bonley	129
Blackburn	67	Bonneau	38, 127
Blackstock	78	Bonnell	132
Blackwell	179	Bonner	42, 108, 174, 198

MISCELLANEOUS ALABAMA NEWSPAPER ABSTRACTS --- VOL 1

Boon	72, 125, 129	Bradshaw	79
Booth	26, 38, 107, 108, 199	Brady	179
		Bragg	160, 161
Boothe	2, 20, 32	Braime	107
Borden	86, 161	Branch	20, 26, 100, 138
Boring	177	Brand	127
Borland	61	Brandon	136, 205
Borum	178	Brant	121
Bostick	67, 158, 159, 161	Brantley	46, 53, 84, 86, 92, 100, 114, 115, 119, 121, 140, 143
Bostwick	121		
Boswell	187	Brantly	20, 26, 32
Bouchillon	169	Brassfield	163
Boundes	78	Brautly	66
Bowan	86	Brazeal	26
Bowden	207	Brazellon	86
Bowdon	182	Breazeal	61
Bowen	120, 175	Breedon	190
Bower	11, 73, 84, 137, 151	Brenere	2
		Brent	46
Bowers	26, 121	Brewer	40, 57, 102, 131, 196, 207
Bowie	40, 46, 55, 56, 114, 135, 143, 177, 194, 208		
		Brickell	150, 204
		Brickley	84
Bowles	20, 51, 79	Bridges	42, 48, 118, 154
Bowman	162	Briggs	6, 171
Boxley	2, 18, 37	Brigman	177
Boyd	44, 143, 147, 173	Bringiet	54
		Brisner	104
Boyken	2	Briston	32
Boykin	11, 15, 137, 174	Britt	134, 177
Boynton	183	Brock	177, 179
Boyter	79, 84	Brogden	50
Bozeman	78, 117	Brookes	20
Bozwell	63, 105	Brooks	8, 11, 46, 57, 61, 92, 100, 124, 143, 179, 210
Brabham	72, 127		
Bracken	177	Brotnam	177
Bradberry	26	Browen	51
Braddum	79	Brown	11, 35, 46, 51, 59, 61, 66, 69, 71, 73, 81, 84, 86, 89, 93, 103, 106, 118, 121, 127, 129, 136, 139, 148, 149, 156, 160, 169, 176, 177, 179, 189, 196, 199, 208, 210
Bradford	51, 99, 177, 179, 194, 199, 202		
Bradley	121, 199		
Bradly	32, 46		

Miscellaneous Alabama Newspaper Abstracts --- Vol 1

Name	Pages
Browning	11, 61, 97
Brummitt	149
Brunson	73
Bryan	73, 127, 179, 197
Bryant	96, 111, 149
Bryon	121
Buanch	55
Buchanan	66, 86
Buck	15, 72
Buckhalter	78, 82
Buckley	72, 161
Buckner	4
Buffington	32
Bugg	117
Buie	179
Bulger	210
Bulla	28
Bullard	40, 63
Bullock	162, 167
Bumgardner	179
Bunn	127
Burch	84
Burgan	139
Burge	51
Burgess	72
Burk	46, 86
Burke	68, 76, 78, 109, 114, 141
Burket	129
Burkit	38
Burkley	79
Burnds	118
Burnes	29, 49
Burnett	100, 193
Burns	100, 179
Burres	121
Burress	92
Burrows	132
Burster	81
Burt	46, 87, 194
Burte	79
Burton	32, 209
Busbee	26
Busby	84, 100
Bush	185
Buster	73
Butler	26, 32, 44, 46, 51, 57, 64, 71, 72, 78, 84, 89, 91, 96, 117, 121, 153, 155, 166, 193
Buttler	193
Buxton	146
Byers	189
Bynd	127
Byran	127
Byrd	73
Byrenheidt	31
Byrne	204
C?rtis	11
Cabaniss	19
Cadle	157
Cadwell	26
Cain	112, 187
Caldwell	11, 20, 132, 197
Cales	179
Calhoon	117
Calhoun	3, 46, 48, 57, 121, 126, 131, 133, 193, 195, 205, 211, 212
Calleham	129
Callen	100, 136
Callender	26
Callens	128
Callilan	11
Callon	121
Calloway	89
Caloway	137
Camack	74
Cambell	100
Camble	38
Camel	179
Cameron	160, 177, 188, 209
Cammack	86
Camp	37, 49, 57, 61
Campbell	12, 24, 26, 30, 33, 34, 37, 38, 51, 52, 55, 57, 61, 66, 72, 74, 78, 84, 86, 92, 100, 103, 112, 125, 128, 129,

MISCELLANEOUS ALABAMA NEWSPAPER ABSTRACTS --- VOL 1

131, 137, 154, 179, 209		Catheart	121
Canady	86	Cathey	61, 155
Candless	72	Cato	18
Cannie	143	Caver	195, 211
Cannte	13, 100, 120, 121, 129, 137	Cawthon	42
		Cawthorn	16
Canterberry	143	Cayol	32
Cantt	149	Cearley	129
Card	79, 121	Chadwick	158, 161
Cardy	12	Chafin	72, 86
Carethers	129	Chalmers	128
Carey	99, 177	Chambers	12, 51, 154, 197
Cargile	198	Chambless	13
Carley	189	Chambliss	137, 143
Carliles	121	Chandler	14, 84, 100, 128, 137, 139, 177, 204
Carlon	92		
Carmichael	87		
Carmichal	128	Chaney	177, 209
Carn	74	Chapin	66, 189
Carnahan	154	Chapins	51
Carney	66	Chapman	11, 15, 18, 26, 29, 30, 34, 37, 74, 136, 145
Carpenter	128, 166, 167, 177, 179		
Carptem	177	Chappell	179
Carr	11, 17, 38, 50, 61, 71, 79, 84, 86, 92, 129, 150	Charlotte	35, 128
		Charrow	184
		Cheek	72
Carrell	20, 128	Cheeseborough	86
Carroll	66, 72	Chesnut	31, 51
Carson	2, 26, 61, 78, 199	Chestina	94
		Child	128
Carter	61, 63, 74, 78, 79, 94, 97, 125, 128, 129, 175, 177, 179	Childers	56, 117, 121, 133, 134, 137, 138, 145
		Childress	121
Cartor	86	Chiles	157
Caruman	79	Chilton	179, 182
Carver	20, 22	Chisholm	61
Carvill	32	Chisolm	61, 74
Cary	92	Chisom	61
Casey	49, 74, 177	Chizm	99
Cash	120, 121	Chocheron	1
Casper	177	Christopher	111
Castleberry	195, 197	Cicero	82

Miscellaneous Alabama Newspaper Abstracts --- Vol 1

Name	Pages
Clanton	66
Clapp	54
Clarh	117
Clark	1, 16, 19, 22, 26, 29, 32, 40, 46, 48, 49, 51, 54, 57, 72, 78, 79, 92, 117, 128, 129, 169, 171, 179
Clarke	2, 38
Claughton	121
Clay	128
Clayton	85
Cleaveland	38
Cleavland	129
Clement	13, 117
Clements	179
Cleveland	11, 32, 46, 60, 65, 69, 72, 117, 121, 127
Cliatt	197
Cliett	208
Clifton	38, 46
Clinron	116
Clinton	145
Clitherall	208
Clrrk	29
Coaker	69
Coalman	74
Cobb	2, 12, 177
Cobbs	177
Cochran	2, 20, 26, 128, 154
Cochrin	2
Cocke	197
Cockran	15
Cockron	129
Cody	100
Coffee	92, 100, 179
Coker	2, 179
Colbert	1, 81
Coldman	128
Coldwell	179
Cole	2, 51, 66, 69, 70, 121
Coleburn	51
Coleman	11, 26, 36, 51, 57, 66, 118, 129, 155, 163, 170, 171, 179, 213
Coley	61
Collins	11, 26, 38, 57, 78, 83, 107, 128, 185
Colly	78, 86
Colman	57
Colwell	117, 128
Comalander	26
Comeandler	11
Comelander	9, 45
Commons	150
Cone	154
Coneuchaker	44
Connally	211
Connell	89
Connely	83
Conner	117, 189
Conoley	48, 53, 147, 211
Conoly	128
Conts	12
Converse	104
Conway	151
Cook	20, 32, 57, 71, 72, 74, 99, 100, 128, 160, 177, 182, 185, 195, 206
Cooke	66
Cooksey	94
Cooper	1, 61, 116
Copeland	177, 190
Corley	63
Cormichael	10, 147
Cornwallis	88
Cortes	2
Cothran	2
Coti	4
Cotten	179
Cotton	74, 86, 189
Couan	84
Covan	11
Coventry	66, 72
Covington	61, 79, 100
Cowan	20, 46, 103, 118, 121, 126, 132, 143, 148, 185

MISCELLANEOUS ALABAMA NEWSPAPER ABSTRACTS --- VOL 1

Cowles	60, 88, 91, 105, 110	Cruikshank	194
Cowsar	188	Crumbly	157
Cox	2, 26, 87, 121, 174, 177, 179, 189, 212	Crumpler	171
		Crumpton	2, 11, 21, 128, 140
		Cuberhouse	128
Craft	117	Culbertson	84, 92, 100
Craig	2, 3, 8, 11, 15, 20, 23, 25, 26, 38, 39, 46, 49, 51, 57, 60, 72, 96, 101, 115, 129, 146, 155, 158, 175	Culbreath	187
		Cullen	31
		Culverhouse	136
		Culverson	202
Crandall	212	Cumberland	128
Crane	55, 97	Cumberlander	104
Cravens	26	Cumings	94
Crawford	12, 32, 34, 66, 74, 78, 79, 88, 100, 121, 124, 167, 202	Cummings	143
		Cunningham	31, 61, 74, 98, 99, 177, 183, 184, 189, 192-194, 197
Crawson	84	Currie	121
Creigk	51	Curry	70, 121, 184, 190, 194, 195, 202, 205
Crenshaw	61, 63, 79, 177		
Creswell	170	Curtis	11, 20, 46, 57, 61, 74, 86, 108, 117, 120, 191, 199
Crim	74, 94		
Criswell	188	Cushman	155
Crittenden	121	Cuthbert	38
Crocher	121	Daffon	92
Crocheron	1, 8, 19, 21, 26, 32, 33, 56, 57, 99	Daily	66, 79, 92
		Dale	78
		Dance	156
Crockett	109	Dancy	179
Crockor	61	Daniel	6, 12, 29, 44, 177
Croheron	86	Dann	48
Croker	79	Danrimple	167
Cronondontholigus	51	Darby	179, 192, 208
Croom	171, 172	Darling	94
Crosby	25, 26, 30, 46, 121, 140	Daugherty	68
		Davenport	151, 173
Crosland	5, 121	Davidson	69, 129
Cross	2, 86, 121, 187	Davie	26
Croswell	115-117, 129, 130	Davis	8, 17, 18, 20, 34, 39, 42, 51, 57, 61, 63, 66, 71, 74, 75, 78-80, 82, 84, 86, 89, 95, 100, 117, 121, 128-131, 135, 139, 159-161, 163-166, 177,
Crow	60, 79, 100, 121, 128		
Crowson	89		

MISCELLANEOUS ALABAMA NEWSPAPER ABSTRACTS --- VOL 1

184, 190, 197-199		Dickey	189
Dawell	32	Dickinson	26, 191
Dawson	128	Dickson	36, 131
Day	26, 32, 50, 51, 57, 61, 79, 86, 89, 100, 124, 148	Diggs	2, 155
		Dillett	51
		Ditmar	175
		Diven	64
Dean	115	Dixon	119, 177, 189, 198
Dear	9, 61, 126, 133		
Deas	26	Dobbins	86
Deason	210	Dodd	179
Deckart	39	Dodson	151, 177
Deckinson	12	Dokeman	121
Deer	72	Doland	107
Degman	46	Dolen	104
Dehay	10	Donaghey	175, 176
Dekle	25	Donald	2, 208
Delane	121	Donley	190
Dellard	129	Donnelly	2
Delony	196	Donohoo	194
Demean	121	Doriah	61
Demming	46	Dorman	192
Denham	12	Dorris	171
Denison	55	Dorroh	27, 121, 141
Dennis	44, 51, 57, 72, 78, 86, 128	Dorsey	179
		Doss	171, 181
Dennison	57, 129, 130	Doubrins	86
Denson	12, 61	Dougherty	56, 160
Dent	6	Douglas	97, 109, 121, 139
Denton	72, 92, 101, 129		
Derden	86	Douglass	177, 179, 194, 207
Derrick	179		
Derry	12, 83	Douthet	121
Deruy	99	Dow	129
Devan	181	Downes	2, 53
DeVaughan	10	Downman	154
Deweecse(?)	86	Doyle	100
Deweese	72, 127	Dozier	49
Dewell	72	Drane	79, 86
Dewey	2	Draper	72, 157
Dexter	39, 141	Dreman	121, 128
Dial	94	Drennon	128
Dick	151	Drew	32
Dickard	117	Driskill	141

MISCELLANEOUS ALABAMA NEWSPAPER ABSTRACTS --- VOL 1

Name	Pages	Name	Pages
Drummond	170		66
Drumond	51	Earles	129
Dubar	51	Easley	189
Dubose	35, 51, 121	Eason	183, 194
Duck	23, 84, 127	Eatman	158, 160
Duckworth	86	Echoles	84
Dudley	17, 20, 124	Echols	48, 68, 80, 128
Dudly	39, 128	Eddins	156
Due	57	Edgerton	128
Duese	78	Edmiston	159
Duest	46	Edmondson	26, 39, 72
Duglass	86	Edney	46
Duke	80	Edomonds	128
Dukes	112, 121	Edves	128
Dulaney	84, 177, 179, 190, 201	Edward	57, 72
		Edwards	2, 40, 56, 84, 94, 110, 117, 122, 128, 176, 177, 203
Dulany	105, 189		
Dun	117		
Dunaghy	92		
Dunaway	46, 118	Eiland	55, 117, 132
Duncan	126, 177, 179, 209	Elder	114, 152
		Elders	94
Dundsons	92	Elkins	66, 72
Dunham	2, 8, 22, 33, 39, 46, 52, 56, 92, 157, 186	Ellerbe	154
		Ellington	177
		Elliot	84, 92
Dunklin	83, 84, 138	Elliott	29, 80, 113, 117, 179, 189
Dunlap	92, 109, 147		
Dunn	66, 78, 79, 109, 110, 128, 192	Ellis	25, 26, 46, 47, 50, 62, 64, 86, 131, 138, 179
Dupree	26, 34, 128		
Durden	74, 141	Elmonson	100
Durham	49	Elmonston	121, 128
Durraw	39	Elmore	51
Duskin	207	Elrod	177, 179
Dye	187, 194, 206, 211	Elston	179, 194
		Embry	177, 179
Dyer	98	Emerson	128
Dyke	60, 62, 79, 103	English	13, 33, 39, 46, 56, 58, 78, 99, 128, 129, 175
Dykes	60		
Earbee	131		
Earl	51	Engoldsby	34
Earle	2, 16, 26, 33, 36, 43, 56-58,	Erwin	6, 11, 62, 82, 132, 147

MISCELLANEOUS ALABAMA NEWSPAPER ABSTRACTS --- VOL 1

Eslave	150	Filinvi	128
Estes	26, 164	Finch	20, 28, 32
Estis	129	Fincher	73, 100, 121
Etherage	2, 26, 49	Finley	185, 196
Ethridge	6, 15, 39, 72, 176	Finly	130
		Fisher	39, 62, 82, 116, 165
Ethrige	78		
Eubank	108, 169	Fiske	94
Evans	8, 26, 31, 38, 43, 55-57, 67, 129, 155, 167, 177, 179	Fitzgerald	32, 174, 185, 195
		Fizzle	2
		Flanagan	66, 100
Eve	177	Flanegan	51
Ewing	71, 74, 87, 96, 99, 108	Flanegin	74
		Flanekin	57
Exell	91	Flanigan	92
Ezell	90	Flanigin	80
Ezrack	128	Flaniken	8
Fain	193, 206, 211	Flanikin	123
Fair	121, 125	Flanniken	28, 29
Fairly	10	Fleming	57
Falconer	32	Flemming	42, 57
Fambro	1, 10, 11, 16, 19, 29, 40	Fleniken	43, 57
		Fletcher	62, 97, 130
Fanin	80	Florence	202, 207
Fant	191	Flourney	210
Farley	84	Flournoy	105
Farness	83	Flurenoy	2
Farrall	74	Foot	100
Fatherlain	20	Forbes	9
Faulk	74	Ford	62, 73, 86, 89, 94, 121, 128
Faulkner	20		
Fay	61	Foreman	177, 179, 189
Fedrick	32	Forman	177
Feicman	73	Forness	137
Fellows	121	Forseth	130
Felton	128	Forsyth	83
Fenimore	92	Forsythe	32
Fergerson	44	Fort	121, 139
Ferguson	110, 114, 121, 143, 179	Forte	57
		Fortson	172
Field	64, 104, 128	Foscue	57
Fike	121, 157	Foster	51, 60, 157, 196
Files	20, 128	Fournier	155

Miscellaneous Alabama Newspaper Abstracts --- Vol 1

Fowler	78, 121, 158	Gamage	67, 93, 128, 135
Foy	26	Gambia	27
Fradly	92	Ganaway	177
Fraley	41	Gannt	100
Franklin	36, 57, 62, 69, 74, 103, 121, 125, 128, 130, 179, 201	Gant	128
		Gantt	25, 55, 71, 84, 92
		Gardiner	27
Frazee	2	Gardner	46, 50, 57, 62, 66, 74, 80, 85-87, 92, 100, 104, 112, 121, 128, 139, 148, 199
Frazer	39, 106, 185		
Frederick	84		
Fredrick	46	Garett	25
Free	171	Garigus	202
Freeman	2, 15, 26, 39, 124, 130, 145, 146, 170	Garner	21, 84, 130, 177, 179
		Garnor	78
Freeze	188	Garret	20, 27, 62, 111, 112
Freman	32		
French	62, 86, 117	Garrett	12, 39, 46, 100, 169, 182
Freudenberger	191		
Friend	158	Gary	117, 121, 128
Frost	39, 121	Gascal	62
Frow	59, 68, 124, 128	Gascoigne	40
Fulford	124	Gaskins	13
Fulgham	166	Gaston	27, 32, 46
Fullenwider	186	Gay	198
Fuller	121, 128, 188	Gayle	2, 8, 12, 15, 26, 28, 29, 32, 39, 41, 45, 46, 59, 62, 74, 78, 82, 86, 90, 99, 103, 110, 111, 137, 154, 199
Fullwood	87		
Funderburg	177		
Funderburgh	135		
Fur	51	Gaylor	177
Furgson	128	Gaylore	128
Furguson	128	Gaynes	99
Furlow	179	Gazzam	118
Furr	29, 130	Gee	1, 42, 44, 52, 86, 151
Fyke	80		
G???	69	Geeghegan	51
G?ge	12	Geiger	57
Ga?away	62	George	32, 57, 62, 73, 128
Gager	32		
Gaillard	102	Getchell	15
Gaines	46, 54, 74, 177	Gewin	157
Gains	99	Ghehegan	28
Galloway	51	Giag	177

Miscellaneous Alabama Newspaper Abstracts --- Vol 1

Gibson	2, 5, 7, 39, 85, 92, 112, 121, 128, 144		125, 128, 152, 190
		Goolsby	62
Gildersleeve	35, 121, 125	Goosa	78
Gill	20, 46, 51, 101, 110, 176	Gordan	20
		Gordon	62, 76, 90
Gillam	119	Goree	20, 152
Gillem	73	Gorman	5, 7, 119, 121, 126, 128
Gillespie	94, 157		
Gillis	72	Gould	172
Gillom	78	Goulding	6
Gillum	79	Gowan	59
Gilmer	74, 98, 123, 128, 140, 175, 176	Grace	161, 183
		Grady	2, 177
		Gragg	188
Gilmore	62, 92, 121	Graham	2, 12, 20, 46, 56, 58, 73, 96, 113, 117, 177
Givban	128		
Givens	177, 185, 187		
Givham	62	Grant	45, 57, 74, 78, 86, 106, 128, 131
Givhan	20, 57, 78, 100, 128		
Glass	61, 66, 128, 147	Graves	14, 107, 114, 120, 121, 128, 131, 136, 137, 139
Glen	12, 73, 117, 207		
Glover	167		
Godfrey	117		
Godhame	12	Gray	27, 92, 177, 179
Goffe	66, 85	Green	50, 74, 105, 133, 136, 143, 198
Goggans	94		
Gol?man	175		
Golden	179	Greene	199
Golding	177	Greening	15, 17, 21, 32, 51, 57, 74, 78
Goldsby	2, 46, 80, 121, 191		
		Greer	60, 67, 84, 159
Golesby	32	Greger	128
Gollsty	130	Gregory	88
Goman	128	Greps	20
Goode	74	Grice	51, 86, 121
Gooden	183	Grier	67
Goodgame	77, 202	Griffice	176
Goodger	128	Griffin	67, 80, 97, 100, 155, 177, 179, 189, 199, 211
Gooding	37, 127		
Goodman	2, 117, 141, 177		
Goodwin	2, 9, 30, 85, 91, 92, 119, 121,	Griffith	207
		Grigg	109

Miscellaneous Alabama Newspaper Abstracts --- Vol 1

Name	Pages	Name	Pages
Grigsby	11, 39, 53, 100, 121	Hammock	32, 176
		Hamner	74
Grimbs	177	Hamon	92
Grimes	92, 121	Hampson	178
Grisby	46	Hancock	179, 191
Grisham	121	Handley	54
Groce	204, 205	Hanford	144
Grumbles	2, 27, 57, 62, 78, 147, 148	Hankins	160
		Hanley	71
Guinn	46, 207	Hanrick	85
Gully	159	Hansborough	32
Gunn	18	Hansbrough	17, 39
Gunter	27, 102	Har?	25
Gurham	2	Harbersham	117
Gurry	128	Hardaway	3, 137, 172
Gustin	11	Hardey	46, 47
Guthere	69	Hardie	177, 179, 203
Guthrie	77, 78, 86, 91, 179	Hardin	78, 85, 117
		Harding	77
Gwin	132	Hardy	61, 148, 154, 161
Gwyn	27		
Habambe	128	Hare	62, 89, 195
Habersham	128	Hargrove	172
Hackworth	94	Harkey	127
Haclow	76	Harkins	86
Haden	32	Harkness	163
Haggard	69, 87, 94, 121	Harky	117
Hagler	73	Harman	178, 179
Haine	61	Harold	62
Hainsworth	63	Harper	171
Halcome	78	Harrel	24, 32
Hale	78, 121, 130, 139, 159	Harrell	26, 39, 57, 59, 60, 108, 175
Haley	200	Harriet	9
Hall	5, 19, 71, 74, 76, 86, 96, 110, 130, 138, 150, 169, 178, 179, 186, 187	Harrington	95
		Harris	20, 46, 51, 62, 63, 78, 80, 85, 91, 92, 96, 105, 107, 108, 114, 115, 121, 128, 137, 141, 154, 162, 172, 185, 187, 189, 194
Halloway	46, 92		
Halmes	4		
Halse	7		
Hamill	183, 201, 202	Harrison	3, 27, 31-33, 39, 40, 77, 78, 89, 91, 94, 96, 97, 100, 117, 119, 130, 155, 157, 171, 177, 178, 203, 205, 211
Hamilton	40, 125, 154, 157		
Hamlett	167		

Harriss	162		71, 121, 192
Harrod	68	Hearn	20, 27, 56, 62, 96, 202
Harroll	2		
Hart	57, 117, 203	Hearne	3
Hartley	95	Heflin	176, 207
Hartman	2	Heice	128
Hartwell	3, 32	Heintz	71
Harvel	121	Helman	25
Harvell	94	Hem	51
Harvey	2, 3, 16, 39, 61, 63, 121, 134	Hemmingray	80
		Henderson	73, 80, 92, 94, 98, 106, 177, 179, 185, 194, 197, 206, 207
Harvill	80, 85		
Harville	84		
Hascall	7	Hendly	164
Haskew	51	Hendon	100, 178
Haskin	130	Hendrich	108
Haskins	94	Hendrick	25, 30, 39, 46, 55, 130, 145, 164, 165
Hassell	160		
Hatch	83, 121, 163	Hendricks	16
Hatche	130	Henry	20, 62, 85, 86, 99, 121, 128, 178, 199
Hatcher	32, 34, 39, 40, 50, 51, 54-57, 62, 78, 123, 128, 133, 146, 154, 175, 176, 199		
		Henstis	27
		Herad(?)	99
Hatfield	43	Herbert	2, 4, 20, 117, 139
Hattox	62		
Haudley	16	Hernden	156
Haughton	178	Herrald	84
Havis	98	Herrell	51
Hawley	133	Herrington	27
Hawthorn	117	Hester	73, 159
Hayes	108, 139	Heustin	62
Hayles	135	Heustis	90, 117
Hayman	74	Hewes	27, 74
Haynes	69, 80, 81, 109, 121, 178, 179	Hewitt	61
		Hewstis	32
Hays	3, 46, 57, 108, 128	Higginbotham	19, 66, 75, 86
		Higginbottom	62
Hazard	92	Higgins	20, 168, 200
Hazle	92	High	25, 29, 74, 160, 167
Headen	179, 185, 203		
Heaggard	27	Higinboatham	99
Heap	74	Hilburn	32
Hearan	86	Hill	12, 16, 23, 27, 39, 57, 61, 62, 64, 72, 75, 80, 87,
Heard	12, 32, 46, 57,		

MISCELLANEOUS ALABAMA NEWSPAPER ABSTRACTS --- VOL 1

	95, 100, 102, 111, 113, 121, 155, 157, 159, 168, 172, 177-180, 182, 207	Holston	80, 100
		Home	174
		Hondley	161
Hillard	80, 92	Honeycut	53
Hillhouse	104, 107, 119	Honsom	128
Hillyard	11	Hood	57, 154
Hinds	24, 92, 143	Hooper	2, 27, 35, 36, 121, 185, 194
Hines	20, 66		
Hinson	9, 74, 85, 121, 128	Hoot	19, 39, 148
		Hope	100
Hinton	80, 174	Hopkins	80
Hitchcock	78, 86	Hopper	80, 94, 128
Hitt	30, 59, 73	Hopson	156
Hobson	20	Hord	158
Hoco poco	51	Horn	46, 94, 162, 172
Hodge	89	Hornbuckle	27
Hodges	71, 96, 136	Horne	69, 130
Hogan	2, 3, 16, 27, 39, 51, 57, 66, 101, 109, 115, 151, 178, 199	Hoss	3
		Hough	3
		Houghton	85
		Houlditch	156
Hogeboom	64	House	2, 106
Hogg	12, 83, 117	Houston	27, 97, 148, 179, 209
Hoggue	94		
Holas	179	Howard	3, 9, 20, 61, 62, 74, 92, 178, 188
Holcomb	121, 128		
Holcroft	155	Howell	12, 15, 42, 186, 202
Holden	30		
Holiness	66	Howie	27, 73, 125
Hollaway	39	Howlett	152
Hollingshead	57	Hoy	98
Hollingsworth	19	Hoyle	189
Hollmark	179	Hoyt	190
Holloway	2, 12, 39, 51, 145, 153, 160	Hubbard	64, 195
		Huckaby	22, 51
Holly	40, 160, 178, 179, 196, 212	Huckeby	46
		Huckster	128
Holman	70, 96	Hudaleston	86
Holmes	4, 20, 27, 39, 40, 49, 57, 73, 92, 177	Huddleston	65, 66, 90, 91, 103
		Hudson	69, 97, 155, 178, 196
Holms	46, 51		
Holo?n	94	Huey	184, 192, 194, 200
Holoway	6, 32, 51	Huff	73, 85

Miscellaneous Alabama Newspaper Abstracts --- Vol 1

Hufford	35
Hughes	11, 39, 57, 78, 113, 163
Hughs	20, 32, 51, 80, 179
Hulbert	32
Hulet	80
Hull	199
Humphrey	85
Humphreys	80, 92
Humphries	150
Huneycutt	117
Hunnicutt	152
Hunt	80, 159
Hunter	25, 35, 57, 105, 130, 136, 179, 186, 199
Huntington	156
Hurlbert	22
Hussey	121
Husted	130
Hustis	57
Hutcheson	3
Hutto	73
Hutton	165
Hyde	74, 121, 156
Hyller	85
Inge	156
Inger	178
Ingram	46, 198
Ingrem	63
Innerally	83
Irby	166
Irvaine	92
Irwin	130
Isbell	183, 184, 194, 197
Isgate	43
Isgett	128
Israel	25, 182
Ivey	7, 122, 134
Ivy	74, 75, 81, 87, 96, 137
Jack???	62
Jackson	3, 27, 39-41, 51, 64, 78, 86, 99, 104, 118, 130, 134, 168, 206
Jacob	20
James	99, 122, 133, 161, 199
Jameson	98
Jarald	74
Jarvis	157
Jay	104
Jemerson	46
Jemison	158, 194
Jenkins	112, 178, 207
Jenning	86
Jennings	60, 74, 189
Jernett	74
Jessup	51
Jeter	20
Jinny	158
John	192
Johnson	1, 3, 6, 8-10, 12, 15-18, 20, 21, 24, 26, 29, 32, 39, 43, 46, 49, 50, 57-62, 67, 70, 74, 90, 92, 101, 108, 109, 117, 122, 128, 130, 140, 143, 152, 165, 173, 176, 178, 179, 193, 194, 198, 199, 209
Johnston	6, 73, 86, 156, 158, 160, 164, 186
Joiner	182, 184, 194
Jonathan	141
Jones	4, 12, 25, 29, 32, 34, 39, 47, 51, 61, 62, 66, 74, 78, 80, 83, 85, 93, 94, 98, 101, 104, 107, 113, 117, 122, 124, 128, 130, 132, 134, 156-158, 164, 168, 174, 175, 176, 178, 179, 182, 201, 202, 204, 210
Jordan	12, 20, 29, 39, 78, 85, 94, 105, 122, 128, 136, 140, 199
Jorden	6, 57

MISCELLANEOUS ALABAMA NEWSPAPER ABSTRACTS --- VOL 1

Name	Pages
Jordon	117
Joseph	80
Judd	103
Jurnet	62
Kallen	135
Kane	34
Kannedy	3
Kave	139
Keaese	122
Keaneer	130
Keating	188
Keats	46
Keenan	13, 64
Keets	12
Keiber	101
Keith	66, 94, 182, 203
Keller	106
Kelly	12, 40, 42, 94, 122, 123, 131, 147, 154
Kemble	23
Kemp	39, 46
Kenan	8, 13, 17, 27, 62, 134, 174, 199
Kendal	12
Kendel	74
Kenedy	120
Kenerly	178, 180
Kenida	178
Kenneda	117
Kennedy	48, 86, 122, 157, 190
Kennon	70, 106, 164, 166
Kenon	74
Kent	78
Kenworthy	27
Keogh	74, 111
Kerr	23, 104
Kervin	3
Key	56, 62, 160
Kidd	90, 168, 209
Kilcrease	80
Kilgore	85, 94, 180
Killgore	78
Killingsworth	80
Kiltrell	19
Kimball	131
Kimble	12
Kimbrough	42, 134
King	3, 12, 19-21, 24, 27, 32, 39, 57, 67, 71, 73, 74, 78, 80, 83, 85, 86, 90, 93, 94, 101, 103, 112, 115, 117, 122, 128, 132, 139, 143, 144, 146, 163, 176, 178, 180, 204
Kinzie	122
Kirk	73, 141, 205, 207, 210
Kirkland	32, 93, 101, 169
Kirkpatrick	51, 135, 165
Kirksey	160
Kissam	33, 68
Knight	19, 201
Knockhimback	51
Knox	115, 176, 209
Kondrid	117
Koonts	128
Koontz	83, 110
Kornega	57
Kornegay	3, 39, 46, 115, 128
Kornigay	130
Kournega	199
Labarre	109
LaBrouse	171
Ladd	105
Ladlon	101
Laferne	122
Lafevre	62
Lake	155
Lamar	87
Lamb	7, 78
Lambert	180
Lambeth	76
Lampley	122
Lancaster	21, 27, 124, 141

Miscellaneous Alabama Newspaper Abstracts --- Vol 1

Land	131	Leffers	27, 143
Lane	85, 151, 180, 192, 195, 198	Leftwich	178, 180
		Leigh	159
Langdon	2, 66, 97	Lemar	12
Langford	32, 51, 55, 61, 80, 133	Lendsy	84
		Lenear	180
Langley	47, 128	Lenel	86
Langston	3, 181	Lenoir	27, 48, 65, 109
Lanksten	66	Lenvir	57
Lapsey	3	Leonard	203
Lapsley	27, 32, 56, 89, 133	Leopard	93, 122
		Leske	51
Larkin	132	Lesley	27, 35, 49
Larkins	138	Leslie	24, 47, 125
Latourrette	57	Lesly	102, 151
Lauderdale	148	Lester	162
Laugher	12	Letcher	122
Laughlin	51, 65, 80	Letters	5
Laughridge	132	Levard	21
Laurence	85	Levenworth	73
Lauson	101	Leveret	178
Law	190, 200	Levie	21
Lawler	112, 177-180, 194, 196, 197	Lewis	5, 27, 31, 47, 62, 73, 102, 117, 122, 124, 127, 131, 137, 159, 161-163, 168, 178, 180, 212
Lawrence	21, 55, 56, 92, 158, 189		
Laws	47	Liber	157
Lawson	85, 104, 196, 213	Lide	3
		Liggin	80
Lay	160, 169	Lightsey	189
Lea	94, 106, 109	Ligon	78
Leach	73	Lile	128
Leachman	159	Liles	180
Leavingsworth	80	Lindsey	44, 73
Leavinworth	85	Lindsy	66
Lebury	99	Linn	21
Ledbetter	12, 180	Linticum	135
Ledlow	12, 21	Linton	185
Lee	3, 10-12, 24, 34, 40, 48, 78, 89, 97, 112, 117, 123, 124, 128, 144, 154, 156, 178, 180, 203	Lipscomb	89
		Little	6, 30, 41, 71, 82, 93, 94, 99, 101, 162
Leech	94	Lively	117
Leer	27	Livespers	51

MISCELLANEOUS ALABAMA NEWSPAPER ABSTRACTS --- VOL 1

Livingston	117	Lyde	12
Loaten	27	Lyggin	66
Lock	27, 111	Lyles	101
Locke	12, 14, 157, 163	Lyman	195
Lockett	152, 175	Lynch	78, 128, 180
Lockhart	2, 94, 107	Lyon	117, 175
Locklin	63	M'Afee	177
Lockwood	38, 47, 62	M'Artha	62
Loco poco	51	M'Bride	62
Lodor	154	M'Connel	94
Loften	150	M'Cord	62
Loftin	149	M'Coroke	62
Logan	3, 13, 21, 27, 38, 130, 156, 157, 159, 161, 172, 202	M'Craw	128
		M'Cullin	103
		M'Cullough	62, 93
		M'Curdy	101
Lolly	84	M'Daniel	106
Lomax	122	M'Duffie	104
Looton	122	M'Elroy	29
Long	6, 10, 39, 130, 159, 180, 189	M'Gea	101
		M'Gill	97
Loocus	80	M'Ginnis	93
Looney	80	M'Ginty	94
Looton	122	M'Gough	97
Loper	122	M'Gran	62
Lord	176	M'Guire	68, 93
Lossy	32	M'Henry	98
Loughridge	133, 136, 142	M'Innis	60
Love	1, 7, 9, 11, 39, 66, 78, 130, 164	M'Intire	105
		M'Intyre	29
Lovely	128	M'Keagg	69
Loving	69	M'Kee	94
Lovly	117	M'Kinley	62, 115
Low	85, 101	M'Kinney	62, 93, 94
Lowry	175, 203	M'Langhlin	93
Loy	117	M'Lendon	94
Loyd	29, 62, 122	M'Leoad	93
Lucas	5, 45, 51, 73, 93, 122, 147	M'Leod	101
		M'Millan	62, 97
Luckie	21	M'Milland	101
Lumpkin	151	M'Neal	62
Lundie	178, 180	M'Neill	109
Lundsay	180	M'Reynolds	93
Lusk	145	M'Wharter	105
Luton	21		

Miscellaneous Alabama Newspaper Abstracts --- Vol 1

M'Whorter	84, 106			132, 146
Maberry	199		Mathis	12, 71
Mabry	170		Matlock	63
Machurn	189		Matteson	122
Mackharm	130		Matthews	27, 40, 42, 47, 74, 78, 79, 86
Macksfield	85			
MacLin	178		Mauldin	206
Madegan	181		Maull	57, 69
Magers	32		Maxwell	66, 85, 109, 172
Maham	189		May	33, 74, 85, 107, 155, 170, 171
Mahan	84			
Mahon	122		Mayer	74
Maker	81, 82		Mayers	74
Mallory	180, 194, 195, 203		Mayes	25, 124, 126
			Mayfield	180
Malory	178, 180		Mayhew	24, 189
Man	51		Mayness	189
Manley	119, 122, 135		Mays	25, 51, 117, 130, 199
Mann	47			
Manning	13, 80, 93, 167		McAdams	86, 205
Maples	17, 25, 112, 122		McAddam	74
Mara	3		McAden	178
Markes	117		McAfee	71, 178, 180, 210
Markham	161			
Marks	174		McAlpin	195
Marr	74, 113		McAlpine	170
Marris	32		McAnana	205
Marsh	91		McAtee	210
Marshal	3, 27		McBride	149
Marshall	27, 80, 122, 144		McBryde	150
Marthhome	130		McCaghran	86
Martin	3, 4, 62, 79, 99, 104, 122, 141, 149, 156, 164, 169, 171, 178, 180, 197, 198, 207		McCaghren	17
			McCain	17, 18, 51, 57, 190
			McCall	117
Mashaw	47, 51		McCamy	78
Mashiere	11		McCane	178
Mason	39, 76, 90, 171, 178, 212		McCann	178, 183, 198
			McCants	39
Massey	41		McCarter	178
Matheson	199		McCarty	73, 80, 165
Mathews	3, 12, 16, 21, 51, 54, 87, 117, 118, 124, 130,		McCaskal	86
			McCaton	39
			McClarde	207

Miscellaneous Alabama Newspaper Abstracts --- Vol 1

McClellan	207, 208		141
McClellen	194	McGeehee	39
McCleod	122	McGehee	152
McClusky	206	McGhee	71
McConnell	179	McGill	12, 57, 59, 122
McConnico	59	McGirty	86
McConok	74	McGlen	3
McCord	32, 69, 79	McGowen	167
McCorkle	183-185, 193, 194, 204	McGraw	73
		McGrew	178
McCormack	74	McGuire	19, 79, 80, 178, 188
McCoullough	14		
McCowalen	128	McHenry	79
McCowan	202	McIlhenny	201
McCoy	73, 130	McIlwaine	85
McCrackin	86, 171	McInnes	27
McCraw	76, 80, 92, 122, 139, 140, 176	McIntire	27
		McIntosh	25, 26
McCrea	39	McIver	128
McCuary	174	McKane	128
McCuller	86	McKeagg	53
McCulloch	178, 180	McKee	74, 157, 180
McCullough	122	McKeller	47
McCurdy	3, 57, 155	McKeney	18
McDaniel	47, 51, 117, 122, 128, 198	McKenny	12
		McKenzie	191
McDonald	3, 32, 59, 130, 140, 178	McKinney	27, 28, 192
		McKinnie	116, 117
McDounal	80	McKinnon	143
McDow	158	McKinny	130, 131
McElderry	210	McKinzey	74
McEldry	180	McKoun	130
McElheney	180	McLarty	122
McElroy	2, 5, 6, 17, 22, 39, 45, 58, 74, 79, 113, 120, 151	McLaughlin	27, 32, 55, 61, 115, 119
		McLaurin	57
		McLean	19, 27, 34, 39, 168
McFail	101		
McFarland	3	McLearin	39
McFarlin	80	McLemore	173, 178
McFarline	130	McLeod	15, 26, 66, 146, 178, 180
McFatter	130		
McGa?a	196	McLeoud	117
McGee	86, 111, 117,	McLoud	85

MISCELLANEOUS ALABAMA NEWSPAPER ABSTRACTS --- VOL 1

McMillam	7	Miers	94
McMillan	57, 85, 122, 143	Miler	73, 126
McMillen	85	Miles	10, 12, 65
McMullen	128	Milhous	54, 55, 59, 119, 125
McNair	21, 32		
McNaire	122	Millan	28, 62, 97
McNalley	206	Miller	21, 32, 66, 88, 101, 122, 128, 130, 133, 135, 136, 148, 171, 178, 180, 189, 212
McNeal	73		
McNeil	140		
McNeill	85		
Mcoker	150	Millhous	122
McPhail	79	Millhouse	40
McPherson	178, 189	Millican	194
McRae	148	Mills	21, 33, 35, 38, 70, 152, 209
McReynolds	68, 70, 80		
McRight	39, 178	Milsted	38
McVail	138	Mim	94
McVey	213	Minor	89
Me?on	62	Minter	3, 5, 7, 8, 21, 27, 32, 86, 93, 120, 122, 128, 130, 143
Meacham	159		
Mead	20, 44, 76		
Meador	12, 117		
Meadows	74, 180	Mitchel	47, 51
Mealy	82	Mitchell	12, 21, 27, 47, 51, 57, 62, 68, 74, 86, 93, 126, 128, 132, 143, 178, 180
Means	149		
Mears	93		
Meek	6, 94	Miux	86
Meken	136	Mixon	173
Melon	80	Mixson	85
Melstead	12	Moads	130
Melton	62, 63, 81, 93, 122	Mobley	15, 74, 120, 128, 159, 163
Meridith	100, 122	Mock	69
Meriweather	146, 165, 167	Moffet	86
Meriwether	168	Moffett	71
Merriweather	34, 181	Moffitt	99
Metcalf	178	Molett	21, 39, 51, 64, 67, 97, 102
Metetheny	128		
Mets	14	Molette	47, 130
Metts	57	Molkey	32
Meux	64, 79	Molton	167
Mickelborough	85, 93	Monk	140, 178
Mickelbury	73	Montgomery	180, 185, 194, 207, 209
Middleton	143		

Name	Pages	Name	Pages
Moody	79, 180	Mowdy	94
Mooney	142	Moxley	200
Moor	59, 62, 74	Moye	12
Moore	10, 12, 27, 47, 51, 57, 63, 74, 77-80, 85, 86, 92, 95, 107, 108, 111, 118, 122, 123, 125, 128, 152, 153, 178, 180, 185, 189, 195, 199	Mozingor	79
		Mulder	21, 55
		Mullen	123
		Mullins	171
		Muncos	206
Mordica	93	Mundine	74
Mordicai	85	Muray	3
Moreng	1	Murchison	17
Moreson	74	Murdock	21
Morgan	3, 6, 7, 12, 15, 29, 40, 57, 62, 81, 108, 117, 130, 137, 152, 174, 178, 180, 182, 184, 200, 207	Murley	48, 140, 143, 146, 147
		Murphey	73
		Murphy	47, 53, 117, 128, 130, 164
Morison	74	Murr	21
Morong	12, 108, 114, 117, 128	Murray	15, 21, 26, 66
		Murry	47, 61, 62, 73, 93
Morris	39, 101, 122, 123, 180, 183, 194, 208	Muse	122
		Mygate	180
Morrison	61, 75, 82, 85, 88, 101, 123, 128, 130, 147	Myres	47
		Myrick	74, 79
		Nace	122
Morrow	64, 95, 128	Naghil	3
Mortow	24	Nall	124, 195
Moseley	9, 35, 36, 39, 41, 74, 84, 103, 137, 205	Nance	32, 47, 147
		Nash	156
		Nave	94
Moselly	108	Neeley	189
Mosely	18, 21, 23, 29, 51, 108, 199	Neighbors	212
		Nelms	74
Moses	13, 21, 25, 62, 66, 67, 79, 83, 117, 130, 199	Nelson	13, 21, 56, 106, 112, 115, 121, 123, 128, 131, 132, 135, 145, 146, 158, 210
Mosher	185		
Mosley	128	Nettles	66
Mosly	130	New	27, 122
Moss	3, 44, 62, 78, 133, 180, 212	Newberry	43
		Newman	121, 122, 142, 143
Motes	153		
Mott	73	Newton	12
Moussune	128	Nichols	63

MISCELLANEOUS ALABAMA NEWSPAPER ABSTRACTS --- VOL 1

Nicholson	178	Ogletree	41
Nickson	27	Ogolvie	27
Nicolson	177	Oharrow	191
Niolep	33	Oldham	187
Niolin	11	Olds	39, 51, 55, 56, 79, 93, 101, 115
Niolon	59		
Nixon	42, 103	Olin	198
Noble	9, 27, 32, 80, 95, 128	Oliver	12, 25, 33, 58, 77, 78, 117, 139, 140, 159, 179, 180
Nobles	62, 85		
Nolen	186, 204		
Noline	130	Olliver	50
Nolly	101	Opelika	206, 212
Norman	26, 51, 101, 105, 157	Ore	128
		Orman	80
Norred	74	Ormand	62, 73, 101
Norris	14, 35, 73, 109, 122, 133, 137, 150	Orr	73, 75, 204
		Orsburn	130
		Osborn	180
Norton	11, 186	Otey	175
Norwood	3, 27, 32, 34, 51, 56, 58, 85, 115, 122, 128, 130, 133, 134, 136, 137, 145, 146, 152, 169, 170	Otley	33
		Otterson	95
		Otts	165, 211
		Outlaw	11, 15, 45, 47, 60, 74, 79, 100, 120, 154
Nowel	58		
Nunellee	41, 43		
Nunilee	21	Overton	3, 12, 99, 117
Nuniley	3	Owen	12, 63, 128, 135, 178, 200
Nunn	12		
Nunnelee	79	Owens	61, 74, 96, 101
Nunnella	62	Owins	130
Nunnelly	173	P?gg	101
Nutting	172	Pace	30, 178
Nye	32	Padget	207
O'Connell	187	Paine	33
O'Donell	58	Painter	42
O'Gilvie	117	Pally	118, 130
O'Neal	10, 74, 79, 166	Palmer	145, 194
O'Sullivan	72	Parham	19, 44, 57
Oden	90, 194, 209	Paris	82, 89
Odom	74, 79, 206	Parish	4, 164
Ogdon	73	Parker	3, 11, 12, 79, 80, 85, 99, 101, 168, 178
Ogelvie	118		
Ogle	198		

MISCELLANEOUS ALABAMA NEWSPAPER ABSTRACTS --- VOL 1

Parkes	3, 47, 118	Peguse	154
Parkham	130	Pelham	33, 59, 86, 101, 122, 186
Parkins	118		
Parkman	66, 88, 97, 136, 143, 151	Pemberson	118
		Penn	180
Parks	14, 21, 129, 145	Pepper	66
Parmer	178	Perine	1, 8, 21, 27, 31, 33, 44, 56, 155
Parnall	12, 33, 41, 52, 58		
		Perkins	3
Parnell	18, 45, 58	Perry	12, 15, 62, 80, 82, 85, 90, 96, 101, 103, 107, 109, 110, 122, 131, 157
Parnold	39		
Parrott	22		
Parry	80	Perryman	27, 150
Parson	29, 118	Persons	27
Parsons	3, 27, 87, 105, 143, 178	Peterson	122
		Pettibone	14, 101, 143, 176
Pas	99		
Paschall	60, 87, 170	Petty	3
Paterson	82	Pew	180
Patrick	74	Phares	157, 159, 161
Patridge	66	Phealden	122
Patten	21	Phelps	62, 74, 79, 109
Patterson	9, 74, 85, 87, 101, 130, 180	Philew	16
		Philileps	180
Patton	62, 120, 167	Philips	1, 12, 40, 85, 101, 116, 163, 178, 180
Paul	52, 76, 79, 126, 129		
		Phillips	21, 27, 56, 58, 73, 74, 80, 89, 93, 95, 101, 106, 110, 114, 116, 122, 130, 136, 141, 143, 163, 164, 189, 204
Paulding	34, 70, 122		
Pauley	180		
Paulling	27, 73, 152		
Payne	79		
Peake	3, 12	Philpot	118
Pearce	33, 169, 192	Pickens	3, 11, 12, 33, 62, 68, 72, 79, 90, 99, 101, 104, 106, 127, 129, 131, 140
Pearse	3, 180		
Pearson	3, 23, 62, 85, 122, 129, 136, 148, 180		
		Pickering	5, 33
		Picket	129
Pease	187	Pickett	15, 26, 70, 84, 105
Peck	8, 14, 15, 22, 33, 39, 164		
		Pierce	62, 80
Peebles	201	Pierson	101, 160
Peeples	66, 68	Pinekney	177
Pegues	27, 39, 59, 120, 129, 137, 145	Pinson	8, 80, 93, 116, 135, 137, 143

MISCELLANEOUS ALABAMA NEWSPAPER ABSTRACTS --- VOL 1

Pippen	162	Prentice	208
Pitman	27, 39, 46	Prentiss	210
Pittes	130	Prestwood	33
Pitts	47, 90, 130, 185, 199	Prevost	40
		Prewett	80
Plant	125	Prewit	85
Plattenburg	129	Price	66, 73, 106, 160, 178, 180
Plattenburgh	107, 108		
Pledger	3	Prichard	21, 40, 41
Ploughman	178	Prickett	70
Plowman	194	Prime	95, 114, 129
Plunket	47, 131	Primm	122
Poe	129	Prinderson	122
Polk	175	Printer	35, 55, 182
Pollard	108, 180	Prior	112, 122, 130
Pomroy	27	Pritchard	14, 34, 44
Pond	111	Pritchett	168
Ponder	125	Pruett	130
Ponsonby	22, 32, 33	Pruit	17
Pool	12, 62, 94, 99, 122	Pruitt	62, 63, 66, 101
		Prun	130
Poole	191	Puckett	26, 191
Poosee	74	Pugg	80
Pooser	86	Pulley	3
Pope	36, 79, 86, 92, 145, 150, 151	Pulmer	86
		Punderson	3, 12, 47
Porter	3, 12, 33, 39, 52, 66, 73, 80, 84-86, 93, 102, 122, 129, 136, 151, 170, 178	Purdue	67
		Purdy	62
		Purple	175
Porterent	129	Purpli	121
Portis	176	Pye	3, 129
Posby	130	Pyles	180
Posonby	52	Quarles	9, 21, 36, 47, 148
Possenby	3		
Potent	129	Quinn	165
Potts	27, 148	Radford	79, 85, 180
Pouncey	12, 118	Rae	27, 64
Pound	203	Ragan	198
Powe	22	Ragland	178, 194
Powell	3, 12, 21, 27, 33, 43, 58, 140, 168, 178, 180, 196	Raiford	25
		Railand	138
		Rainer	15, 62, 74
		Raines	27, 47
Powers	26	Rains	129

MISCELLANEOUS ALABAMA NEWSPAPER ABSTRACTS --- VOL 1

Name	Pages
Rakestraw	103
Rambart	141
Rambo	93
Ramsey	9, 37
Randall	122, 180
Randle	39, 86, 95, 99, 151
Randolph	27, 162, 177
Rane	39
Rariner	45
Rasco	21, 59, 118
Ratcliff	110
Ratcliffe	158
Rather	101, 129, 178
Ravenel	31
Rawls	18
Ray	80, 101
Rayford	178
Razer	39
Rea	74
Read	65, 74, 92, 123, 130, 140, 141
Reavis	178
Reece	74
Reed	79, 110, 142, 153, 178
Reeder	94
Rees	21, 73
Reese	118, 139
Reeves	24, 113, 124, 129
Reid	27, 64, 93, 94, 103, 126
Reisor	55
Renalde	86
Renfro	175, 183, 203
Renfroe	195, 196, 204, 206, 207, 210
Rennolds	58
Renoulds	74
Rentfrow	180
Reves	129, 130
Reynolds	33, 59, 62, 79, 85, 86, 91, 93, 96, 107, 112, 115, 121, 129, 194
Rhea	180
Rhem	58
Rhinehart	69
Rhoden	180
Rhodes	194, 199
Rhortridge	124
Rice	39, 47, 79, 91, 120, 178-180, 186, 187, 213
Rich	66
Richardson	62, 63, 94, 152, 153, 167, 169
Richey	27, 80, 178, 189
Richy	76
Riddle	80, 122, 130, 157, 180, 183, 188, 190
Ridgway	162
Riesor(n?)	137
Rieves	27, 130
Riezer	180
Rigby	58
Riggins	62
Riggs	62
Rigly	86
Riley	31, 33, 188, 196
Rinaldi	79
Rion	122
Rippetoe	189
Ritchey	92
Rivers	130
Rives	57, 129, 148, 173
Rixey	176
Roach	54
Roads	180
Roark	125
Robberson	180
Robbs	189
Roberson	68, 70, 71, 73, 79, 81, 103, 120, 183
Roberston	96

Miscellaneous Alabama Newspaper Abstracts --- Vol 1

Roberts	3, 9, 21, 26, 37, 41, 47, 58, 62, 72-74, 79, 86, 122, 137, 155, 159, 189, 202	Ruesum	66
		Rumph	17, 74, 111
		Rush	61, 122
Robertson	52, 81, 96, 129, 147, 207	Russel	39, 73, 122
		Russell	21, 66, 129, 152, 198
Robeson	4, 36, 41, 99, 180	Russum	101, 134
Robinson	36, 62, 80, 147, 178, 180, 186	Russum(?)	101
		Russun	80
Robison	101	Rutherford	11, 14, 27, 35, 47, 74, 83, 86, 93, 122, 131, 137
Robson	87		
Rochell	33		
Rockell	47		
Rocket	139	Rutledge	79, 85, 129, 178, 180
Rodgers	79, 130, 178, 180	Rutlege	46
Rogers	47, 52, 80	Rutlidge	80, 178
Roland	85	Ruttendge	129
Rolies	178	Ryan	180
Rolines	130	Rynolds	129
Roller	142	S?liman	162
Rollins	85, 178	Sadrick	129
Rombo	93	Saffold	3, 22, 33, 39, 52, 56, 58, 59, 62, 73, 74, 80, 85, 105, 130, 155, 174
Root	5		
Roper	27, 32, 39, 46, 52, 74	Safford	8, 12, 33, 127, 129, 154
Rosaman	188		
Rose	27, 36, 70, 80, 82	Safield	129
		Sage	22, 52
Roseman	180	Salter	40
Ross	31, 39, 52, 79, 94, 97, 106, 129	Salters	101
		Saltmarsh	37, 47, 56, 58, 86, 108, 114, 118, 155
Rosser	4-6, 57, 129		
Roundtree	80, 86		
Rountree	3	Saltonstall	12
Routh	189	Sample	83, 88, 93, 101
Rowan	27	Samplee	73
Rowden	178	Samson	43
Rowe	154, 178, 180	Samuel	194
Rowell	31	Sanders	21, 58, 74, 75, 94, 170, 171, 180
Rowndtree	129		
Rowsey	79		
Roy??ter	103	Sandlin	3, 12
Royle	62	Sanfley	21

Miscellaneous Alabama Newspaper Abstracts --- Vol 1

Sanford	48, 121, 204			81, 85, 93, 101, 115, 133, 137, 144
Sargent	3			
Satterwhite	25, 210			
Satterwhitt	86		Sharpe	105
Saunders	3, 20, 39, 77, 94, 105, 122, 140, 166, 173		Shaw	21, 62, 66, 74
			Shearer	3, 60, 65, 91, 98, 109, 110
Savage	33, 39, 129		Sheldon	122, 166
Savery	184, 194		Shelley	178, 180, 192, 194
Sawyer	80, 178, 180, 202		Shelton	43, 73, 80, 169, 178, 180
Saxon	5, 103			
Saxton	52		Sheperd	66
Sayre	187		Shephard	62
Scales	188, 201		Shepherd	73, 74
Scarbro	101		Sheppard	12, 38, 62, 129, 130
Scarbrough	172			
Scever	146		Shepprard	39
Schofield	80		Sherrer	86
Schoppert	167		Sherrod	94, 200
Scott	12, 52, 79, 87, 89, 122, 142, 154, 178, 185		Shields	70, 73, 101, 122, 129, 135, 138
Scripter	45		Shipman	62
Scull	16		Shoat	66
Seales	178		Sholes	130
Seaman	16, 20, 135		Shores	141
Searle	47		Short	12, 27
Sears	94		Shortridge	112
Seawell	79		Shouse	212
Seay	207, 209, 211		Shulz	86
Seligman	157		Shuney	118
Sellers	44, 46, 154		Si?on	101
Sellzer	11		Sigler	73, 93
Seltzer	53, 106		Siks	130
Sewel	14, 74		Silvers	127
Sewell	14		Simes	62
Shackelford	62, 76, 90, 94		Simmons	79, 101, 127, 129, 155, 180, 183, 188, 194, 195
Shaddock	28, 104, 106			
Shaffer	43, 180		Simms	33, 60, 113, 122, 132
Shanklin	205			
Shannon	89		Simons	130
Sharber	129		Simpkins	37
Sharp	69, 74, 76, 79,		Simpson	54, 58, 61, 65,

MISCELLANEOUS ALABAMA NEWSPAPER ABSTRACTS --- VOL 1

Sims	74, 103, 104, 117, 122, 129, 133, 204 62, 66, 79, 80, 86, 93, 129, 134, 151, 153, 178, 180, 189	Snow Sobury Sol Soles Sorals Sorell	21, 175 187 19 74 86 18, 20, 21, 40, 109, 129, 130
Singleton	39, 104, 135	Sorells	130
Sisor	129	Sorrell	10, 21, 43, 47, 52, 74, 76
Sizemore	196		
Skaggs	194	Sorsby	168, 169, 172
Skeen	118	Spaight	154
Skelton	122	Sparks	74
Skinner	62, 73, 79, 86, 155, 191	Sparman Sparran	101 58
Slaughter	193	Sparrow	52, 122
Sledge	122	Spears	118, 173
Sloan	71, 180	Speed	12
Slone	4	Spence	73, 101, 178, 180, 201, 208
Small	25, 29-31, 39, 41, 42, 44, 49, 58, 59, 67, 76, 77, 81-83, 102, 106, 114, 118, 119, 125-127, 136, 144, 150, 170, 173, 202	Spencer Spensby Spinks	64, 130, 167, 195 12 199
Smedley	74, 80, 124	Spinnacuta	55
Smiley	3, 12, 31, 58, 60, 95, 96	Sponsonby Sprate	52 9
Smily	130	Springs	164
Smith	7, 12, 13, 19, 21, 22, 27, 29, 33, 39, 47, 55, 58, 60, 62, 63, 66, 74-76, 79, 84, 86, 90, 92, 94, 96, 101, 114, 118, 122, 123, 126, 129, 130, 132, 140, 146, 159, 170, 171, 178, 180, 190, 203, 204, 206, 211	Spyker Sreaoman Stabler Stachan Stamps Stanton Stapler Stapleton	194 18 74, 86 18 74, 84, 86 3, 12, 108 158 16
Smitherman	199	Starkey	72, 95
Smoot	180, 198	Starr	122
Smyley	3, 47, 52, 174	Stebbins	82, 151
Snead	30	Stedman	122
Snedecor	166	Steed	178
Sneed	21, 143	Steel	156
Sneider	199	Steele	47, 152
Snell	20	Steitz	152

MISCELLANEOUS ALABAMA NEWSPAPER ABSTRACTS --- VOL 1

Step	41	Sulivan	12
Stephens	3, 27, 33, 47, 52, 73, 80, 118, 151	Sullivan	33, 39, 72, 122, 138, 140, 148
Stephenson	183	Summers	181
Sterrett	126, 133	Summons	95
Sterritt	203	Sumners	180
Stevens	101	Supple	21
Steward	44	Sutliff	135
Stewart	3, 12, 21, 73, 140, 181, 183, 189, 211	Suttle	142, 199
		Suttles	77
Stickney	165, 166	Sutton	145
Stidman	27, 39	Swain	194
Stinnett	180, 188	Swan	183
Stinson	122	Swepson	39
Stockdale	206	Swift	58, 101, 122
Stocks	106, 183	Swingston	36
Stokes	66, 93, 160	Swope	192, 212
Stone	4, 11, 12, 80, 101, 129, 175, 180, 195, 196, 206, 208	Symmes	105
		Taber	60, 99
		Tait	116
		Talene	12
Stoner	122	Taliaferro	190
Storey	184, 193	Talmage	178
Story	4, 164	Tanner	13, 189, 204
Stoudemire	129	Tant	178
Stout	41	Tarrant	76, 84
Stovall	205	Tarrence	133
Stover	180	Tarver	47, 69, 79, 93, 103, 122, 139
Strachon	39		
Strambler	52	Tasker	158
Street	28, 64, 122, 160, 192	Tate	67, 79, 87, 94, 106, 116, 141, 145, 182
Stribling	165		
Strictland	180	Taul	194, 202, 208
Stringfellow	24, 60, 85, 94, 156	Taulon	129
		Taylor	3, 12, 40, 53, 62, 65, 75, 76, 79, 80, 87, 97, 101, 102, 105, 109, 110, 119, 120, 122, 126, 130, 136, 148, 167, 178, 180, 182, 184, 199, 212
Strong	93, 113, 147		
Strothers	59		
Strudwick	94		
Stuart	59, 162, 186		
Stubblefield	180	Templin	173
Sturdivant	39, 85, 94, 95, 132	Terry	21, 27, 33, 99, 147, 178, 180, 194, 207, 211
Suddth	129		

MISCELLANEOUS ALABAMA NEWSPAPER ABSTRACTS --- VOL 1

Terryman	91	Topp	201
Th?rp	12	Torrans	12
Thaxton	76	Towchets	129
Thetford	160	Townsend	3, 180, 187, 188, 212
Theus	189		
Thomas	12, 21, 23, 50, 85, 106, 122, 130, 135, 146, 165	Tpincutoperitatus 52	
		Trammel	4, 63, 195
		Trarer	39
		Trarers	64
Thomason	78, 82, 154, 178, 180, 182, 184	Traun	48, 53
		Travis	47, 62, 166
		Traylon	52
Thominson	93	Traylor	3, 39, 60, 87, 130, 139
Thompson	3, 12, 21, 22, 27, 58, 62, 66, 72, 85, 118, 122, 130, 144, 157, 166, 171, 178, 204, 206		
		Tredwell	123, 133
		Tredwill	115
		Tremore	180
Thomson	81	Trewitt	201
Thornton	165, 170, 183, 185	Trigg	62, 75, 77, 79
		Trippe	17
Thrash	22, 58, 199	Troup	78, 211
Thurber	56	Trowel	87
Thurmond	47	True	161
Thweatt	79	Tubb	87, 94
Tichinor	167	Tucker	73, 80, 93
Tierce	171	Tueman	58
Tigner	87	Tulson	118
Tignor	67, 82	Tunstall	202
Tillmon	73, 130	Turnbough	94
Tilman	30, 162	Turner	5, 63, 67, 71, 77, 106, 123, 161, 170, 180, 184, 191, 193, 194, 196, 200
Tilton	67		
Tinsley	79		
Tippett	73, 75, 101, 122	Tuthill	31
Tipton	21, 139, 148, 194	Twiggs	88
		Tyler	202
Tittle	61	Tynes	171
Todd	33, 87	Tyrce	160
Toler	75	Tyus	90, 139, 152
Tolson	47, 124	Ullman	171
Tome?	118	Ulmer	12, 20, 27, 56, 58
Tomkies	178		
Tomme	47	Underwood	3, 12, 21, 27, 31, 37, 47, 52, 58, 127, 148,
Tompkins	93		
Toomer	52		

MISCELLANEOUS ALABAMA NEWSPAPER ABSTRACTS --- VOL 1

	154	W?????	94
Upfold	118	Waddell	67, 129
Utley	94	Waddill	115
Va?er	62	Waddle	27, 122
Vaescr	3	Wade	15, 16, 21, 33,
Vail	39, 47		105, 130, 143
Vallient	122	Wadkins	21, 27, 33, 47
Valts	118	Wadsworth	13, 52
Van	8, 62, 79, 103,	Wakeley	75
	125, 159, 192	Walden	194
Van De Graff	8	Waldron	7, 189
Van Doorn	159	Walice	101
Van Dyke	62, 79, 103	Walker	3, 13, 18, 21, 33,
Van Ness	125		39, 47, 49, 52, 55, 58, 63, 73,
Vandeford	129		75, 79, 84, 85, 87, 93, 95, 97,
Vanderford	122		100, 101, 109, 112, 113, 118,
Vanderslice	27, 85		123, 129, 131, 132, 134, 143,
Vann	3, 75		145, 149, 154, 162, 167, 170,
Vanpelt	18		171, 182, 188, 189, 192, 198,
Varnell	39, 47, 101		212
Vassar	89	Wallace	63, 64, 79, 94,
Vasser	27, 45, 58, 62,		96, 101, 110
	75, 80, 91, 93,	Wallas	130
	95, 122, 127,	Wallis	28, 195
	135, 174	Walters	94
Vaughan	56, 148	Walton	13, 64, 79, 145
Vaughn	80, 146, 191	Wanan	58
Vedge	13	Ward	8, 13-15, 21, 87,
Veglen	13		91, 114, 176
Venable	193	Wardwell	28
Vensey	178	Ware	105, 118, 120,
Verell	129		123, 125, 153,
Vernon	10, 75, 91, 104		156, 179
Verrell	21, 39	Warford	40
Vickers	13, 21	Warnock	85
Vincent	11, 153, 188	Warre	118
Ving	129	Warren	14, 67, 80, 94,
Visher	197		131, 145
Voegelin	14	Warrin	94
Vogelin	8	Warters	33
Vogeline	122	Warwick	182
Volentine	52	Waters	94, 105
Volly	21	Watkins	13, 22, 40, 87,
Voultz	75		88, 122, 156,

MISCELLANEOUS ALABAMA NEWSPAPER ABSTRACTS --- VOL 1

	164, 170, 179, 180, 189		75, 79, 85, 87, 101, 113, 129, 130, 151, 153, 158, 174, 180, 183, 208
Wats	189		
Watson	13, 47, 50, 55, 67, 81, 101, 124, 130, 155, 170, 179, 180, 188, 200, 212	Whitehead	131
		Whiting	58
		Whitlock	13, 27, 101
Watt	171	Whitman	57, 105
Watters	123	Whitmore	129
Watts	1, 3, 13, 21, 27, 33, 47, 52, 58, 87, 127, 147, 154	Whitney	54
		Whitted	13, 25, 27, 40, 47, 52, 58
Waugh	13, 130		
Wear	109, 122, 129, 143, 146	Whitten	13, 21, 207
Weatherly	186, 204	Whitworth	179
Weathers	188, 212	Wiggins	56
Weaver	3, 11, 21, 27, 40, 83, 91, 98, 112, 122, 129, 131, 132, 145, 179	Wilbanks	27, 40
		Wilcox	47, 58
		Wilde	185
Webb	13, 38, 39, 73, 94, 122, 157, 164	Wilder	40, 180
		Wiley	3, 11, 12, 17, 26, 27, 47, 52, 70, 71, 75, 79, 87, 93-95, 101, 106, 109, 129, 149, 154, 158, 160, 163, 167, 170
Webster	31, 122, 129		
Weeks	83		
Weissenger	152		
Weissinger	27, 152	Wili?	80
Welch	13, 39, 47, 67, 85, 125, 129, 179, 180, 194, 195, 197, 203	Wilkerson	26
		Wilkins	27, 122
		Wilkison	67
		Willey	63
Welcker	179	Williams	3, 7, 13, 25, 27, 33, 40-43, 47, 49, 52, 58, 59, 67, 71, 75, 78, 79, 84, 87, 94, 101, 112, 122, 129-131, 138-140, 145, 158, 159, 165, 179, 180, 198
Wells	120, 184		
Wessenger	33		
Wesson	180		
West	3, 13, 27, 33, 40, 42, 52, 79, 84, 115, 122, 123, 129-131, 151, 179		
		Williamson	20, 27, 31, 47, 79, 118, 122, 139, 188
Westbrook	35	Williford	63, 167
Weyman	132	Willis	28, 118, 143, 150, 166
Whaley	157		
Whaples	47		
Whatley	3, 21, 75, 97, 129, 157	Willman	194
		Wills	115, 129, 133
Wheeler	26, 75, 179, 180	Willson	56, 58, 85, 179, 180
Whisenant	193		
White	1, 3, 13, 27, 33, 34, 40, 47, 52, 58, 61, 63, 64,	Wilmer	175
		Wilson	3, 13, 14, 20, 28,

Miscellaneous Alabama Newspaper Abstracts --- Vol 1

	29, 40, 50, 67, 73, 75, 79-81, 94, 97, 98, 101, 119, 122, 139, 164, 180, 194
Wilton	80
Winbourn	184, 192
Windham	39, 63, 75
Windsor	127
Winham	64
Winn	170, 208
Winter	1, 80, 116, 181
Wisinger	58
Withers	144
Witherspoon	89
Witt	32
Wittich	79
Wolfe	40
Womack	23, 29, 43, 47, 105, 131, 141, 148, 157
Wood	21, 22, 27, 33, 40, 67, 87, 122, 136, 139, 179, 180, 188, 189, 202
Woodall	118
Woodard	179
Woodbry	80
Woodruff	13, 199, 203
Woods	63, 95, 106, 109, 118, 125, 146
Woodward	93, 101, 122, 185
Woolley	69, 97
Wooten	149
Wooter	89
Worley	100, 104
Wrabon	79
Wren	3, 29
Wrenn	27
Wright	3, 27, 33, 43, 44, 53, 75, 80, 109, 123, 130, 143, 163, 167, 198
Write	81, 123, 141, 180, 181
Wyatt	87, 123, 189
Wyckoff	99, 104
Wyett	75
Wyman	58
Wynn	99, 101, 199, 201
Wyott	75
Yale	123
Yampert	193
Yancey	3, 21, 28, 29, 35, 36, 50, 54, 182
Yarborough	180
Yateman	199
Yeates	95
Yeldell	20
Yeldill	46
Yongue	58
Yost	115, 123
You	38
Young	21, 52, 63, 76, 89, 93, 95, 137, 180
Youngblood	87, 93
Zimmerman	81, 129

MISCELLANEOUS ALABAMA NEWSPAPER ABSTRACTS --- VOL 1

SLAVE NAME INDEX

Name	Pages
Aaron	7, 142
Abby	52
Abraham	110
Abram	5, 6, 38
Aggy	52
Alabama	65
Albert	201
Alfred	14, 125
Amey	13
Amy	52, 65, 158
Andrew	65
Ann	52
Anne	52
Anthony	58
Barbary	52
Barscna	65
Batts, Nathan	16
Beckey	142
Ben	52, 119
Betsey	158
Betty	52, 65
Biddy	52
Bill	1, 16, 41, 71, 144
Blythe, Webster	200
Bob	107
Boston	168
Brittan	159
Bruce	202
Bryant	166, 186
Burill	111
Buster	131
Calvin	143
Carolina	136
Caroline	158, 163
Carter, John	125
Cash, Hiram	107
Casy	52
Cely	65
Charles	1, 49, 54, 90, 97, 153, 158
Charlotte	158
Christian	202
Ciawley	158
Cornelius	65
Cresey	119
Cyrus	52
Daniel	52, 65, 98, 102, 182
Dave	99
Drucilla	103
Easter	65
Edmund	158
Ellick	5, 137
Ely	199
Emily	52
Erronia	163
Fanny	52
Fed	200
Felix	191
Frances	186
Frank	45, 49, 158
Frederick	75
French	158
Gee, Billy	52
George	52, 70, 99, 126
Green	52, 182
Greer, Nancy	159
Griffin, Alex	211
Hagar	45
Hannah	52, 54
Harma	71
Harriet	19
Harriett	52
Harry	7, 77
Henry	45, 50, 52, 65, 101, 168
Hester	30
Holly, George	212
Honry	153
Hugh	163
Isaac	56, 58, 76, 140, 185, 193, 201
Isabella	36

254

MISCELLANEOUS ALABAMA NEWSPAPER ABSTRACTS --- VOL 1

Isam	156	Maria	36, 65, 149, 158
Island	163	Mariah	52
Isobel	52	Martha	52
Jack	91	Martin	65
Jackson	19	Mary	19, 52, 65, 103, 145, 166
Jacob	65, 76		
Jane	52, 65, 146, 163, 181, 186	Matilda	163
		Melissy	142
Jeffrey	65	Milly	19
Jeffry	52	Milo	72, 89
Jery	52	Minty	144
Jesse	144	Mitchell	152
Jesse Tom	52	Monroe	65
Jessey	112	Morning	4
Jim	6, 52, 58, 149, 150, 163	Moses	65, 69, 119, 158, 173
Jimmy	158	Nan	112
Jinny	158	Nancy	65, 112, 140
Joe	30, 137	Nathan	9
John	31, 52, 65, 110, 123, 125, 163, 196, 201, 202	Natt	71
		Ned	52, 149
		Nelly	150
Jonathan	141	Orin	68, 103
Jordan	104	Othello	65
Josephine	158	Peter	5, 52, 91
Joshua	112	Phil	153
Judah	65	Philip	192
Judy	52	Phillis	11
King, Lewis	83	Phoeby	52
Lary	112	Phyllis	52
Levi	201	Piley	112
Lewis	13, 83, 156	Pompey	69
Limus	141	Pondy	199, 201
Lizzy	112	Poydere	52
Lloyd	52	Prince	52
LoLo	31	Priscilla	52
Louisa	52, 65	Rachel	52, 65
Lucretin	19	Rafe	99
Lucy	45, 52, 65, 103, 158, 160	Randell	144
		Ransom	65, 126
Luke	65	Reuben	6, 7, 126
Lydia	52	Richard	65, 166
Madison	65	Robert	45
Margaret	125, 163	Robin	65

Sally	65, 163
Salor	112
Sam	52, 58, 110
Sanno	67
Sarah	65, 99, 134, 163
Scott	9
Shadrick	116
Silas	6
Silsina	65
Simon	36
Smith	149
Sol	19
Solomon	52, 196
Sophia	45
Sophonia	52
Sophy	125
Squire	186
Stapleton, John	16
Stapleton, Seaborn	16
Stapleton, Zeno	16
Stapleton, Zenothan	16
Stapleton, Zenothen	16
Stephen	54, 99, 116, 200
Stewart, John	181
Sue	65
Suky	65
Susannah	119
Tempy	158
Tener	158
Tom	64, 158, 163
Ursey	158
Viney	163
Viny	158
Wappin	71
Washington	107
Webb, William Wesley	197
Webster	200
Will	153
William	65, 116, 158, 168, 193, 201, 202

www.ingramcontent.com/pod-product-compliance
Lightning Source LLC
Chambersburg PA
CBHW071329190426
43193CB00041B/1040